SO YOU WANNA SEE COWBOY STUFF?

The Western Movie/TV Tour Guide

by Boyd Magers

**With Special Movie Locations Contributions
by Tinsley Yarbrough**

Published by:

Empire Publishing, Inc.
PO Box 717
Madison, NC 27025
336-427-5850

Empire Publishing, Inc.
PO Box 717
Madison, NC 27025-0717
phone: 336-427-5850
fax: 336-427-7372
email: movietv@pop.vnet.net

Library of Congress Control Number 2002116141
ISBN Number 0-944019-39-0

Published and printed in the United States of America

1 2 3 4 5 6 7 8 9 10

Dedication

To Evy—who was there at the beginning and still is 43 years later.

TABLE OF CONTENTS

Acknowledgments to a Gathering of Friends

A book this far-reaching would not have been possible without the unselfish input and knowledge of a host of people. Primary among them is Tinsley Yarbrough for all his expert contributions to nearly all of the filming location entries in this tour guide. This guide would not be nearly as thorough on the background of these historic sites without his expertise. He is truly a locations archeologist. Portions of the locations covered in this tour guide originally appeared in Tinsley's "Those Great B-Western Locations" column published bi-monthly since 1994 in WESTERN CLIPPINGS and the one-shot THOSE GREAT B-WESTERN LOCATIONS published in 1998. They are reprinted here in somewhat edited or altered form with Mr. Yarbrough's permission.

This book or any other project I'm involved in would not be possible without the expert help of my wife and partner, Donna.

The Audie Murphy entries simply would not have been as thorough—many even possible—without the research, time and knowledge of Rolla Mires, an Audie Murphy aficionado par-excellence. When it comes to Audie, if Rolla says it, you can take it to the bank.

Larry Jensen's knowledge of movie railroads and trains is unfathomable. He spent seven years researching for his 1981 book, THE MOVIE RAILROADS, and has learned even more since its publication. His input was invaluable to this tour guide.

Without the untiring help of Bryan Burgess many entries on this tour would be sadly lacking. Bryan spent hours checking facts and tracing footprints to help us with this book.

Billy Holcomb's generosity is as big as his state of Texas. And his state is better represented because of his help.

Laura Bates provided nearly all of the Hopalong Cassidy data for the Cambridge area.

There are so many others who provided help in one way or another that it would take a chapter to detail their assistance. But we offer our sincere "Thanks" to: Hoyt Adams, Leith Adams, Rose Marie Addison, Chris Alcaide, Susan Anderson, Sam Austill, Wade Austin, Bonita and Gregg Barton, Julie Baumer, Judith Beck, Earl Bellamy, Jack Bennett, Phyllis Berlin, Joe Binski, Jay Black, Karla Buhlman, Linda Burke, Jerry Campbell, Joe Caro, Sharon Carter, Jim Clark, Bobby Copeland, Roger Crowley, Jim Curry, Brent Davis, Jim Derr, Margie Earlywine, Brian Eider, Ken Espiau, Walt Farmer, Tommy Farrell,

Michael Fitzgerald, Elvis Fleming, Norman Foster, Keith Foster, Georgia Furr, Brian Gardner, Jimmy Glover, Noretta Glup, Jim Goldrup, Ray Goldrup, Tom Goldrup, M. David Gonzalez, Alex Gordon, Paul Grimes, Louis Guili, Roger Hall, Jim Hamby, Maxine Hansen, Loyal Haun, James Henager, Kelo Henderson, A. J. Higgenbottom, Graham Hill, Larry Hopper, Tommy Ivo, Michael Johnson, Dick Jones, Elmer Kelton, Don Key, Jim Kocher, Rhonda Lemons, John Leonard, R. Phillip Loy, Lou Mallory, Stanley Martin, Merrill McCord, Teri McKeating, Tom McLaughlin, Doug Miller, Hal Miller, Janey Miller, Bob Nareau, Don Nelson, Tom Nichols, M. G. "Bud" Norris, Vern O'Dell, Milton Obrock, Parmly-Billings (Montana) Library, Elvin Pettet, Roy Rogers Jr., David Rothel, Bill Russell, Jim Ryan, Elizabeth Salome, Jerry Schneider, John Sents, Leslie Shores, Richard Simmons, David Scott Smith, Richard Smith III, Ann Snuggs, Jennifer Stewart, Karen Stewart, Ken Stier, Frank Story, John Stovall, Neil Summers, Ken Taylor, Harold Tedford, Harvey Tedford, Everett Templeton, Howard Thomas, Burchell Thompson, Shane Van Ausdal, Herb Wagner, Suzanne M. M. Warner, Kurt Wenner, Johnny Western, Ray White, Adrien Witkofsky.

Introduction

In preparation for this book, we contacted nearly 300 readers of our own WESTERN CLIPPINGS publication, readers in virtually every state in the Union, to obtain leads on western movie related museums, displays, monuments, restaurants, etc. The response was outstanding. We thank all who helped, even if it was only to say, "There's nothing I know of in my state." However, I'm certain there are other sites we have overlooked that should be included in this tour guide. If you know of any, contact us at 1312 Stagecoach Rd SE, Albuquerque, NM 87123 and we'll include them when a revised second edition is printed.

We're providing as detailed and as complete information as we could obtain on each entry. We found some sites and museums to be helpful, others never returned our calls. Some (such as the Country Music Hall of Fame) wanted to charge a $50 research fee (?) For free publicity? Therefore, we have given you as much information on each site as we could gather. Bear in mind, things change, in particular, phone numbers (especially area codes) and museum hours. It's always a good idea to double check by phoning ahead of your visit. Also bear in mind, exhibits at museums do rotate or change from time to time.

This tour guide is not intended as a history book or comprehensive treatise on western stars, instead it will guide you to museums and areas where you can learn more about the stars we enjoyed on the screen. For the most part, we are assuming you know who Ken Maynard, Hoot Gibson, Gene Autry etc. are or you wouldn't be interested in this book, therefore we are not going into a detailed history or description of their lives and work. However, on some of the lesser known players we will give you a brief accounting of their contribution to westerns.

Not mentioned in this book are many fabulous private collections belonging to long-standing collectors. These are not included for obvious security factors.

As we travel state by state, we are *not* defining birthplaces of western celebrities unless we know of a home with a significant distinguishing marker. Also not listed are the various burial sites (with a few important exceptions) of the western stars. For those desiring that information, it's well detailed in B-WESTERN BOOT HILL by Bobby Copeland (Empire, 1999) or you may check <www.findagrave.com> on the internet.

We apologize for the lack of clarity on some photos in this tour guide. Obviously, we were unable to personally visit all the sites included and were forced to rely on secondary sources for some photos.

For the L.A./San Fernando Valley portion of your tour, we suggest you purchase THE THOMAS GUIDE: LOS ANGELES COUNTY STREET GUIDE AND DIRECTORY (published by Rand McNally). It's practically indispensable, especially if you've never driven in the L.A. area before. It *will* make your life easier! About $20 at many bookstores and newsstands—but Laurel Park News at the corner of Laurel Canyon and Moorpark always has a supply on hand.

When you're reading about filming locations in California you should be aware of the "30 Mile Hollywood Studio Zone", an area within a 30 mile radius of Beverly and La Cienega Boulevards in Los Angeles agreed upon by the motion picture and TV producers and industry unions as a clearly defined boundary to determine various logistical issues in the production of films as to pay scales, working conditions and travel time. Locations within the zone were considered local, outside the zone were considered distant. Staying inside the zone means flexibility and economy. You'll find most filming activity for budget westerns stayed within this zone.

Many of the movie location sites listed are open to visitors, others are private. Feel free to visit and take a discreet look, but please don't disturb residents or trespass on private property. Often a little charm and explanation of why you're there will go a long way.

Remember too, when it comes to western movie filming locations, space limitations make it practically impossible for one guide book such as this to pinpoint every specific filming location or film made there. For example, hundreds of westerns were made at Iverson's and Corriganville in California. We cannot list them all. Then too, a film such as "Outlaw Josey Wales" was shot in several different states—often a scene here, a scene there. "Flap" ('70) with Anthony Quinn utilized at least six different locales within New Mexico and "Showdown" ('73) with Dean Martin traveled to five different New Mexico areas. We will guide you to the primary locations and give you a representative sampling of movies lensed there, but there are plenty more—and certainly hundreds of unlisted titles. Therefore, for more detailed information on filming locations we suggest you consult all of these reference works.

Tinsley Yarbrough's "Those Great B-Western Locations" bi-monthly column in WESTERN CLIPPINGS, 1312 Stagecoach Rd SE, Albuquerque, NM 87123.

Tinsley Yarbrough's five-volume videotape set of "Those Great B-Western Locations". Available from VideoWest, Inc., 1312 Stagecoach Rd SE, Albuquerque, NM 87123.

AN AMBUSH OF GHOSTS ('91) by David Rothel (Empire Pub.)

ON LOCATION IN LONE PINE ('90) by Dave Holland (Holland House).

THE MOVIE RAILROADS ('81) by Larry Jensen (Darwin Pub.).

OLD TUCSON STUDIOS FILM HISTORY (Old Tucson bookshop).

THE WORLD'S MOST FAMOUS MOVIE RANCH—CORRIGANVILLE ('99) by William Ehrheart (Ventura County Historic Society).

WESTERNS OF THE RED ROCK COUNTRY (SEDONA) ('91) by Bob Bradshaw (Bradshaw Color Studios).

IN SEARCH OF HOLLYWOOD, WYOMING 1894-1929 ('85) by William Huey (Huey Pub.).

QUIET ON THE SET ('84) by Robert Sherman (Sherway Pub.).

FILM IN ARIZONA ('01) (Arizona Film Commission).

SHOT ON THIS SITE ('95) by William A. Gordon (Citadel Press).

THE CONEJO VALLEY ('89) by Carol A. Bidwell (Windsor Pub.).

CINEMA SOUTHWEST ('00) by John A. Murray (Northland Pub.).

WHERE GOD PUT THE WEST—MOAB/MONUMENT VALLEY ('94) by Bette L. Stanton (Four Corners Pub.).

HOLLYWOOD GOES ON LOCATION ('88) by Leon Smith (Pomegranate Prod.).

FAMOUS HOLLYWOOD LOCATIONS ('93) by Leon Smith (McFarland).

A FIELD GUIDE TO MOTION PICTURE LOCATIONS AT RED ROCK CANYON, MOJAVE DESERT, CA by Richard J. Schmidt (Canyon Two Pub.).

HOLLYWOOD OF THE ROCKIES ('97) by Frederic Wildfang (Rochester Hotel in Durango, Colorado).

100 YEARS OF FILMMAKING IN NEW MEXICO ('98) published by NEW MEXICO MAGAZINE.

THE WORLDWIDE GUIDE TO MOVIE LOCATIONS ('01) by Tony Reeves (Titan Pub.).

ALABAMA

Johnny Mack Brown Mural

Johnny Mack Brown was born September 1, 1904, in Dothan. He attended public school and graduated from Dothan High in 1922. Johnny's father owned a family clothing store. In 1926 Johnny graduated from the University of Alabama where he was an All-American halfback.

Brown parlayed his football heroics into a long-lasting B-western screen career. He died in 1974 but his legend lives on in Dothan where a 20 ft. tall mural, by artist Susan Tooke, on the side of a S. St. Andrews Street downtown building.

Dothan is in the extreme southeast corner of Alabama.

Johnny Mack Brown mural.

★★★

Johnny Mack Brown Birthplace

The birthplace of Johnny Mack Brown is at 513 South St. Andrews Street in Dothan, just four blocks from the downtown Brown mural.

Birthplace of Johnny Mack Brown.

★★

"Bear" Bryant Museum

Items pertaining to cowboy star Johnny Mack Brown's football days are housed at the Coach Paul "Bear" Bryant Museum at the University of Alabama in Tuscaloosa. (205) 348-4668.

Selected captain of the 1925 University of Alabama football team, on New Year's Day in 1926 Brown attained national fame for his catch of the longest pass yet thrown in a Rose Bowl game. The 65 yard pass urged Alabama on to defeat Washington 20-19. In 1957 Johnny Mack Brown was inducted into the National Football Hall of Fame.

★★

ALASKA

Sergeant Preston's Trading Post

Although Sergeant Preston of the Yukon (Richard Simmons) is not there, nor was he ever there for filming, Sgt. Preston's Trading Post is still a well-known gift shop in Skagway (in the southeastern peninsula) and is still paying tribute to the great Northwest Mounted TV series.

Sergeant Preston's Trading Post.

★★★

Will Rogers Monuments

A monument memorializing the spot where Will Rogers and aviator Wiley Post died in a tragic plane crash is at Walakpa Bay near Point Barrow. The cement and rock shrine with brass spires on top can only be reached in the summer by four wheel drive vehicles or in winter by snowmobile or dogsled.

There is also a monument to Will across the road from the Barrow airport, southeast corner of Momeganna and Airport Road in Barrow. This is an engraved granite monument with a bronze replica of Will and Wiley Post's plane in the center.

Monument to Will Rogers and Wiley Post.

★★

ARIZONA

Yuma

Yuma has a long history as a filming site and titles shot there include a couple of classic B-westerns as well as one of the Duke's Mascot cliffhangers.

According to local historian Frank Love, the first film lensed in the area was "Bandit Joe and the Lovely Heroine's Rescue" starring future Mack Sennett comedian Ben Turpin. The first major film lensed at Yuma was the Ronald Colman version of "Beau Geste" ('26), followed the same year by Valentino's "Son of the Sheik" and in 1929 by "The Desert Song" with John Boles as well as the William Powell/Richard Arlen rendering of "Four Feathers".

In 1930, a town set was built on the banks of the Colorado River near Yuma for John Wayne's "Big Trail", with the Colorado substituting for the Mississippi River at the beginning of the settlers' trek west.

By 1990, Yuma had played host to more than 40 titles, including the 1939 Gary Cooper version of "Beau Geste", Tyrone Power's "Suez" ('38), Bogart's "Sahara" ('43), Jimmy Stewart's "Flight of the Phoenix" ('66), desert scenes for the superb political thriller "Seven Days In May" ('64), the "Return of the Jedi" ('82) entry in the "Star Wars" series, Stallone's "Rambo III" ('88), a couple of the Hope/Crosby "Road" pictures, and such A-westerns as Alan Ladd's "The Badlanders" ('58) and "Last of the Comanches" ('52) with Broderick

Crawford. The John Wayne "Three Musketeers" serial ('32) and Gene Autry's "Red River Valley" ('36) lensed in part at the area's most frequently used locale—Buttercup Valley in California's Imperial Sand Dunes, a few miles northwest of Yuma and the Arizona border.

"Three Musketeers" and "Red River Valley" also included another familiar Yuma landmark, the old territorial prison. More than 3,000 inmates were

Gates of now abandoned Yuma Prison.

confined in Yuma's prison from its opening in 1876 until 1909 when the last convicts were transferred to a new facility at Florence. The local high school then occupied those buildings from 1910 to 1914. During the depression it became a shelter for the homeless. The prison, including its impressive main gate, played a variety of roles in "Three Musketeers" with its cell row and other facilities being put to excellent use in "Red River Valley".

The latter title also featured Yuma's Laguna Dam, on the spillway where Gene and an apparently hung-over George Chesebro staged an exciting and dangerous fight sequence.

The small train that figured prominently in the "Red River Valley" plotline was used in "real life" to haul ore from area mines. The engine or one like it (or perhaps the same engine, modified in appearance over the years) is now on display on the lawn of a Yuma museum.

Scenes from Tom Mix's "Rider of Death Valley" were shot at Black Butte and Telegraph Pass, east of Yuma as well as in Buttercup Valley.

★★

Gene Autry Park

The Anaheim Angels Spring training is held at Tempe Diablo Stadium, 2200 W. Alameda in Tempe. A "Gene Autry Park" minor league training field was established in 1999 at 4125 E. McKellips in Mesa.

★★

May West Restaurant

When in Tempe, check out the May West Restaurant (a low budget Denny's) which serves a "Tom Mix" (corn beef hash breakfast) and a "Chill Wills" (omelet with homemade chili) among its many movie star monikered meals. There's also a "Duke" (hamburger topped with bacon and cheese). Tom Mix is pictured on their menu.

1825 E. University Drive (480) 966-2761.

★★

Arizona In The Movies Gallery at the Mesa Southwest Museum

Definitely worth a visit is the Arizona in the Movies Gallery at the Mesa Southwest Museum in Mesa. Curator Keith Foster displays many (and is constantly seeking more) Arizona movie-related artifacts. The exhibits explain how filmmaking in Arizona began in earnest with examples from the 1940 film "Arizona." Fact verses fiction is examined. They display Joanne Dru's riding coat from "She Wore a Yellow Ribbon", Rex Allen's "Frontier Doctor" TV series doctor's smock and britches, a Gene Autry hat, Gene Hackman's outfit from "Geronimo," memorabilia from "Tombstone," "Ballad of Cable Hogue" and other Arizona lensed pictures. Foster places an emphasis on women in Arizona and John Ford (a small section of "Stagecoach" was shot near Mesa). Bear in mind some of these exhibits do rotate.

Be sure to take note of the superbly preserved stagecoach that traveled the historic Apache Trail from Mesa to Roosevelt in the early days. The ongoing exhibitions elsewhere in the resplendently impressive museum are actual territorial jail cells (the museum was technically built around them), a copper mine, a Lost Dutchman mine replica, and the absolutely stunning (!) dinosaur hall unlike any I've seen, depicting the prehistoric development of Arizona on land and sea. For children there's a hands-on adventure center while you explore the Sonoran desert walk, the hall of minerals, the Spanish Colonial period, the hall of astronomy, and historic courtyard. At least allow yourself a good portion of a day to wander the winding corridors and multi-levels of this exceptional museum.

Open Tuesday-Saturday 10-5, Sunday 1-5. 53 N. MacDonald Street (southeast corner of MacDonald and 1st). (480) 644-2230.

★★★

Ben Johnson Memorial Barn

The Ben Johnson Memorial Barn is at Sunshine Acres Children's Home in Mesa. Johnson held rodeo benefits to raise funds for the home. During visits he became interested in their 4-H program and construction of the new barn (erected in the mid '90s) caught his eye. Ben's name is on the barn with a large painting of the friendly cowboy inside.

Tours available 8-5 Monday-Friday, 10-4 Saturday, 1-4 Sunday. 3405 N. Higley Rd. in Mesa. (480) 832-2540.

★★★

Cudia City

Tris Coffin and Kelo Henderson's popular "26 Men" TV series ('57-'59) utilized Cudia City, a movie studio on the northeast corner of Camelback Rd. and 40th St. in Phoenix. The studio site became a dinner theatre in the '50s and in the '60s was torn down to make way for an apartment complex.

★★★

Los Dos Molinos

The places Tom Mix purportedly slept are beginning to rival those of George Washington!

Los dos Molinos, rated one of Arizona's "most fun" restaurants by GOURMET magazine, states in its publicity it serves its fiery Mexican-style food "within the white adobe house once owned by Tom Mix."

Mix authority Bud Norris says there is no confirmation of this. But, what the heck, you gotta eat while you're in Phoenix anyway.

8646 S. Central. (602) 243-9113.

★★★

Happy Trails Resort

A small collection of Roy Rogers and Dale Evans items are on display in the office of the Happy Trails Resort in Surprise. The western duo were original investors in this mobile home/manufactured homes and RV resort.

Streets inside the resort bear names like: Palomino, Roy Rogers, Cool Water, Dale Evans, Trigger, Buttermilk, Tumbleweed, Pat Brady, Nellie Belle (sic), Six-Shooter, etc.

This resort caters to 'snowbirds' and is crowded during the winter but almost empty in the summer. 17200 West Bell Rd. in Surprise (a suburb of Phoenix on its northwest edge). (623) 584-6645.

★★

Ben Johnson Days Rodeo

Ben Johnson Days rodeo is held every November in Apache Junction to raise money for some of Johnson's favorite charities, including the Sunshine Children's Home.

★★

Apacheland

A principal filming site in the Phoenix area is Apacheland. Originally constructed for episodes of "Death Valley Days", the site also hosted episodes of "Wyatt Earp", "Have Gun Will Travel", "Gunsmoke" and other TV series, as well as portions of several features, including the town portions of Jason Robard's "Ballad of Cable Hogue" ('70) and Elvis' "Charro" ('69).

When demand for the site as a filming location declined in the early '70s, Apacheland, near the famed Superstition Mountains—home to the Lost Dutchman mine—became an amusement park featuring public appearances by such stars of TV oaters as Peter Brown of "Lawman", Robert Fuller of "Laramie" and Doug McClure of "The Virginian". The amusement park closed in 1984 and, since that year, the area has been seen primarily in commercials, which had begun lensing there as early as 1958 and include the famous Volkswagon spot featuring a minister in front of the Apacheland church set, as well as commercials for Toyota, Dodge trucks, the GM Montana, Jeep and Colt 45 malt liquor. Features have occasionally lensed there in recent years, too.

In 1969, a fire caused by a discarded cigarette set the town ablaze, destroying all the sets but its barn, church and the original structures on the property. The sets were rebuilt on the same foundations with essentially the same designs, albeit with some modifications. Other fires, including one in 1999, caused less damage to the property. When first built, Apacheland included a soundstage but a tornado blew off its top years ago and it gradually deteriorated.

In 1996, a large restau-

Apacheland filming site with the Superstition Mountains as a background.

rant and bar with facilities for catered affairs was opened.

On occasion, major corporations have rented Apacheland to shoot day-long comic western videos featuring their top salesmen and executives. But the site's moneymaking days seem largely a thing of the past.

For a visit to one of the few surviving western sets, take U.S. 60 (the Superstition Fwy) east from Phoenix to Apache Junction, take a right there onto Kings Ranch Rd. Apacheland is at 4369 S. Kings Ranch Rd. A restaurant at Apacheland features a memorabilia display.

Sampling of Westerns Filmed in APACHELAND

- Wanted Dead or Alive (TV): Fourth Headstone ('58)
- Wanted Dead or Alive (TV): Crossroads ('59)
- Four Fast Guns ('60)—James Craig
- Stagecoach West (TV): Stock exteriors used throughout series ('60-'61)
- Purple Hills ('61)—Gene Nelson
- Have Gun Will Travel (TV): The Siege ('61)
- Broken Land ('62)—Jody McCrea
- Blood On the Arrow ('64)—Dale Robertson
- Arizona Raiders ('65)—Audie Murphy
- Death Valley Days (TV): Temporary Warden ('65)
- Death Valley Days (TV): Brute Angel ('66)
- Death Valley Days (TV): Kid From Hell's Kitchen ('66)
- Dundee and the Culhane (TV): various episodes ('67)
- Death Valley Days (TV): The Friend ('68)
- Death Valley Days (TV): Great Diamond Mines ('68)
- Charro ('69)—Elvis Presley
- A Time For Dying ('69)—Audie Murphy
- Ballad of Cable Hogue ('70)—Jason Robards
- Guns of a Stranger ('73)—Marty Robbins
- The Gambler–The Adventure Continues (TV) ('83)
- Blind Justice ('93)—Armand Assante

★★

Tom Mix Monument

About 15 miles south of Florence (headed toward Tucson) on two-lane Hwy. 79 (the Pinal Pioneer Parkway, near mile marker 116) is the spot where Tom Mix was killed October 12, 1940, while driving at a high rate of speed. As Tom came upon road detour signs, he zigzagged and flipped into a dry wash. His Cord automobile overturned, pinning him underneath. A large metal suitcase (on display at the Tom Mix Museum in Dewey, Oklahoma) vaulted forward, striking Tom in the neck and head, killing him.

Signs now mark Tom Mix Wash where his Cord turned over in the dry creek bed. Nearby is the 10 foot Tom Mix monument and roadside park which presents a riderless horse in silhouette atop a stone base. A plaque is inscribed: "In memory of Tom Mix whose spirit left his body on this spot and whose characterization and portrayals in life served to better fix memories of the Old West in the minds of living men."

Gene Autry was present at the 1947 dedication. The horse figure atop the monument has been stolen and replaced several times over the years.

Tom Mix Monument.

★★

Gammon's Gulch

Gammon's Gulch Ghost Town Movie Set is in Pomerene, about 12 miles north of Benson.

Although we can verify no films or TVers shot there, the authentic mine, saloon, and other buildings are impressive. Inside the Grandview Hotel you'll find a collection of John Wayne memorabilia.

Take Pomerene Rd. to Cascabel Rd, continue to mile marker 7. Shortly you'll come to E. Rockspring Rd. Turn left. Gammon's Gulch is the first gate on the left. Open 9-5 Wednesday-Sunday. (520) 212-2831.

★★★

Tombstone

Walk through a door to the Old West! No town captures the imagination of western enthusiasts like Tombstone. Once the roughest, toughest mining camp on the western frontier, the historic district of town is preserved in appearance much as it was at the height of the silver boom in 1879. The ghosts of Wyatt Earp, Doc Holliday, the Clantons and Big Nose Kate still haunt the town's main thoroughfare, Allen Street.

There's so much to see and do—the famous O.K. Corral where the Earps fought the Clantons in the West's most famous gun battle (recreated on screen in "My Darling Clementine", "Gunfight At O.K. Corral" and several others)...the Bird Cage Theatre, the wildest, most famous honky-tonk in America in 1881 (and it has the bullet holes in the wall to prove it)...Boothill Cemetery where many authentic notorious gunslingers are buried...the Tombstone Epitaph features the newspaper's original 1880s printing press...and so much more history.

Be sure to stop in the Tombstone Mercantile Co. (720 Fremont St.) to view over 16,000 square feet of merchandise from movie memorabilia and vintage clothing to Native American art and jewelry. A western collector's paradise. (520) 457-1489. On the back wall of the Tombstone Mercantile, note the cast bronze plaques in which WESTERN CLIPPINGS magazine (1312 Stagecoach Rd. SE, Albuquerque, NM 87123) honors the movie stuntmen who have appeared at each year's Tombstone Film Festival. The plaque for 2001 honors Whitey Hughes, Dean Smith, Bobby Hoy, Bobby Herron and Neil Summers. The 2002 plaque honors Whitey Hughes, Jack Williams, Joe Canutt, Roydon Clark and Chuck Bail.

Hugh O'Brian places his hands in wet cement during the Tombstone Western Film Festival in July 2001. The handprints of O'Brian, Will Hutchins, Harry Carey Jr. and others are now on display at the Tombstone Mercantile Company.

With as many westerns made *about* Tombstone as there were, you'd expect the area to be a hotbed of film activity. Oddly, it was not. Scant few were lensed there...train scenes for John Wayne's "McLintock!" were shot in nearby St. David (which can be seen in the background); the mudfight scene was filmed on private property right outside of Tombstone; the hunting scenes with Wayne and Stephanie Powers were shot somewhere along the San Pedro River. Meanwhile, the river crossing scenes for "Red River" were filmed at Fairbank, a few miles northwest of Tombstone on Hwy. 82, along with the early scene where John Wayne meets the young version of Montgomery Clift. Filming also took place in the Coronado National Forest south of Benson. Recently, Danny Glover's "Buffalo Soldiers" shot in the Dragoons northeast of Tombstone as did the TV pilot for "The Magnificent Seven." Tom Selleck's "Ruby, Jean and Joe" used local roads including the Charleston rest stop at the San Pedro River west of town. Glenn Ford stayed in Tombstone in the '50s while he was working on "3:10 To Yuma" which lensed around nearby Benson and Willcox (to the north) and Sonoita (to the west). Given the lack of motels then, Tombstone was probably the best central location. Speaking of the Sonoita area, the railway station, scene of a big musical number in "Oklahoma" ('55), is in Elgin, 20 some miles west of Tombstone off Hwy. 82.

Most importantly, the CBS telefilm "Return to Tombstone" in 1994 with Hugh O'Brian was filmed right in Tombstone amidst dozens of film clips from his "Life and Legend of Wyatt Earp" TV series ('55-'61).

For general information on Tombstone, call the Chamber of Commerce (888) 457-3929.

★★★

Rex Allen Museum

The Rex Allen Museum is dedicated to the life of the Willcox native who became the last of the silver screen singing cowboys. It houses memorabilia from all facets of Rex's career—his years at Republic, rodeo trophies, his Disney work, the buggy used on his TV series "Frontier Doctor" and more. Sequined cowboy suits, guns, guitars, plaques and honorariums, recordings, comic books, movie posters etc.

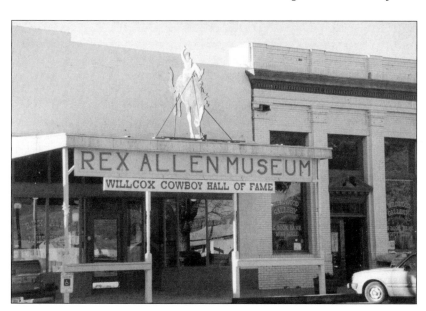

Rex Allen Museum.

Across the street, a larger-than-life bronze statue of Rex, created by artist Buck McCain, signifies the importance of Willcox's favorite son.

Rex Allen (1920-1999), born to homesteader parents, went on to stints on radio, including the National Barn Dance at WLS, Chicago, which led to a film and recording career. His bigget Decca Record hits ("Crying In the Chapel", "Money, Marbles

A Rex Allen guitar and other memorabilia on display at his museum.

and Chalk", "Streets of Laredo") came after he'd signed with Republic in 1949.

Rex's TV series "Frontier Doctor" came along in '57, one of the few TV series produced by Republic. In 1960 the Arizona Cowboy began a long, fruitful association with Walt Disney, narrating films and "Wonderful World of Color" shows for NBC. He continued to appear at fairs and rodeos for years, being named Mr. Cowboy by the Rodeo Producers Association. Rex wrote a regular column for HORSE AND HORSEMAN magazine for years and became a highly paid voice-over commercial spokesman for Purina, Honda and others. Rex also hosted the West Texas Rehab telethon for years.

Opened in 1989, the Rex Allen Museum is at 150 N. Railroad Ave. in Willcox. (877) 234-4111.

Rex Allen Days Celebration is held annually.

While in Willcox, be sure to notice Pedro Gonzales-Gonzales Alley, named in honor of Rex's long-time amigo.

Rex Allen's son, Rex Jr., penned the official state song, "I Love You Arizona."

★★

Tucson Rodeo Parade Museum

The Tucson Rodeo Parade Museum is located at 4823 S. Sixth Ave. (northeast corner of Sixth Ave. and Irvington) in Tucson. The large metal building, originally the first city airport hanger, was developed as a museum to house many historic stagecoaches, ore wagons, milk wagons, surreys, buckboards, conestoga wagons and coaches of all types used in Tucson's annual Fiesta de Los Vaqueros parade, presented annually since 1925.

It's known as the longest non-motorized parade in the country.

While the museum is not yet finished, it can be improved on only as funds are developed. Open to the public 9-4 in January and February, with hopes of a year-round schedule soon. Admission is free, but donations are welcomed.

Set among a typical western street is Duncan Renaldo's Cisco Kid aqua-blue horse trailer for transporting his horse Diablo.

Over the years, various western stars who rode in the parade include Gary Cooper (1937), William Boyd as

Duncan Renaldo's horse trailer.

Hopalong Cassidy (1951), Rex Allen (1957 and several other times), Chill Wills, stars of TV's "High Chaparral" (1969), Michael Landon (1970), Montie Montana (1973), Ben Johnson (Grand Marshal in 1996), Don Collier (Grand Marshal in 1997), Rex Allen Jr. (1997). Photos of all these stars and others from the various parades can be seen at the museum. (520) 294-3636. (520) 294-1280.

★★

Locomotive #1673

A Southern Pacific Railroad locomotive #1673 used in "Oklahoma" and "3:10 To Yuma" is now on static display at the Amtrack station in Tucson, 400 E. Toole Ave. (520) 623-4442.

★★

Old Tucson

In 1939, an unprecedented set was built for the Columbia Pictures epic "Arizona." Director Earl Bellamy was a 22 year old assistant director to director/producer Wesley Ruggles on the filming of "Arizona." Earl recalls, "We put in a street Wesley Ruggles wanted where the pioneers were coming into this village. This was shot June and July and I remember at 11am we called a siesta 'cause it was so hot. From 11-2pm nobody did anything. That lasted about a week and a half, then (studio head) Harry Cohn said, 'Enuf of that fellas. You shoot sunshine, rain or what have you.' As to actual building, Jim Pratt was head of construction at Columbia Pictures for years. He later became Production Manager at Universal. There was nothing Jim didn't know about building anything. He could build the moon if you had to. He was a crackerjack. Jim was right down there (on the desert) with 'em to show the workers what the studio wanted. When the picture was done, Columbia turned it over to Pima County."

Forevermore dubbed Old Tucson after "Arizona," it was a hit-and-miss operation with the county overseeing use of the crumbling site. Then, in 1959, Bob Shelton saw its potential, leased the site and formed Old Tucson Development Company. He refurbished old buildings and built new ones. In January 1960 he threw open the doors to an anxious public. Shelton continued to develop Old Tucson as the tourists flocked in along with movie production. A 13,000 square foot sound stage was built in 1968. In 1970 a complete wardrobe department was purchased from MGM. By 1980, Old Tucson was the third most popular paid attraction in Arizona. In all, over 300 productions have lensed at Old Tucson, most importantly the "High Chaparral" TV series. Old Tucson was sold to DRD Venture II in 1986, but Shelton remained as a vp of motion pic-

Harness shop at Old Tucson can be seen in "Ten Wanted Men", "Arizona Raiders" and others.

tures and TV.

On April 24, 1995, a fire of unknown origin ravaged the site destroying three quarters of the "Arizona" townsite. Many pieces of priceless memorabilia and costumes were also lost. Thankfully, the "High Chaparral" sets were spared as was the Southern Pacific train depot and the ex-Virginia and Truckee Railroad engine #11 which is now on static display at Old Tucson. Owned by MGM from 1945

"High Chaparral" ranch house.

to 1970 and by Old Tucson since, it can be seen in "Union Pacific" ('39), "The Sheepman" ('58), "Horse Soldiers" ('59), "Man Who Shot Liberty Valance" ('62) and "How the West Was Won" ('63)...a total of 60 films in all.

Rebuilding began by fall of '95, and by January 1997, Old Tucson was once again flourishing with 16 new buildings, albeit this time more of a western amusement park than a true location. Still, with the "High Chaparral" ranch house and other original buildings, it's a must on your western movie tour. Located at 201 S. Kinney Rd. in Tuc-

The Reno, used in "3:10 to Yuma" among others.

son. (520) 883-0100. Open year round except Thanksgiving and Christmas.

Sampling of Westerns Filmed in OLD TUCSON

- Arizona ('40)—William Holden
- Last Roundup ('47)—Gene Autry
- Last Outpost ('51)—Ronald Reagan
- Violent Men ('54)—Glenn Ford
- Ten Wanted Men ('55)—Randolph Scott
- Reprisal ('56)—Guy Madison
- Walk the Proud Land ('56)—Audie Murphy
- Gunfight at OK Corral ('57)—Kirk Douglas
- Gunsight Ridge ('57)—Mark Stevens
- Guns of Fort Petticoat ('57)—Audie Murphy
- 3:10 to Yuma ('57)—Glenn Ford
- Buchanan Rides Alone ('58)—Randolph Scott
- Lone Ranger and the Lost City of Gold ('58)—
  Clayton Moore
- Posse ('75)—Kirk Douglas
- Rio Bravo ('59)—John Wayne
- McLintock ('63)—John Wayne
- Arizona Raiders ('65)—Audie Murphy
- El Dorado ('67)—John Wayne
- Hombre ('67)—Paul Newman
- Last Challenge ('67)—Glenn Ford
- Return of the Gunfighter (TV)—Robert Taylor ('67)
- Winchester 73 (TV)—Tom Tryon ('67)
- High Chaparral (TV) ('67-'71)
- Heaven With a Gun ('69)—Glenn Ford
- Rio Lobo ('70)—John Wayne
- Bonanza (TV): Power of Life and Death ('70)
- Bonanza (TV): Top Hand ('71)
- Bonanza (TV): Desperado ('71)
- Yuma (TV)—Clint Walker ('71)
- Joe Kidd ('72)—Clint Eastwood
- New Maverick(TV) ('78)
- Young Riders (TV) ('89-'92)
- Border Shootout ('90)—Glenn Ford
- Dead Man's Revenge ('94)—Bruce Dern
- Quick and the Dead ('94)—Sharon Stone

★★★

Mescal

Erected for "Monte Walsh" ('69) with Lee Marvin, Mescal is the home of Old Tucson's second western movie town location. Since the devastating fire at Old Tucson in 1995 and the subsequent rebuilding of Old Tucson into more of a tourist site, Mescal now sees most of the western film production—when there is any. Mescal is situated on 60 acres leased from the state. MGM invested over $200,000 into the sets for their "Young Riders" TV series, adding new storefronts and new buildings.

Unfortunately, the location is not open to the public unless you're lucky enough to catch a groundskeeper who will let you in. 35-40 miles east of Tucson near Benson.

Sampling of Westerns Filmed in MESCAL

- Life and Times of Judge Roy Bean ('72)—Paul
  Newman
- Hanged Man ('74)—Steve Forrest
- Buffalo Soldiers ('79)—John Beck
- Tom Horn ('80)—Steve McQueen
- Desperado (TV) ('87-'89)
- Monte Walsh ('89)—Lee Marvin
- Young Riders (TV) ('89-'92)
- Tombstone ('93)—Kurt Russell
- Quick and the Dead ('94)—Sharon Stone

★★★

Prescott

One of the most scenic sites in the Grand Canyon state for filming was Prescott, Yavapai County, in the hill country of northwest Arizona.

In 1912 Romaine Fielding did 15 silents in Prescott for the Lubin Company. The next year, Selig Polyscope opened a satellite studio at 712 Western Ave. and began work on a series of shorts directed by silent star William Duncan at Selig's Diamond S Ranch east of town. Duncan starred in several of those titles with future cowboy super-star Tom Mix in a supporting role. Soon, Mix became the star in over 60 one-reelers circa 1913. These were shot primarily in the Diamond Valley area and its Slaughterhouse Gulch, a dry wash east of Prescott.

The ranch house Mix and his family occupied, much modified in appearance, now serves as the community clubhouse for the Yavapai Hills subdivision out Hwy. 69 at 5010 Bear Way. Tom lost the ranch in the 1929 Wall Street crash. A "hanging tree," a 200 year old maple often seen in Mix flicks, stands in the area on lot 30. The dry wash that runs through Yavapai Hills, known as Slaughterhouse Gulch, was also used in films including "Sheriff of Yavapai County" ('13). The hanging tree is at the bottom of this gulch. The sales office as you enter the subdivision houses much Mix memorabilia (including the original door to the ranch house) so be sure to stop. Many of the street names in Yavapai Hills have Mix connections such as Tony Trail, Miracle Rider Rd., Thundering Herd, Tom Mix Trail, Purple Sage, etc.

In mid 1915, the Selig operations moved to Las Vegas, New Mexico, for filming, but Mix returned to Prescott for filming for several years.

In 1939, Ben Judell, independent film distributor and producer of several exploitation quickies, formed Producers Distributing Corporation with ambitious production plans, including a Tim McCoy series and The Sagebrush Family, a western version of Fox's popular Hardy Family series. Perhaps at the suggestion of PDC, contract director Robert Tansey, whom the Prescott newspaper would later dub the community's "Ambassador to Hollywood," Judell also decided to establish a studio in Prescott. By late November, PDC had completed initial construction of a western street on a clearing in the Granite Dells five miles northeast of town, a picturesque collection of rock formations amid scattered pines.

In early December, the company filmed "The Sagebrush Family Trails West", first in a planned series of eight titles starring 13-year-old junior rodeo champion Bobby Clark. Later that month, Tim McCoy arrived for work on "Texas Renegades" telling a reporter he intended to make Prescott his motion picture headquarters. How-

Granite Dells area of Prescott. Note the western street set (now gone) in the background with Watson Lake in the foreground.

ever, the PDC chapter in Prescott's film history was short lived. The Sagebrush Family series was a flop and bit the dust after one entry. PDC, facing financial difficulties, was forced to reorganize and became PRC (Producers Releasing Corporation). PRC worked on the cheap and deemed locations as distant as Prescott too expensive.

Prescott native and leading lady Dorothy Fay encouraged filmmakers to come to Prescott and other Arizona locations. She and future husband Tex Ritter lensed three B's

Painting of Tom Mix which now hangs at the Ramada Inn.

there in '39-'40. They were married in Prescott's First Congregational Church on June 14, 1941.

Director Robert Tansey interested producer Scott Dunlap of the Rough Riders series in the area. Tansey filmed a Tom Keene there (making effective use of Watson Lake on "Dynamite Canyon") and Dunlap brought Buck Jones, Tim McCoy and Raymond Hatton to town for the first Rough Riders, "Arizona Bound", filming around the Granite Dells. Other scenes featured plains areas near the street set and along what is now Hwy. Alt. 89 northeast of Prescott.

One impressive shot in "Arizona Bound" pictured a closeup of Buck on Silver, posed before a chimney rock formation. That rock formation can be seen in the distance on the right along Hwy. Alt. 89, in a plains area a couple of miles beyond the point where Alt. 89 breaks off from Hwy. 89 northeast of town.

Parts of later flicks also lensed in the area, including Steve McQueen's "Junior Bonner" ('72), "Wanda Nevada" ('79), "Billy Jack" ('71), the '94 version of "The Getaway" with Alec Baldwin and establishing scenes for the Lloyd/Beau Bridges TV series "Harts of the West" ('93) (although most exteriors for that series were actually shot at Sable Ranch and Rancho Maria north of Los Angeles, not in Arizona).

Incidentally, the Ramada Resort across Hwy. 69 from Yavapai Hills subdivision sports a large painting of Tom Mix in their lobby. Mix is also pictured on their brochures. 4499 Hwy. 69.

Sampling of Westerns Filmed in PRESCOTT

- Range Law ('13)—William Duncan
- Sallie's Sure Shot ('13)—William Duncan
- Law and the Outlaw ('13)—Tom Mix
- Made a Coward ('13)—Tom Mix
- Sheriff of Yavapai County ('13)—Tom Mix
- Rollin' Westward ('39)—Tex Ritter
- Sagebrush Family Trails West ('40)—Bobby Clark
- Junior Bonner ('72)—Steve McQueen

- Rainbow Over the Range ('40)—Tex Ritter
- Rollin' Home to Texas ('40)—Tex Ritter
- Texas Renegades ('40)—Tim McCoy
- Arizona Frontier ('40)—Tex Ritter
- Dynamite Canyon ('41)—Tom Keene
- Arizona Bound ('41)—Rough Riders
- Wanderers of the West ('41)—Tom Keene

★★★

Sedona

Some of the most gorgeous country in the west is around Sedona. Western filmmakers learned this early with the first western lensed in Sedona being Zane Grey's "Call of the Canyon" with Richard Dix in 1923.

Coffee Pot Rock north of Sedona. Look for it in "Relentless", "Station West" and others.

Sedona is surrounded by sunset-colored flanks that rise 2,000 feet or more above the floor of the town. Every spire, every butte, every canyon wall has a slightly different tinge of color or character to it. Truly, Sedona could be a national park, rivaling Zion, Bryce or even the Grand Canyon for beauty were it not for the fact real estate brokers have already staked a considerable claim on the area. However, most of the land is owned by the Forest Service, resulting in semi-wilderness butting up against shops, restaurants and outlet malls. Downtown Sedona is a cluster of shops, art galleries and hotels in the valley with Capitol Butte towering over the west end of town. The climate draws many wealthy retirees to the area while many of the trophy homes around Sedona are summer escapes for the rich and famous.

You'll notice Coffee Pot Rock, a well-known formation north of town in Oak Creek Canyon which was the backdrop for many westerns, in particular "Station West" ('48) with Dick Powell. The town's sprawling growth (now 15,000 or more) sadly prevents film crews from ever capturing certain scenes again such as when Dick Powell rides away at the end of that film with Coffeepot Rock in the background. That area is now beset by homes and condos.

North of Sedona, along Hwy. 89A, is Oak Creek Canyon, about 20 miles out of

Gorgeous Red Rock Crossing seen in "Broken Arrow" and many others.

town. The Canyon is a deep cut in the Colorado Plateau, about 2,500 feet at its maximum depth, stretching for nearly 15 miles. What makes it an oasis are the forests of green rising on either side of Oak Creek.

West and north of Sedona is the Red Rock country, mostly wilderness only a few miles out of town run by the Coconino National Forest. The Ranger station in town provides maps and suggestions for short hikes or lengthy excursions.

One of the most popular filming sites was Red Rock Crossing with magnificent Cathedral Rock in the background. Scenes from "Broken Arrow" ('51), "Copper Canyon" ('50), "Apache" ('54) and others were done here.

Sedona Chamber of Commerce—(800) 288-7336.

Sampling of Westerns Filmed in SEDONA

- Call of the Canyon ('23)—Richard Dix
- Last of the Duanes ('30)—George O'Brien
- Riders of the Purple Sage ('31)—George O'Brien
- Robber's Roost ('33)—George O'Brien
- Stormy ('35)—Noah Beery Jr.
- Texas Trail ('37)—William Boyd
- Billy the Kid ('41)—Robert Taylor
- Tall In the Saddle ('44)—John Wayne
- California ('46)—Ray Milland
- Angel and the Badman ('47)—John Wayne
- Cheyenne (aka Wyoming Kid) ('47)—Dennis Morgan
- Gunfighters ('47)—Randolph Scott
- Fabulous Texan ('47)—Bill Elliott
- Coroner Creek ('48) Randolph Scott
- Strawberry Roan ('48)—Gene Autry
- Albuquerque ('48)—Randolph Scott
- Blood On the Moon ('48)—Robert Mitchum
- Relentless ('48)—Robert Young
- Hellfire ('49)—Bill Elliott
- The Gunfighter ('50)—Gregory Peck
- Comanche Territory ('50)—Macdonald Carey
- Broken Arrow ('51)—James Stewart
- Flaming Feather ('51)—Sterling Hayden
- Indian Uprising ('52)—George Montgomery
- Half Breed ('52)—Robert Young
- Pony Soldier ('52)—Tyrone Power
- Gun Fury ('53)—Rock Hudson
- Johnny Guitar ('53)—Sterling Hayden
- Outlaw's Daughter ('54)—Bill Williams
- Shotgun ('55)—Sterling Hayden
- Last Wagon ('56)—Richard Widmark
- Yellowstone Kelly ('59)—Clint Walker
- Rounders ('65)—Glenn Ford/Henry Fonda
- Fire Creek ('68)—James Stewart
- Wild Rovers ('72)—William Holden

★★

Cottonwood Hotel

John Wayne and Gail Russell had a secret, but not so secret, romance during the filming of "Angel and the Badman" in 1946.

While filming around Sedona, the couple courted at the Cottonwood Hotel in Cottonwood some 25 miles south of Sedona. They were seen on occasion holding hands in the lobby and dress shop below the hotel where one employee recalled Wayne picking out a dress for Russell. There's memorabilia from the western in the hotel.

"Desert Fury" ('47) with Burt Lancaster was partially lensed in Old Town Cottonwood.

The set for Elvis Presley's "Stay Away, Joe" was built on Bypass 89A and later became a dancehall. It's now the Shepard of the Valley Lutheran Church. The Cottonwood Hotel and old jail from the prohibition era were also utilized.

The charming circa 1925 Cottonwood Hotel and Gift Shop is at 930 N. Main St. in Cottonwood on 89A between Prescott and Sedona. (520) 634-9455.

★★

Page

Warner Bros. erected an authentic looking $1 million western street on the shores of Lake Powell near Page for "Maverick" with Mel Gibson and James Garner. Locals can point out the precise spot.

Some scenes for Clint Eastwood's "Outlaw Josey Wales" were shot in the area also.

Page is in north-central Arizona near the Utah border.

★★

Painted Desert

The remnants of a mine set built for William Boyd's "The Painted Desert" (31) are still in existence at the Painted Desert off I-40 25 miles east of Holbrook. The desert stretches 150 miles from the Grand Canyon to Petrified Forest National Park and has an area of about 7,500 sq. miles, so you need to check with a park ranger for directions to the old site. Apparently, a special effects man used too much dynamite in one of the last scenes...not adequately testing the softness of the sandstone into which he placed the charges...thereby not only destroying the set but killing one of the extras and injuring several other people. Other scenes were shot in nearby Dinosaur Canyon and in Tuba City (north of Flagstaff, off Hwy. 89.)

Sampling of Westerns Filmed at **PAINTED DESERT**

- Painted Desert ('31)—William Boyd
- Stormy ('35)—Noah Beery Jr.
- Texas Trail ('37)—Hopalong Cassidy
- Virginia City ('40)—Errol Flynn
- California ('47)—Ray Milland
- A Distant Trumpet ('64)—Troy Donahue

★★

Andy Devine Museum

Andy Devine (1905-1977), Kingman's favorite son, was born in Flagstaff but grew up in Kingman when his family moved there in 1906.

Andy injured his larynx as a child when he fell on a curtain rod, giving him a distinct gravelly voice that served him well later in motion pictures.

Before entering films Andy was a pro football player in 1925 for the Los Angeles Angels, worked as a telephone lineman, lifeguard and news photographer.

By 1926 Andy was being featured in silent 2-reel comedies. He later appeared on Jack Benny's radio show. Earnestly beginning in feature films in 1931, few were westerns until 1939's "Stagecoach".

Andy is well remembered as Jingles P. Jones, Guy Madison's sidekick ("Hey, Wait for me, Wild Bill!"), on TV's "Wild Bill Hickok" (1951-1958).

In 1955 a street was named after him in Kingman on the "This is Your Life" TV

31

Portrait of Andy Devine that welcomes visitors to his Kingman museum.

program.

Andy appeared in many parades in Kingman during the annual Andy Devine Days Roundup (still held each September. 928-757-7919).

The Mohave Museum of History and Art devotes a large section of its 12,000 square feet to Andy Devine, exhibiting his

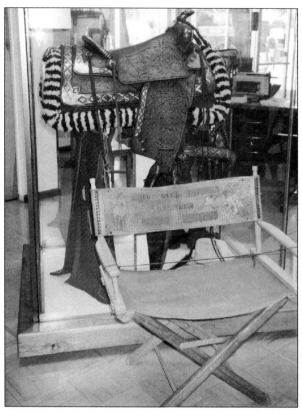

Andy Devine's saddle and extra-wide director's chair on display at the Mohave Museum.

saddle, oversized director's chair, dozens of family photos, movie stills, letters and much more. A large portrait of Andy by artist Mildred Wheeler, commissioned by Andy's widow, welcomes visitors to the museum at 400 W. Beale (right by Andy Devine Dr.). Open Monday-Friday, 9-5, 1-5 on weekends. (928) 753-3195.

★★

ARKANSAS

Jimmy Wakely Birthplace

Monogram B-western singing cowboy Jimmy Wakely was born in Mineola and went to school there before moving to Oklahoma where he began his singing career.

Mineola no longer exists, but to see Wakely's boyhood home, take the second drive to the left if you take the Mineola Road north from Hwy. 84 (between Umpire and Athens in west central Arkansas). There is a vacant mobile home on the site presently. A post office was also once there.

★★★

Gail Davis Childhood Home

We know Gail Davis as TV's "Annie Oakley". Gail's childhood home stands at 401 Colonial Court in Little Rock.

Gail's father, Dr. W. B. Grayson, was a noted doctor and when Gail was two her Dad was appointed head of the state health department causing the family to move to Little Rock. Gail once pointed out to Tom Nichols the two doors you see facing the street. The door on the left is the entrance to the living room, the door on the right led to Gail's bedroom in the front of the house that allowed her to sneak out during her teen years unnoticed by her parents.

★★★

Arkansas Walk of Fame

Gail ("Annie Oakley") Davis and Alan Ladd are the primary western names included in the Arkansas Walk of Fame in downtown Hot Springs (619 Central Ave.), Ladd's hometown.

The Walk of Fame is a series of brass plaques set in the sidewalk honoring Arkansans who have achieved national fame.

Glen ("True Grit") Campbell and Johnny Cash are also included. But where's Slim Andrews and Jimmy Wakely?

★★★

Stoby's

While in Hot Springs drop by Stoby's for a bite to eat. The booths of the restaurant include photos of Gene Autry and Roy Rogers. 5110 Hwy. 7 North (North of Hot Springs Village on Hwy. 7.)

★★★

Arkansas Entertainers Hall of Fame

The first western star, Broncho Billy Anderson, is enshrined at the Arkansas Entertainers Hall of Fame at the Pine Bluff Convention Center and Visitor's Bureau in downtown Pine Bluff. Along with Anderson are Julie Adams, Alan Ladd, singer Patsy Montana, Dick Powell, William Grant (composer of the "Gunsmoke" theme) and many other performers from Arkansas not associated with westerns.

Displays chronicle their careers with memorabilia belonging to the stars. Hours: Monday-Friday 9-5, Saturday and Sunday (seasonal—call.) (800) 536-7660.

★★★

Pine Bluff Mural

Film pioneer Freeman Owen and the first cowboy star, Broncho Billy Anderson, on the Pine Bluff mural.

While you're visiting the Arkansas Entertainers Hall of Fame in Pine Bluff, seek out the mural at 209 Main in the downtown area. It portrays Broncho Billy Anderson as well as Freeman Owen who perfected a sound-on-film process allowing movies to talk. Both grew up in Pine Bluff.

★★★

Daisy Air Rifle Museum

"It's a daisy!"

BB guns from around the world, some more than a century old, grace the display cases of the Air Rifle Museum in the Daisy Manufacturing factory in Rogers. Red Ryder, Buck Jones, Buzz Barton—they're all here in the Air Gun Museum which first opened in 1966.

Open weekdays, no charge. Rogers is in the very northwest corner of Arkansas, above Springdale on BR71.

★★★

CALIFORNIA

Edendale

Before there was Hollywood, there was Edendale. Hoot Gibson, in his memoir tape, stated, "I came back to Los Angeles (in 1910) and Selig Polyscope had just come into a town called Edendale at the time. They needed cowboys in their pictures. I did the first stunts out there."

Today, visitors who navigate the eastern part of Silver Lake should be aware they are traversing the crossroads of cinematic history. William Selig opened his mission-style studio at Clifford St. and Glendale Blvd. in 1910 and opened the gates to what would become the film capital of the world.

In the decade after Selig set up shop, half a dozen other film companies opened studios in Edendale, clustering on Branden, Aaron and Effie streets. A few blocks north, Teviot St. became Mixville after Tom Mix who established his operation there.

The Keystone Kops ran rampant on Effie St. and Glendale Blvd. Mack Sennett stayed in the area until 1928 when he moved to Studio City. By the '30s the studio had become a roller-skate palace. Later it became the Palace Dance Barn where Tex Williams and his Western Caravan held forth.

Today, the last remaining concrete structure is a public storage facility at 1712 Glendale Blvd.

But just drive or walk the streets of the area—you'll feel the history in the air.

★★★

Patriotic Hall

A bronze plaque in Audie Murphy's honor hangs in Patriotic Hall, a veteran's memorial building on South Figueroa St. in downtown Los Angeles. Dedicated in 1971, the plaque depicts a profile of Audie's head and his medal of honor, proclaiming him "the Most Decorated Soldier of World War II."

★★★

Sportsmen's Lodge

One of Hollywood's old time institutions is the Sportsmen's Lodge at 12825 Ventura Blvd. in Studio City. The coffee shop is still a meeting place for old timers, decorated with western star photos and one-sheets.

Dick Jones ("Buffalo Bill Jr.", "Range Rider") portrait in tile-art by Katie West at Sportsmen's Lodge.

A new western memorial wall in the patio section of the coffee shop was designed, engraved in granite and emblazoned in full color tiles by artist Katie West. The 8x30 ft. tile-art wall encompasses granite engravings of Monte Hale, Dick Jones, Jocko Mahoney, Sam Elliott, James Drury, Tom Selleck, Dale Robertson and Jon Locke. Above the tiles are other photo memorials to Richard Farnsworth, Burt Kennedy, Clayton Moore, George Montgomery, Iron Eyes Cody, Eddie Dean, Chuck Connors, Jocko Mahoney, Pat Buttram, Doug McClure, Ben Johnson and Denver Pyle. The wall is designed in honor of Jim Roberts' Roundup, also known as the pre-Golden Boot Party which is held poolside annually in August the day before the Golden Boot Awards.

Many other Hollywood functions are held here also, such as Pacific Pioneer Broadcasters meetings and honorariums and Michael Fitzgerald and Gary Bell's Hollywood Reunion (aka Jivin' Jacks and Jills Party). (818) 769-4700.

★★

Republic Studios

The 43-acre Republic Studio in north Hollywood arguably produced the best B-westerns during the movies' golden age. Located at 4024 Radford Avenue off Ventura Blvd. in Studio City, the San Fernando Valley thrill factory produced 386 series westerns and 66 serials, many of them classics, as well as a host of A-westerns and many B and A non-westerns during its comparatively brief history. Republic was home to Gene Autry, Roy Rogers, Bill Elliott, Don Barry, 3 Mesquiteers, John Wayne (for a period), Allan "Rocky" Lane, Monte Hale, Rex Allen, Rough Ridin' Kids and Sunset Carson.

Bordered on the south by Ventura Blvd., west by Radford Avenue, east by

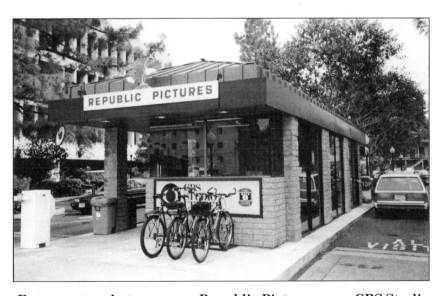

Entrance to what was once Republic Pictures, now CBS Studio Center. The sign with the Republic eagle was erected for a special luncheon tribute to seven of Republic's Sweethearts— Dale Evans, Peggy Stewart, Adele Mara, Adrian Booth, Vera Ralston, Ruth Terry and Helen Talbot.

Colfax Avenue, and north by the Los Angeles River (now long part of L.A.'s concrete aqueduct system), studio facilities, first constructed in 1928, were originally home to comedy king Mack Sennett. When Sennett went into bankruptcy in 1933, Mascot Pictures became a major tenant for two years. Then, in 1935, Herbert J. Yates, owner of Republic Film Laboratories and the American Record Company, joined with Mascot, Monogram and Liberty Pictures to form Republic Pictures Corporation. Its first two pictures, "Westward Ho" ('35) and "Tumbling Tumbleweeds" ('35), and stars John Wayne and Gene Autry, were instant hits and, in 1937, Yates assumed sole control of studio operations.

Over the years, Yates gradually added new sound stages. By 1950, the lot comprised many sound stages, two dubbing and musical scoring stages, a large carpentry/miniature building, scene docks and a blacksmith shop, as well as other facilities and many permanent exterior sets.

The '50s would be witness to Republic's decline and fall—a consequence of the rise of television, Herbert Yates' failure to move aggressively into TV production, and big-budget flops starring Yates' wife Vera Ralston, whom the mogul was obsessed with making into a big star caused Republic's B-western era to end with the early '54 release of Rex Allen's "Phantom Stallion." Although the studio's "Stories of the Century" series won an Emmy, Republic's other TV product was confined to "Adventures of Fu Manchu" and Rex Allen's "Frontier Doctor".

In 1959, Republic released its last western feature, "Plunderers of Painted Flats", and in May of that year Yates called it quits, leasing the studio to Lippert Pictures. CBS Television became the studio's principal lessee in 1963, renaming the facility CBS Studio Center. CBS purchased the property in April of 1967 and two years later built a four-story office building near the original Radford Avenue entrance to Republic. In July of 1982, CBS and 20th Century Fox entered a joint venture that included ownership and operation of the studio as CBS/Fox.

In the mid-'80s Fox sold its interest to Mary Tyler Moore. Then, in 1992, CBS acquired MTM's interest and the CBS Studio Center sign went up over the main gate once again. In 1995, the studio began construction of several new sound stages in an area north of the Los Angeles River occupied for years by a studio parking lot.

Western productions, including "Wanted Dead or Alive", "Tales of Wells Fargo" and color episodes of "Gunsmoke", figured prominently in studio productions for many years. In '67-'68, many of the sets on the western street were moved to a sound stage. A new, smaller, decidedly less impressive street was constructed roughly parallel to Colfax Ave. for the Stuart Whitman "Cimarron Strip" series. The opening scene to color "Gunsmoke" episodes gave viewers perhaps their last look at the western street of the Republic era; otherwise, that series, as well as "Big Valley" and others, mainly used the sound stage street exteriors and "Cimarron Strip" sets, including some remaining from the old days.

Shortly thereafter, the street fell victim to bulldozers, providing more space for production facilities. What of the great Duchess Ranch house/relay station, frequently seen on color "Gunsmoke" episodes but in later years tragically altered in appearance to satisfy whatever limited filming use it was expected to serve? It later became a storage shack for the studio's nursery or green department. A sad end to the most wonderful thrill factory of them all.

The lot is not open to tour, but you can at least see where the fabulous studio that gave us so much excitement once held forth. 4024 Radford Ave.

★★★

Beverly Garland Holiday Inn

Beverly Garland co-starred in westerns with Bill Elliott, Wayne Morris and Rory Calhoun and on TV with the Lone Ranger, Clint Eastwood, Jocko Mahoney, Robert Culp, Dale Robertson, James Arness, her good friend Robert Horton, Lloyd Bridges and several others.

The 255 room Beverly Garland Hotel (a Holiday Inn at 4222 Vineland Ave.) is widely known around the country as *the* place to say in North Hollywood. The idea to use her name was a mutual agreement with her husband, the late Fillmore Crank, when they bought the seven acre property from Gene Autry for $100,000 over 28 years ago. At that time the property was a treeless seven acre field overrun by chickens.

Special parking space reserved for Republic star Monte Hale at Beverly Garland's hotel.

The Beverly Garland features a beautiful courtyard, several meeting rooms (where the Hollywood Collectors and Celebrity Show is staged four times annually) and a very nice restaurant—outside of which you'll spot a reserved parking space for "Texas 9—Monte Hale". The restaurant entranceway features a photo montage of Whip Wilson, Tom Tyler and Ken Maynard.

Large photos of Beverly are situated throughout the hotel and lobby area. Souvenir T-shirts are on sale in the gift shop including a shirt with a one-sheet repro from her "Gunslinger."

Beverly herself welcomes you to the hotel on a special TV channel in your room which features clips from many of her films and TV series, including an episode of "Yancy Derringer."

For reservations, (800) 238-3759, (818) 980-8000.

★★★

Universal Studios

Universal's founder Carl Laemmle consolidated Imp, Bison 101 and several other companies to form Universal Pictures in 1912. In 1915, he bought a 410-acre chicken ranch in what was to become North Hollywood and built Universal City.

Western stars, both A and B, were a Universal staple—from the Duke, Jimmy Stewart and Jock Mahoney, to Hoot Gibson, Tom Mix, Buck Jones and Ken Maynard, to Bob Baker, Johnny Mack Brown and Tex Ritter, to Rod Cameron, Eddie Dew and Kirby Grant. In fact, the first filming on the lot apparently took place at what was to become the elaborate "Six Points, Texas" streets, the core of the studio's western sets.

Especially in the early days, production crews sometimes used location town sets, such as Kernville's western street. But most Universal titles used Six Points. As its name suggests, the Six Points set consisted of six streets running out from a square roughly like the spokes on a wheel. A large livery stable is perhaps the most recognizable Six Points set. Park Lake, a large pool, served as the western street dock. A large riverboat set was at the end of one street. Another set was a large Mexican village. A street identified on studio maps as Denver St. played Medicine Bow, Wyoming, on TV's "The Virgin-

Six Points western street on the Universal backlot, so named because six streets come together to form a town square. *(Photo by Ken Taylor).*

ian". West of Denver St. and the railroad set was the oft-seen Falls Lake. During the western feature and TV era, a fake mountain with dirt-filled roads sturdy enough for horseback riding served as a backdrop to the lake and also included a waterfall that could be activated at the call of a plotline.

In a 1946 merger, Universal became Universal-International and dismantled its B-western, B-feature and serial units, choosing to focus its assets entirely on higher budget titles. Financially, that move proved a near-disaster. But MCA (Music Corporation of America) eventually rode to the rescue.

In 1950, the talent agency giant formed its television arm, Revue Productions, and acquired space at Republic (now CBS Studio Center) on Radford Avenue in North Hollywood, where Revue began churning out dozens of TV series: "Tales of Wells Fargo," "The Deputy," "State Trooper," "Alfred Hitchcock Presents" and "Leave It to Beaver."

In 1959, MCA moved its productions to Universal, purchasing the lot and dubbing it Revue Studios. In 1964, Revue was renamed Universal City Studios and its TV production arm became Universal Television.

From 1950 to 1980 the company produced more than 200 series, among them such favorites as "The Virginian," "Wagon Train" and "Laramie." For "The Virginian", star James Drury recalls that the impressive Shiloh Ranch set was developed east of the Hollywood Freeway. In an effort to keep the freeway out of camera range and cut down on traffic noise, the studio built a 150-200-foot high berm, or hill, about 100 yards from the freeway. The hill served its purpose reasonably well. But the valley it created with adjacent hills on the lot also trapped smog and intense heat, making filming on the Shiloh spread, Drury remembers, uncomfortable at best.

Unfortunately, the roads, settings for many western and serial chases, are now paved and used mainly by the trams carrying thousands of riders daily over the lot on Universal's highly profitable studio tour, while the site of the Shiloh spread now hosts the tour parking lot. A 1990 fire destroyed four acres of sets (about 20 percent of the studio's backlot facades), but the Little Europe sets, scene for the "Frankenstein" flicks, among many others, escaped damage, as did the hillside residences used in countless sitcoms and, most important, the western and Mexican sets.

The studio tour is worth the price of admission for western, serial and TV fans. Enter from the south end of Lankershim Blvd. in N. Hollywood. 100 Universal City Plaza, Universal City. (818) 508-9600.

★★

King's Western Wear

The famous King's Western Wear of California is at 11450 Ventura Blvd. in Studio City. The store is decorated with autographed photos of the numerous movie and TV cowboys who shopped at King's since 1946 when it was located in Van Nuys.

★★

Nudie's Custom Java

Drop in to Nudie's Custom Java for java, tea, soups, sandwiches and Nudie Western Wear memorabilia. 11651 Riverside Dr. (at Colfax) in Studio City. (818) 753-9966.

Nudie custom tailored western wear for Roy Rogers, Gene Autry, Rex Allen, Duncan Renaldo and dozens more western players.

★★

Autry Museum of Western Heritage

The (Gene) Autry Museum of Western Heritage is truly preserving the past and the history of the West for future generations. Since the world class, tri-level museum opened

Kirby Grant and Gloria Winters' costumes worn on TV's "Sky King" as Uncle Sky and niece Penny.

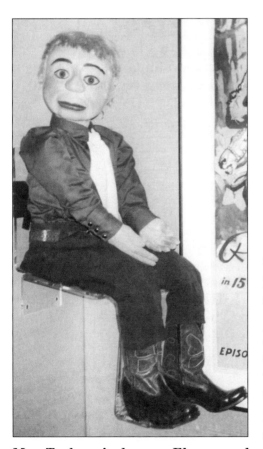

Max Terhune's dummy Elmer used in Three Mesquiteers and Range Busters B-westerns.

in November 1988, hundreds of thousands of people have passed through the entrance to the finest gathering of real and reel West artifacts ever imagined, over 60,000 objects.

This state of the art facility is truly a magnificent legacy to Gene Autry's love of the west. The superior staging of art and artifacts is at once obvious to the viewer. What is not so apparent, is the incomparable white glove care to which each artifact entering the museum is treated. The preservation, care and safety of the Autry is matchless.

Until you've been to the Autry, a thrill every western fan should experience, you cannot realize the scope of its many galleries. It is not just a loving memory to

Gene and other cowboys, but a fully developed history of the entire westward expansion. One trip alone cannot do the Autry justice.

For movie and TV fans, housed in the 'Spirit of Imagination' section are clothing, boots, guns, spurs and various items owned by Hoot Gibson, Tom Mix, Buck Jones, Ken Maynard, Bob Livingston, Tim Holt, Charles Starrett, Herb Jeffries, Tim McCoy, Max Terhune, Rex Allen, Ben Johnson, Carolina Cotton, Johnny Mack Brown, James Arness, Kirby Grant, John Bromfield, Jimmy Wakely, Gabe

A Gene Autry display at his world class museum.

Ward of the Hoosier Hot Shots, Monte Hale, Michael Landon, Gloria Winters, Noah Beery Jr., Wallace Beery, Rex Rossi, director Bob Totten, Patsy Montana, Hugh O'Brian, Steve McQueen and *many* others. The mind boggles at the artifacts.

It boggles ever further to witness the material not yet on display currently housed in the enormous lower floor basement collections warehouse. As well cared for as exhibits on display are hundreds of items of clothing worn by Gene Autry, Clayton Moore, Roy Rogers, Kirby Grant, Jimmy Wakely, Peggy Stewart, etc.; saddles belonging to Fred Thomson and Ken Maynard; the original Melody Ranch firewagon and other items from Melody Ranch; hats, boots, guns, gunbelts (Duncan Renaldo)—too much to describe.

The Autry has never been a stagnant once-you've-seen-it-why-go-back museum. Its exhibits are ever evolving. The Autry has film series, lectures on the west, workshops, western music concerts in the Wells Fargo Theatre; an excellent research center and a well-stocked museum store.

The entire staff of the Autry is doing an absolutely magnificent job. Your window into the west is in Griffith Park, 4700 Western Heritage Way, adjacent to the L.A. Zoo, where I-5 and State Route 134 meet. Open Tuesday-Sunday, 10-5, Thursdays til 8. (323) 667-2000. Wonderful gift shop with many Gene

(L-R) Dale Robertson outfit and gunbelt from "Tales of Wells Fargo", Clint Eastwood shirt from "Rawhide", John Bromfield outfit from "U. S. Marshal" and Hugh O'Brian's gunbelt (with a holster for the Buntline special) in the center foreground.

Michael Landon's gunbelt used on "Bonanza" for 14 years.

Autry related items.

An impressive, magnificent bronze of Gene, playing his guitar sitting beside Champion, greets you in the courtyard of the Autry Museum. Artist DeL'Esprie spent three years creating the magnificent work and was paid $300,000.

Larger than life bronze of Gene Autry and Champion greets you in the courtyard of the Autry Museum.

★★

Griffith Observatory

The very first film to use Griffith Observatory in Griffith Park was Gene Autry's "Phantom Empire" serial in 1935, filmed the year construction was completed. It stood in for the underground city of Murania. Gene did battle with the baddies on various exterior

walkways and steps and against the backdrop of the facility's copper roof and art deco wall.

In 1912, land speculator Griffith J. Griffith offered the city of Los Angeles $100,000 to build an observatory on the 3,015 acre park property he had donated to the city in 1896. However, by 1912 Griffith had served a year in San Quentin for shooting out his wife's eye during a drunken argument, so Los Angeles city fathers would accept no gift from the convicted felon.

After his death, however, a trust the philanthropist had established turned his dream into reality on the slope of a park mountain. Construction began in December 1933 and was completed seventeen months later at a cost of over $655,000. The facility is a huge concrete structure topped by three

Griffith Observatory stood in for the underground city of Murania in Gene Autry's "Phantom Empire" serial.

copper-clad domes, the largest and most familiar a hundred feet across and the smaller two each 30 feet wide.

Griffith Observatory can also be seen in many non-westerns such as "Rebel Without a Cause", "Superman" TV show, "War of the Colossal Beast" and the Republic serial "Purple Monster Strikes" ('45). 2800 Observatory Rd. in Griffith Park.

★★

Gene Autry Memorial Interchange

The intersection of the Golden State (I-5) and the Ventura (134) freeways was re-named the Gene Autry Memorial Interchange at dedication ceremonies September 29, 1999, following a measure passed by the California Senate. Jackie Autry unveiled the new highway sign. Monte and Joanne Hale were in attendance along with city and state dignitaries as the children's chorus from Castelar Elementary School sang "Back In the Saddle."

★★

Gene Autry Cutout

A life-size two-dimensional cutout figure of Gene Autry greets passengers at the Burbank Airport Southwest terminal. Several celebrity cutouts (bolted to the walls) rein-forces the fact the San Fernando Valley boasts a variety of entertainment. The photo of Gene (circa 1939) stepping off a train was originally supplied to Gene Autry Entertain-ment by longtime Autry devotee, Lillian Spencer. A plaque beneath the figure details Gene's five stars on the Walk of Fame.

On Hollywood Way off I-5 in Burbank.

★★

Gene Autry burial site at Forest Lawn.

Gene Autry Burial Plot

Gene Autry was laid to rest October 2, 1998, in a custom-made western suit, beside his first wife, Ina, at Forest Lawn cemetery with several personal items—his pilot's license, American League baseball pass, a copy of "The Showman's Prayer", his favorite hard candy, a tiny stuffed teddy bear he liked and pictures of his special friends. Sheltering Hills, Lot 1048. Forest Lawn, Hollywood Hills, 6300 Forest Lawn Dr., Glendale. Open 8-5, 7 days a week.

★★

Warner Bros. Studios

The history of Warner Bros. studio began, in a sense, in early 1905, when Harry Warner established a 90-seat nickelodeon in Newcastle, Pennsylvania, and brought brothers Sam, Abe and Jack into the business. Soon the brothers Warner were involved in film distribu-tion and, in 1913, moved into film production with the formation of Warner Features.

After World War I, they bought a ranch off Sunset Blvd. and built their first studio. Incorporated as Warner Bros. in 1923, the company released 14 pictures that year, including the first in the Rin Tin Tin series.

In 1925, the brothers acquired Vitagraph and began experimenting with sound. Achieving instant success, they released "The Jazz Singer" in 1927 and in July 1928, "Lights of New York", the first all-talking motion picture. That same year they acquired a theater circuit with 250 screens and also bought First National Pictures, including its 135-acre Burbank studio and back lot.

In 1926, Warner Bros. had also purchased a studio ranch in Calabasas, about 20 miles west of Los Angeles, on property now south of the Ventura Fwy. between Los Virgenes Road and Lake Calabasas and occupied largely by the Calabasas Country Club. The 2,800-acre Warner studio ranch in Calabasas featured rolling hills and scattered trees. Its many permanent sets included a stockade fort, a Mexican hacienda seen in "The Lash" ('30) and "Ride Him, Cowboy" ('32), the first entry in John Wayne's WB B-western series, and a western street set seen in such big budget features as Errol Flynn's "Dodge City" ('39) and Gary Cooper's "Springfield Rifle" ('52), which also featured the fort set. That street was also used for several entries in Dick Foran's short-lived B-series for the studio.

The Burbank lot also included many permanent exterior sets, including New York and Midwestern streets, which are still there, a tenement street, English, Norwegian and Viennese streets and an ocean liner/pier set.

Distinguishing the ranch western street set from that on the lot in WB films and TV series was not easy, but occasionally the rolling hills of the Calabasas area could be spotted in the background of street scenes shot at the ranch, as in "Springfield Rifle."

Warner Bros. sold its Calabasas property in the '60s and a fire destroyed the studio movie western set during the filming of "Gremlins" ('84), leaving only a livery stable, which now stands next to Warner Bros.' Midwestern street. The back lot also included a Mexican set seen in the "Sugarfoot" episodes "Outlaw Island" and "Canary Kid, Inc.," among others.

In the '50s the studio began to build sets in a wooded area along the studio's southeastern boundary. Thereafter known as "The Jungle," part of that area became, in 1958, the site for a second studio western town to be used primarily in TV productions. Constructed for the "Lawman" series with John Russell and known as Laramie Street after that series' Laramie, Wyoming, locale, the set is still standing and its general outline, if not its specific facades, remains today much as it did in Warner Bros.' TV-western heyday. It has played host not only to "Lawman" ('58-'62) but also to "Cheyenne" ('55-'63), "Maverick" ('57-'62), "Sugarfoot" ('57-'61), "Colt .45" ('57-'60), "Bronco"

Laramie Street on the Warner Bros. backlot tour.

('58-'62) and "The Dakotas" ('63) in the old days and "Adventures of Brisco County, Jr." ('93-'94) in recent times. With a unique arrangement of streets, the Laramie set could pose as two or three or more towns in a single TV episode.

The farmhouse and general store sets for "The Waltons" ('72-'81) were situated in woods north of the Laramie set and scenes for that series also occasionally used the Laramie street as well as Warner Bros.' Midwestern and New York streets.

Saloon on Laramie Street at Warner Bros.

Western TVers and features sometimes used the studio's Midwestern street. John Wayne's "The Shootist" ('76) gave prominent display to a house on that set and two "Sugarfoot" entries set in San Francisco ("Highbinder" and "Fernando") used houses on the Midwestern set. With the demise of the TV western in the '60s and early '70s, Laramie Street was used less frequently, but still makes an occasional appearance in TV shows, commercials and even features.

No doubt by popular demand, Laramie Street is now a regular part of Warner Bros.' excellent schedule of small-group tours that also includes a visit to the studio's fine and growing Warner Bros. museum.

Take Vineland Ave. in North Hollywood to Riverside Dr., Riverside east to Hollywood Way and Hollywood Way south to the Warner Bros. gate.

★★

Warner Bros. Museum

The Warner Bros. Museum opened in 1996 on the lot of their Burbank headquarters. The 7,000 square foot, two-story museum contains more than 650 artifacts and is the first such collection to be created by a studio. Visitors will see costumes, props, letters, production notes and much more.

Corporate archivist Leith Adams told us about some of the items housed in a special western exhibit: John Wayne's buckskin shirt from "Hondo", his hat from "Rio Bravo", the rifle he used in "Rio Bravo," "Searchers" and "Red River"...the one with the rounded-out lever so Wayne could cock it in motion, Wayne's chaps from "Red River," "Searchers" and others, a stove and chair from "Rio Bravo" and personal letters from Wayne revealing the intelligence and humor of the man. Much of this is on loan to WB from Michael Wayne.

There's also Gary Cooper's shirt from "Distant Drums," Randolph Scott's cavalry shirt from "Thunder Over the Plains", Alan Ladd's costume from "Iron Mistress" along with

Ladd's 1935 payroll records when he started as a grip on the lot for $1 an hour.

Other exhibits encompass WB's first fifty years (1919-1969) in animation, musicals, James Dean, "Casablanca" etc. Visitors view film clips on TV monitors documenting the artifacts on display.

Eventually, the next twenty-five years of WB history will be unveiled as well as Warner's TV history. Be aware, these displays are subject to change from time to time.

The museum is the first stop on the two hour 15 minute WB studio tour. For western fans, the highlight of the 40 acre backlot tour is Laramie St., one of the last standing western towns on a studio lot.

Guests can walk the dusty streets, peek inside the jail, and order a drink in the same saloon where Will Hutchins, Clint Walker and Ty Hardin bellied up to the bar.

Advance reservations are required, (818) 954-1744.

★★★

Tom Mix Hunting Lodge

The remains of a 8,800 sq. ft. hunting lodge once owned by Tom Mix are at the corner of Lookout Mountain and Laurel Canyon (2401 Laurel Canyon Blvd.). Laurel Canyon is a busy, narrow, winding street. You come upon the corner unexpectedly and will need to park on Lookout Mountain or another side street and walk back to view the Mix property.

The hunting lodge was built in 1915. An underground tunnel built for the cabin still

Remnants of a once gorgeous fireplace inside the Tom Mix hunting lodge.

exists but is now blocked at both ends for safety purposes after the 18 room, lavish, log cabin became a crash pad for the human debris of the '60s social explosion.

Inhabited in the '70s by non-rent-paying street-level pilgrims, the lodge burned down when a deadbeat banjo player fell asleep with a lighted cigarette in his hand shortly after sunrise on Halloween morning, 1981. Losses were set at $210,000.

According to actor Jan Merlin, who then lived nearby, the lot where the lodge stood served as a Christmas tree lot for several years. All of the area is in a badly tended overgrown state these days. The Mix place is surrounded by a chain link fence, but can often be found open. You'll have to check with caretakers on the premises to be able to look around.

Incidentally, a legendary meeting between Tom Mix and Wyatt Earp took place at the Laurel Canyon Tavern up Laurel Canyon Blvd. The tavern burned in 1923 and was rebuilt in 1928 and exists today as the Caiote Restaurant and Canyon Country Store. Parts of the original foundation are still visible.

★★★

Tom Mix Homes

There are several former homes of Tom Mix which look much the same today as they did in the '20s.

5845 Carrollton Way—a modest frame dwelling.
3456 Floyd Terrace, between Universal and Burbank Studios.
1024 Summit Dr., Beverly Hills (The mansion can only be approached by a private
   drive.).
24248 Walnut, Newhall.

★★

Museum of TV and Radio

The west coast installation of the Museum of TV and Radio opened in 1996 at 465 Beverly Dr. in Beverly Hills on the corner of Beverly Drive and Santa Monica Blvd. The east coast museum was established in New York in 1976 at 47-50 St./Rockefeller Center. Both provide access to an extensive collection of classic TV and radio programs, apparently relying more on big hit shows than lesser known and cult favorites. Don't go expecting to locate every episode of, for instance, "Sgt. Preston" on radio and TV. One member of Pacific Pioneers Broadcasters told me the museum centers much more on TV than it does radio. How much western material contained is unknown at this time. Beverly Hills hours Wednesday-Sunday Noon-5, Thursday evening til 9. New York hours Tuesday-Sunday Noon-6, til 8 on Thursday, 9 on Friday.

★★

Ellison Drive

Ellison Drive in Beverly Hills was named for James (Jimmy) Ellison who, as a developer following his film work, built many of the homes in the area. Ellison was Hopalong Cassidy's sidekick in the early Hoppys, starred in "The Plainsman" and in the '50s co-starred in westerns with Johnny Mack Brown and Russell Hayden.

★★

Franklin Lake

"Bonanza" watchers will recognize serene Franklin Lake as an oft-used location. TV's "How the West Was Won" and especially "The Andy Griffith Show" used it as well. Seen in these "Bonanza" episodes: "The Savage" ('60), "Star Crossed" ('68), "A Dream To Dream" ('68), "Little Girl Lost" ('68), "My Friend, My Enemy" ('69), "Old Friends" ('69) and "A Place to Hide" ('71).

Go west on Sunset Blvd. from Hollywood. Turn right on Beverly Dr. where Beverly Dr. and Coldwater Canyon Dr. meet. Turn right on Franklin Canyon Dr. Go past the lower Franklin Canyon reservoir. At the upper reservoir (Sooky Goldman Nature Center) turn right and follow the road until you reach the parking lot.

★★

Beverly Hills Hotel

Your California tour isn't complete without lunch at the exquisite Beverly Hills Hotel which saw a $100 million remodeling in 1995 by the current owner, the Sultan of Brunei, one of the richest men in the world. It has long been "The" place to dine for the Hollywood elite.

Angie Dickinson says it was at the hotel where she got her first kiss from the man who later became her husband, Burt Bacharach...Robert Culp ("Trackdown") admitted the hotel's Polo Lounge was his favorite "watering hole," adding, "but I don't do any watering anymore." ...Ernie Borgnine recalled an incident at the Polo Lounge when he challenged John Wayne with, "Are you afraid to work with *real* actors?" ...Robert Stack reminded he was one of the polo players who bent an elbow at the Polo Lounge after matches at Will Rogers Polo Field. In fact, it is said the lounge got it's name because Will and his friends used to stop at the hotel restaurant for drinks after their polo games at the ranch.

9641 Sunset Blvd., Beverly Hills. (310) 276-2251.

★★

Will Rogers State Historic Park

Will Rogers lived at what is now Will Rogers State Historic Park until his death in 1935 after which time the family home was donated to the state of California by his widow in 1944.

Tours of the historic sprawling ranch house are available and you can take long walks around the beautifully landscaped polo grounds and stable area. The park is also a trailhead for hiking into the Santa Monica Mountains.

Polo matches still take place on the grounds that Rogers installed and played on with friends like Big Boy Williams.

Personal belongings of Will and his family are just as they left them. The home is filled with western art (Charles M. Russell, etc.), souvenirs, photographs, books and Indian artifacts.

Open 8am-sunset daily; house tours hourly on the half hour, 10:30-4:30. Gift shop adjoining. 1501 Will Rogers State Park Road in Pacific Palisades off Sunset Blvd. (310) 454-8212.

Will Rogers home at what is now a state historic park.

★★

Hoppyland Amusement Park

Hoppyland Amusement Park once stood at 400 Washington St., in Venice. The 80 acre site had picnic grounds, a baseball diamond and more than 20 thrill rides. Boat races and water ski shows were held at the 17 acre Lake Los Angeles, a remnant of the Ballona Wetlands (later Marina del Rey) where film pioneer Thomas Ince once shot silent western films in the teens. Hoppyland opened in 1951 and closed in 1954 as Hoppymania began to fizzle out with the advent of the Davy Crockett boom.

Long ago torn down and replaced with modern buildings.

★★★★★★★★★★★★★★★★★★★★★★★★★★★★★★

John Wayne Statue

Western legend John Wayne rides his horse in an excellent larger-than-life bronze statue (approximately 25 ft. tall) directly in front of the Washington Mutual offices at the corner of Wilshire Blvd. and La Cienega Blvd. (8484 Wilshire.) This was formerly the Great Western Savings Bank for whom the Duke was a spokesperson on radio and TV commercials for several years.

John Wayne bronze on Wilshire Blvd.

★★★

Murals

Artist Kent Twitchell specializes in larger-than-life photo-realist portraits of people, often celebrities. He was active in the creation of the Mural Conservancy of Los Angeles and serves on its advisory board.

Perhaps Twitchell's most unusual work is the 40 x 56 ft. Holy Trinity With the Virgin. The three standing figures wearing white scientific lab coats are meant to be Mother Mary, God and Jesus Christ. As models, the artist chose three TV personalities who represent traditional values—Jan Clayton (as Mother Mary) played the mother on "Lassie." Clayton

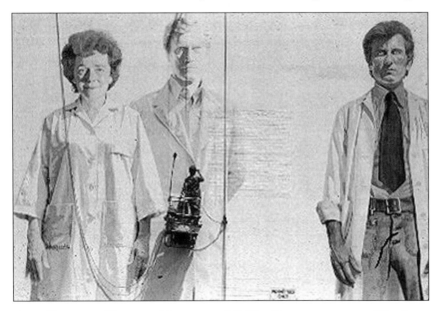

Jan Clayton, Clayton Moore and Billy Gray represent Mother Mary, God and Jesus Christ on Kent Twitchell's mural at Otis/Parsons School of Art.

Moore (God) was the "Lone Ranger" and Billy Gray (Jesus) was the son, Bud, on "Father Knows Best." Located at 2401 Wilshire Blvd. (near Carondelet St.) on the exterior of the Otis/Parsons School of Art and Design.

Twitchell also did a 20 x 15 ft. portrait in blue of Steve McQueen on the exterior of a building on 1151 Union St. near 12th.

An 11 x 45 ft. mural of character actor Strother Martin is the southwest exterior of a building at 5200 Fountain Ave. at Kingsley Dr. in East Hollywood.

★★★

Tom Mix Stutz Racing Car

Tom Mix's 1915 Stutz racing car, seen in Tom's "The Road Demon" ('21), is on display at the Peterson Automotive Museum in Los Angeles. The car was once featured on an AMC "Hollywood Hot Wheels" documentary.

The curator told us Leo Carrillo's convertible (with steer horns on the hood) was currently (December '01) on loan to them but not on display. That car usually resides with the Imperial Palace auto collection in Las Vegas, Nevada. (702) 794-3174.

6060 Wilshire Blvd. (at Fairfax). Open 10-6 Tuesday-Sunday. (323) 964-6331.

★★★

Hollywood Walk of Fame

One of the most popular and free things to do when you're in Hollywood is to walk along Hollywood Blvd. and Vine St. and check out the 2,150 stars honored along the 41 block Walk of Fame whose gateway begins at LaBrea and Hollywood Blvd. and goes east 18 blocks to Gower St. with stars on both sides of Hollywood Blvd. The Walk of Fame is also on Vine St. going from Yucca St. to Sunset Blvd. (about 3 blocks).

In 1958 the Hollywood Chamber of Commerce voted to memorialize stars past and present on Hollywood Blvd. Joanne Woodward, Burt Lancaster, Preston Foster, Olive Borden, director Edward Sedgwick and Louise Fazenda were the elite group of six selected from a list of over 1,000 personalities to begin the process—representing old and new. Within 16 months 1,558 luminaries had been forever immortalized in one sweeping, continuing installation. The official dedication took place on February 8, 1960. Eight years passed before a new star was placed into the terrazzo walkway.

The Walk of Fame has five categories for inclusion—motion pic-

Dick Jones star on Hollywood Walk of Fame.

ture, TV, recording, radio and live theatre (which includes rodeo).

Of the 2,150 stars recognized, most are honored in only one category, although some have two. Only a few have three or four, but Gene Autry is the only star to be honored with all five categories. Gene is also the only star to reproduce the stars around the base of the life size Gene Autry statue at Edison International Field.

There is a walking tour booklet for the Hollywood Walk of Fame listing all the stars honored. It's available free from the Hollywood Chamber of Commerce at 7018 Hollywood Blvd. (323) 469-8311.

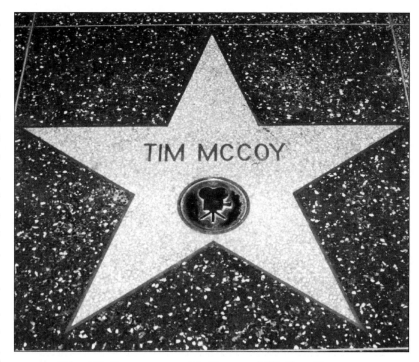

Tim McCoy star on Hollywood Walk of Fame.

In addition to the primary western stars listed on the following page, many stars who worked sporadically in westerns are honored, such as Barbara Britton, David Brian, Lloyd Bridges, Judy Canova, Macdonald Carey, David Carradine, Jeff Chandler, Jan Clayton, James Coburn, Spade Cooley, Arlene Dahl, Cecil B. DeMille, Dan Duryea, John Ericson, Rhonda Fleming, Texas Guinan, Alan Hale, Barbara Hale, Jon Hall, Stuart Hamblen, Howard Hawks, Charlton Heston, Marsha Hunt, Walter Huston, Pee Wee King, Pinky Lee, Joan Leslie, Burt Lancaster, A. C. Lyles, Vaughn Monroe, Jack Mulhall, Paul Newman, Maureen O'Hara, Gregory Peck, House Peters Sr., Snub Pollard, Mala Powers, Jane Russell, Tom Selleck, James Stewart, Barry Sullivan, Kent Taylor, Robert Taylor, Ernest Tubb, Richard Webb, Richard Widmark, Jane Withers and others.

★★

Here is a list of the *primary* western stars included in your walking tour and their locations.

Art Acord	1709 Vine St.	Raymond Hatton	1708 Vine St.
Rex Allen	6821 Hollywood Blvd.	Gabby Hayes	1724 Vine St., 6427 Hollywood Blvd.
Broncho Billy Anderson	1651 Vine St.	Earl Holliman	6901 Hollywood Blvd.
Michael Ansara	6666 Hollywood Blvd.	Jack Holt	6313 Hollywood Blvd.
Richard Arlen	6755 Hollywood Blvd.	Anne Jeffreys	1501 Vine St.
James Arness	1751 Vine St.	Ben Johnson	7083 Hollywood Blvd.
Gene Autry	6384, 6520, 6644, 6667, 7000 Hollywood Blvd.	Buck Jones	6834 Hollywood Blvd.
Gene Barry	6555 Hollywood Blvd.	Dick Jones	7042 Hollywood Blvd.
Warner Baxter	6284 Hollywood Blvd.	Victor Jory	6605 Hollywood Blvd.
William Beaudine	1777 Vine St.	Alan Ladd	1601 Vine St.
Noah Beery Jr.	7021, 7047 Hollywood Blvd.	Michael Landon	1500 Vine St.
Monte Blue	6290 Hollywood Blvd.	Guy Madison	6333, 6933 Hollywood Blvd.
Ward Bond	6933 Hollywood Blvd.	Lee Majors	6931 Hollywood Blvd.
Bill Boyd	6101 Hollywood Blvd.	Ken Maynard	6751 Hollywood Blvd.
William Boyd	1734 Vine St.	Doug McClure	7065 Hollywood Blvd.
Walter Brennan	6501 Hollywood Blvd.	Joel McCrea	6241, 6901 Hollywood Blvd.
Charles Bronson	6901 Hollywood Blvd.	Tim McCoy	1600 Vine St.
Harry Joe Brown	1777 Vine St.	Steve McQueen	6834 Hollywood Blvd.
Johnny Mack Brown	6101 Hollywood Blvd.	Robert Mitchum	6240 Hollywood Blvd.
Smiley Burnette	6125 Hollywood Blvd.	Tom Mix	1708 Vine St.
Pat Buttram	6382 Hollywood Blvd.	George Montgomery	6301 Hollywood Blvd.
Rory Calhoun	7007 Hollywood Blvd.	Clayton Moore	6914 Hollywood Blvd.
Rod Cameron	1720 Vine St.	Audie Murphy	1601 Vine St.
Yakima Canutt	1500 Vine St.	Hugh O'Brian	6613 Hollywood Blvd.
Harry Carey	1521 Vine St.	Dave O'Brien	6251 Hollywood Blvd.
Harry Carey Jr.	6363 Vine St.	George O'Brien	6201 Hollywood Blvd.
Leo Carrillo	1517, 1635 Vine St.	Jack Perrin	1777 Vine St.
Andy Clyde	6758 Hollywood Blvd.	Denver Pyle	7083 Hollywood Blvd.
Iron Eyes Cody	6655 Hollywood Blvd.	Vera Ralston	1752 Vine St.
Chuck Connors	6838 Hollywood Blvd.	Duncan Renaldo	1680 Vine St.
Gary Cooper	6243 Hollywood Blvd.	Tex Ritter	6631 Hollywood Blvd.
Buster Crabbe	6901 Hollywood Blvd.	Dale Robertson	6500 Hollywood Blvd.
Gail Davis	6385 Hollywood Blvd.	Roy Rogers	1620, 1733, 1752 Vine St.
Jim Davis	6290 Hollywood Blvd.	Will Rogers	6401, 6608 Hollywood Blvd.
Andy Devine	6258, 6366 Hollywood Blvd.	Gilbert Roland	6730 Hollywood Blvd.
Richard Dix	1608 Vine St.	Cesar Romero	6615 Hollywood Blvd., 1719 Vine St.
Jimmy Dodd	1600 Vine St.	Henry Rowland	6328 Hollywood Blvd.
Buddy Ebsen	1765 Vine St.	Randolph Scott	6243 Hollywood Blvd.
Dale Evans	6638 Hollywood Blvd., 1737 Vine St.	Jay Silverheels	6538 Hollywood Blvd.
Dustin Farnum	6635 Hollywood Blvd.	Sons Of The Pioneers	6845 Hollywood Blvd.
William Farnum	6322 Hollywood Blvd.	Milburn Stone	6823 Hollywood Blvd.
Dick Foran	1600 Vine St.	Gale Storm	6119 Hollywood Blvd., 1519, 1680 Vine St.
Scott Forbes	1650 Vine St.	Forrest Tucker	6385 Hollywood Blvd.
John Ford	1640 Vine St.	Elena Verdugo	1709 Vine St.
Glenn Ford	6933 Hollywood Blvd.	Jimmy Wakely	1680 Vine St.
Robert Fuller	6608 Hollywood Blvd.	Clint Walker	1505 Vine St.
Beverly Garland	6601 Hollywood Blvd.	John Wayne	1541 Vine St.
James Garner	6927 Hollywood Blvd.	Dennis Weaver	6822 Hollywood Blvd.
Hoot Gibson	1765 Vine St.	Stuart Whitman	7083 Hollywood Blvd.
Don Haggerty	6140 Hollywood Blvd.	Bill Williams	6145 Hollywood Blvd.
William S. Hart	6363 Hollywood Blvd.	Tex Williams	6412 Hollywood Blvd.
John Hart	6432 Hollywood Blvd.	Marie Windsor	1549 Vine St.

Grauman's Chinese Theatre

(L-R) Pvt. Inga Boberg, John Wayne and Sid Grauman at the Duke's foot and handprinting at Grauman's Chinese Theatre.

Grauman's Chinese Theatre in Hollywood is famous for the scores of celebrity foot and hand prints in cement outside the theatre. The tradition started in 1927 (when the theatre was opened by founder Sid Grauman) purely by accident when silent screen star Norma Talmadge accidentally stumbled into the fresh cement that had been poured for a sidewalk out front. The first "official" prints were on April 15, 1927. Now, close to 200 foot and hand prints are in the Forecourt of the Stars which draws around 2,000,000 tourists a year, second only to Disneyland. In 1973, the late theatre exhibitor, Ted Mann (Rhonda Fleming's husband) became sole owner of Grauman's, renaming it Mann's Chinese.

Among the celebrities in the forecourt are a number who are western stars: Gene Autry and Champ, Bill (William S.) Hart, John Wayne, Roy Rogers and Trigger, Tom Mix and Tony, Gary Cooper, Clint Eastwood, Barbara Stanwyck, James Stewart, Rhonda Fleming (of course!), Alan Ladd and Steve McQueen.

The theatre is in the 6900 block of Hollywood Blvd.

★★

Debbie Reynolds Hollywood Motion Picture Collection

In Debbie Reynolds' words, "It's a dream come true." The (literally) tons of movie memorabilia she has carefully collected since 1970 now have a permanent home at the Debbie Reynolds Hollywood Motion Picture Collection on the top floor penthouse at the all-new $615 million block-long Hollywood and Highland Complex.

Debbie's collection, for which she's paid hundreds of thousands of dollars over the years, was so large that only a fraction of it was ever displayed at her now-defunct Las Vegas hotel which only had 6,000 square feet of exhibition space. Her new location has 20,000 square feet.

Over the years, Debbie bought prop and costume treasures galore from the MGM, 20th Century Fox and Columbia auctions. Managed by Debbie's son Todd Fisher, the Collection, valued conservatively at $30 million, consists of more than 3,400 costumes, sets and props from over 650 motion pictures and/or TV series. The memorabilia represents all film eras from silent epics like "Ben Hur" and "Mark of Zorro" to musicals like "Singin' In the Rain" and the more recent "Godfather" gangster classic.

Besides the permanent displays (which will rotate as there is simply too much to display at any one time), three uniquely designed theatres have been created to display various items along with corresponding clips from the movies in which they appeared.

As to western items, Todd tells us they have two Richard Dix costumes from "Cimarron" as well as one of Glenn Ford's from the remake; an elaborate collection of costumes worn by Debbie, Gregory Peck, John Wayne, James Stewart and Carroll Baker in "How the West Was Won"; a Cesar Romero Cisco Kid costume; items from "Butch Cassidy and the Sundance Kid"; Henry Fonda and Edna Mae Oliver costumes from "Drums Along the Mohawk"; Marilyn Monroe's costume from "A Ticket To Tomahawk"; Betty Grable's dance hall costume from "Beautiful Blonde From Bashful Bend"; Douglas Fairbanks'

Debbie Reynolds amidst the thousands of items of clothing and props on display at her new museum.

"Mark of Zorro" costume; and other costumes from "Four For Texas", "Giant", "River of No Return", "Gone With the Wind", "Annie Get Your Gun", "Sheepman", "Brigham Young", "Raintree County", "Outcasts of Poker Flats" and the "Wild Wild West" TV series.

Todd says they have a 28,000 square foot warehouse where all the material is stored. Included is an enormous paper collection of six-sheets, one-sheets, lobby cards. Then there are the artifacts and props.

Debbie and her children, Todd and Carrie Fisher, are truly dedicated to bringing this collection into the open at Hollywood and Highland for the public to enjoy.

Across the street from Mann's Chinese, Hollywood and Highland's massive Egyptian-themed arch connects the 75 varied retail shops and restaurants as well as a large-event ballroom. Also located here is the glitzy new 3,300 seat Kodak Theatre, the new home for the Academy Awards.

Certain to be a major stop on your Hollywood tour. Opening in 2003.

★★★

Hollywood Roosevelt Hotel

In the middle of the shabbiness of Hollywood Blvd. in Hollywood, standing like a beacon beckoning us back to the glory days of old Hollywood, is the historic Hollywood Roosevelt Hotel, 7000 Hollywood Blvd. (323) 466-7000.

Located just a block west of the Chinese Theatre, the hotel was founded in 1927 by a syndicate of Hollywood luminaries to house east coast movie makers who were working on the west coast. Will Rogers was on hand for the inaugural celebration. The hotel's Blossom Room hosted the first ever Academy Awards on May 19, 1929.

The hotel was featured in 1988's "Sunset" with Bruce Willis as Tom Mix and James Garner as Wyatt Earp attending the first Academy Awards.

The Roosevelt went into a decline in the '50s and was nearly torn down in the '80s before the Radisson chain rescued the historic site and set out to restore it to its former glory. Armed with original blueprints and historic photos, they undertook a $35 million renovation.

Stepping off the Boulevard's dirty sidewalk into the Roosevelt's elegant lobby is like stepping back in time. Climb the tiled stairway to the upstairs mezzanine and you'll find historic photos lining the walls and the original movie camera used to film "Gone With the Wind" on display. There's a rumor the ghost of Montgomery Clift ("Red River") haunts the 9th floor (suite #928) where he used to pace the halls back in '53 learning his lines for "From Here to Eternity".

★★

Hollywood Wax Museum

Cowboys standing tall at the Hollywood Wax Museum include Roy Rogers, John Wayne, Clint Eastwood, Butch and Sundance (Paul Newman and Robert Redford), Will Rogers, and Ben, Hoss and Little Joe (Lorne Greene, Dan Blocker, Michael Landon) from "Bonanza" (Pernell Roberts never grants his likeness. Interestingly, Greene told the museum if Roberts' likeness was to be included, he wouldn't grant them *his* permission!) Kevin Costner from "Dances with Wolves" is also included.

Open Sunday-Thursday 10-Midnight, Friday-Saturday 10-1am. 6767 Hollywood Blvd. in Hollywood. (323) 462-5991.

★★

The Lasky-DeMille barn used in "Squaw Man" (1913) is now the Hollywood Heritage Museum.

Hollywood Heritage Museum

Originally built in the 1880s, the Hollywood Heritage Museum (aka Hollywood Studio Museum) is housed in the Lasky–DeMille barn leased in 1913 for "The Squaw Man". Then at Selma and Vine, in 1927 the barn was moved to Melrose Ave., now Paramount. The barn was later a train station on the set of "Bonanza".

The museum was established in 1980 when it was moved to its present location in a large parking lot across from the Hollywood Bowl at 2100 N. Highland Ave. in Hollywood. (Enter the parking lot on Milner Rd. off Highland.)

The building contains Delmar Watson's football helmet from George O'Brien's "Gay Caballero" ('32); a rare photo from the premiere of "Dodge City" ('39) shows Buck Jones (with a cigarette), Hoot Gibson, Wayne Morris and Big Boy Williams; a fire proof 35 nitrate film storage can from the William S. Hart Company; several tomahawks and arrows—props from "Squaw Man" and lots of rare photos of historic Hollywood.

Open Saturday and Sunday only from 11-3:45.

★★

Hollywood History Museums

The Max Factor Beauty Museum is now the Hollywood History Museum. The Max Factor building and museum collection was sold by Proctor and Gamble in 1996 to a developer and the Max Factor Museum was closed with the new owner planning to open the Hollywood History Museum in 1999, however, that opening was pushed back several times, finally opening in 2002. Some pieces from the Max Factor exhibit remain in this new museum while others are currently on display at the Hollywood Entertainment Museum which opened in 1996 at 7021 Hollywood Blvd. in Hollywood. (323) 465-7900. This small, modest museum is located in the basement floor of the modern Galaxy Center and movie multiplex. Open Tuesday-Sunday, 10-6. They feature a display of costumes from Paramount, some of which are western. A nearby bank of telephone receivers allows you to listen to Hollywood legends discussing the industry, among them John Wayne. (323) 960-4833.

The Max Factor Hollywood History Museum is at 1666 N. Highland Ave., in Hollywood.

★★★

Gower Gulch

The corner of Sunset and Gower in Hollywood was the center of activity for Poverty Row producers. Many of them had offices or soundstages in the area. In the '20s, '30s and

'40s, cowboys used to gather at that historic corner to hopefully be selected as "day players" for low budget cheapies, hence the nickname Gower Gulch.

Since then, developers of the shopping center that now occupies the corner have designed it to resemble a western street. Large colorful portraits of Roy Rogers, Gene Autry, Dale Evans and John Wayne decorate one wall.

Large sign at Sunset and Gower shopping center denotes where the original Gower Gulch once was.

★★★

Gene Autry's Golden West Studios

The building which now houses the Old Spaghetti Factory restaurant was once Gene Autry's Golden West Studios from which Gene and people like Johnny Bond ran much of Gene's music publishing. 5939 Sunset Blvd. (Exit Hwy. 101 at Sunset.)

★★★

Bronson Canyon

Originally a quarry for construction of Los Angeles's first street-car system, Bronson Canyon has been a favorite filming site at least since 1919, when the Jack Hoxie silent serial "Lightning Bryce" lensed in the canyon while some of the quarry equipment was

I'm kneeling at the west, and main, entrance to Bronson Canyon.

still in place.

Bronson is part of the 4,000-acre Griffith Park, largest municipal park in the nation. The horseshoe-shaped canyon hosts four tunnel entrances—two large entrances, one at each end of the main tunnel, as well as a medium-size tunnel entrance and very small cave opening with short tunnels merging with the main tunnel near its east end. The walls of the canyon are steep but were accessible to production units for rare shots near or at the top of the canyon.

Used in varying ways in countless western, sci-fi and gangster films as well as serials, its most famous appearance remains as the entrance to the underground city of Murania for Gene Autry's futuristic "Phantom Empire" serial in '35. The strangely shaped mid-sized tunnel was the one used.

Bronson's smallest cave opening made a rare appearance in a scene with Tom London for Columbia's "Superman" serial ('48). In another scene for the same title, heavies drove into the west tunnel entrance after driving up the tree-lined road leading to the canyon entrance road (in perhaps the only film use ever of that tree-lined road) and stopping at what appeared to have been the actual chained entrance to the canyon.

But B-western stars were the canyon's most frequent visitors. Buck Jones made impressive use of the east entrance to the main tunnel in "Hello Trouble" ('32), wagons raced through the tunnel in an exciting scene for John Wayne's "Sagebrush Trail" ('33), Hoppy put it to use in "Leather Burners" ('43) and, in a beautifully photographed scene, the Durango Kid fought off bandits in the Bronson caves below villainess Mary Newton's ranch house (actually the middle Iverson ranch set at Chatsworth) in the climax to "Desert Vigilante" ('49).

A-westerns and TVers were hardly strangers to the area either. While most of Wayne's "The Searchers" ('56) was filmed at exotic locales, the crew returned to Bronson for its exciting and moving climax. Not only did such sci-fi classics as "Invasion of the Body Snatchers" ('56) lense there, but also such Grade Z clunkers as "Robot Monster" ('53), featuring the space-helmeted gorilla Ro-man, and "It Conquered the World" ('56).

East side of the Bronson Cave area with the entrance to the underground city of Murania for "Phantom Empire" on the right.

Bronson Canyon is very close to Hollywood & Vine, so close, in fact, a slight upward tilt of a moviemaker's camera would bring Tinseltown's famed "HOLLYWOOD" sign into view. To reach the canyon, take Hollywood Blvd. east to Bronson Ave., Bronson north until it becomes Canyon Blvd. then Canyon north to the end of the road and a small parking area on the left. Walk up the gravel entrance road and enter one of the few sites that still looks almost exactly as it did in the golden era.

 Sampling of Westerns Filmed at BRONSON CANYON

- Lightning Warrior ('31)—George Brent (serial)
- In Old Cheyenne ('31)—Rex Lease
- Three Musketeers ('33)—John Wayne (serial)
- Gordon of Ghost City ('33)—Buck Jones (serial)
- Terror Trail ('33)—Tom Mix
- Man From Hell ('34)—Reb Russell
- Honor of the Range ('34)—Ken Maynard
- Mystery Mountain ('34)—Ken Maynard (serial)
- Phantom Empire ('35)—Gene Autry (serial)
- Rancho Grande ('40)—Gene Autry
- Land of the Six Guns ('40)—Jack Randall
- Adventures of Capt. Marvel ('41)—Tom Tyler (serial)
- Under Fiesta Stars ('41)—Gene Autry
- Man From Cheyenne ('42)—Roy Rogers
- Call of the Canyon ('42)—Gene Autry
- Desert Vigilante ('49)—Charles Starrett
- Lone Ranger (TV): Enter the Lone Ranger ('49)
- Roy Rogers (TV): Train Robbery ('52)
- Hellgate ('52)—Sterling Hayden
- Range Rider (TV): Hideout ('53)
- Great Jesse James Raid ('53)—Willard Parker
- Kit Carson (TV): Counterfeit Country ('54)
- Thunder Pass ('54)—Dane Clark
- Massacre Canyon ('54)—Phil Carey
- Lone Ranger ('56)—Clayton Moore
- Tales of the Texas Rangers (TV): Riders of the Lone Star ('57)
- Californians (TV): Regulators ('57)
- Return to Warbow ('58)—Phil Carey
- Texan (TV): Border Incident ('59)
- Rough Riders (TV): Ransom of Rita Renee ('59)
- Bonanza (TV): Saga of Annie O'Toole ('59)
- Rawhide (TV): Incident in No Man's Land ('59)
- Bat Masterson (TV): High Card Loses ('60)
- Bonanza (TV): Thunderhead Swindle ('61)
- Ride the High Country ('62)—Randolph Scott/Joel McCrea
- Gun Hawk ('63)—Rory Calhoun
- Virginian (TV): Hour of the Tiger ('64)
- High Chaparral (TV): Terrorist ('67)
- Bonanza (TV): To Die In Darkness ('68)
- Bonanza (TV): War Bonnet ('71)

★★★

KCET-TV/Monogram Sunset Studio

KCET-TV, the L.A. PBS station at 4401 W. Sunset Blvd., once housed Monogram Pictures and a host of other studios. It first became the setting for filmmaking in 1912 when one of the Lubin Co. units opened a small studio there for filming instructional titles featuring local tourist attractions. It was replaced the next year by the Essanay (S & A) Film Company, founded by George K. Spoor and "Broncho Billy" Anderson for production of one-reel westerns. After making some 20 titles, Essanay vacated the property in April of 1913.

The following October the Kalem Company moved onto the lot with a unit that included director, and later western heavy, J.P. McGowan in its ranks. Following Kalem's departure in 1917, Willis and Inglis, a theatrical agency and story brokerage firm, acquired the property as a rental studio.

By the beginning of 1918, its facilities included an enlarged outdoor stage and an

58

Inside KCET-TV which was once Monogram.

indoor stage, as well as offices, scene docks, property shop, dressing rooms and carpentry shop. For the next two years several companies leased the facilities.

In 1920, silent star turned producer Charles Ray purchased the property and established a company on the lot for the production of films to be released through First National. By July Ray had completed construction of a new stage (with pool beneath the stage), still in use today as Stage A.

By October of 1922 the lot boasted a Spanish-style administration building, which is still standing, as well as backlot sets, including a very narrow western street with a backdrop of buildings and an exiting or entering side street, camera left, at the street's one end. Ray's company went bankrupt in 1923 and for several years the studio went largely unused.

By 1927 it was again active as a rental studio operated by Jean Navelle, with Tiffany and other small companies leasing its western set and other props.

In 1931, recording engineer Ralph Like purchased the lot for leasing, revamped Stage A for sound and the next year erected what is now Stage B on the current property.

Throughout the '30s a number of independents produced cheapie features on the western street, utilizing a tiny saloon set with balcony seen in many titles. Although headquartered at a lot nearby, Trem Carr's Monogram studio also used the Like lot frequently and, in 1942, purchased the studio as well as adjoining property to be used for additional scene docks, a New York street and offices.

In 1943, a building on Sunset Blvd., which bordered the studio on the south, was acquired to house the studio's costume department and, by 1946, Monogram had bought bungalows on Commonwealth Street for use as offices. During the '40s and early '50s, the little studio was kept busy with a seemingly endless outpouring of western titles as well as its Charlie Chan, Bowery Boys, Bomba the Jungle Boy, Jiggs and Maggie, Latham Family, Kirby Grant/Chinook and Bill Elliott detective entries, along with a few B+/A Monogram features.

The studio's long-term lease in 1937 of Ernest Hickson's Newhall ranch, thereafter called the Monogram Ranch until Gene Autry's purchase of the property as his "Melody Ranch" in 1952, eliminated the need for the studio's tiny western set, which was later dismantled. Stage A hosted a tiny jungle set for the Bomba entries but the studio's limited back lot facilities obliged much location shooting. With the rise of television and decline in demand for B-product, the studio in 1952 dropped the Monogram logo and became Allied Artists. In 1970, KCET's parent company purchased the studio.

To reach KCET (which does offer tours—[323] 666-6500), go west on Sunset after exiting the Hollywood Fwy. The studio is on the left.

Sampling of Westerns Filmed at MONOGRAM SUNSET STUDIO

- The Sheriff's Story ('13)—Broncho Billy Anderson
- Light of Western Stars ('18)—Dustin Farnum
- Courtship of Miles Standish ('23)—Charles Ray
- Overland Bound ('29)—Leo Maloney
- Ridin' Fool ('31)—Bob Steele
- Scarlet Brand ('32)—Bob Custer
- Guns for Hire ('32)—Lane Chandler
- Border Guns ('34)—Bill Cody
- Way of the West ('34)—Wally Wales
- Six Gun Justice ('35)—Bill Cody
- Wild Mustang ('35)—Harry Carey
- Rider of the Law ('35)—Bob Steele
- Rough Riding Ranger ('35)—Rex Lease
- Pals of the Range ('35)—Rex Lease
- Cowboy and the Bandit ('35)—Rex Lease
- Vanishing Riders ('35)—Bill Cody
- Ghost Town ('36)—Harry Carey
- Desert Justice ('36)—Jack Perrin
- Custer's Last Stand ('36) serial—Rex Lease
- Headin' for the Rio Grande ('36)—Tex Ritter
- Rollin' Plains ('38)—Tex Ritter
- King of the Wild Stallions ('59)—George Montgomery

★★★

William S. Hart Park

The small but unique William S. Hart Park is at 8341 De Longpre Ave., one block south of Sunset Blvd. in West Hollywood. Although you can enter via the steps on Sunset, it's easier to park on De Longpre. The former residence of the silent western star now houses the Actors Studio.

Former residence of William S. Hart is now the Actors Studio.

★★★

Silent Movie Theatre

When in Hollywood, check out the Silent Movie Theatre at 611 N. Fairfax Ave. (323) 655-2510. You might catch a silent western with William S. Hart or Tom Mix.

★★★

Chapel In the Canyon

The familiar Chapel in the Canyon, a landmark on Topanga Canyon Blvd. in Canoga Park since 1957, is now owned by the Chatsworth Christian Church. One of the complex's assembly halls is named after Roy Rogers and Dale Evans who joined the chapel's congregation around 1962 when they lived on a ranch west of Chatsworth and became active in the church. Dale took part in 1958 groundbreaking ceremonies for a 100 seat add-on to the original structure.

★★★

Calabasas Pet Cemetery

Other than Roy and Dale, Gene Autry and John Wayne, we aren't going to get into the whereabouts of cowboy star gravesites in this book. That subject is well covered in Bobby Copeland's B-WESTERN BOOT HILL (Empire Publishing) and you can check

<www.findagrave.com>. However, we will mention the Los Angeles Pet Memorial Park at 5068 N. Old Scandia Lane in Calabasas, commonly known as the Calabasas Pet Cemetery. In operation since the '20s, caretakers seem to have meticulous records. William Boyd's Topper is interred in an undated grave. Nearby is the grave of Smoke ('31-'54) owned by Chief Thundercloud and ridden by Dick Foran in his '35-'37 Warner Bros. B-westerns. Also a horse named Sunny ('25-'52) owned by Chief Thundercloud. Tonto's Scout is also buried here.

William Boyd's famous horse Topper is interred at Calabasas Pet Cemetery.

★★★

Century Ranch

With rugged Santa Monica mountains and rolling hills surrounding it, plus a creek and lake, the area known as the 20th Century Fox/Century Ranch came into play when Fox bought the property in 1946, after leasing the area since 1941. It's perhaps best known as doubling for Korea on TV's "M*A*S*H", but it did see duty in quite a few western films or TV series. "Butch Cassidy and the Sundance Kid" has a snippet of a famous scene that featured the Century Ranch, where Butch and Sundance jump off a cliff and into a raging river to avoid capture by the pursuing posse.

The ranch grew in size over the years to 6,000 acres. In 1974, Fox sold the Century Ranch to the state who opened up the property to the public as Malibu Creek State Park.

To reach Fox Century Ranch, take Ventura Freeway west from North Hollywood about 20 miles to the Las Virgenes Rd. exit and Las Virgenes south to the ranch entrance, now a park, on the right.

 Sampling of Westerns Filmed at CENTURY RANCH

- My Friend Flicka (TV): series ('55-'56)
- Love Me Tender ('56)—Elvis Presley
- Broken Arrow (TV): various episodes ('56-'58)
- Flaming Star ('60)—Elvis Presley
- Daniel Boone (TV): various episodes ('64-'70)
- Loner (TV): various episodes ('65-'66)

- Legend of Jesse James (TV): various episodes ('65-'66)
- Custer (TV): various episodes ('67)
- Lancer (TV): various episodes ('68-'70)
- Cade's County (TV): various episodes ('71-'72)
- Kung Fu (TV): various episodes ('72-'75)

★★★

Joel McCrea Ranch

Frances Dee, Joel McCrea's widow now in her 90s and a star in her own right ("Four Faces West" etc.), still lives on the McCrea Ranch on Moorpark Rd. in Thousand Oaks.

The fabulous ranch is now listed on the National Register of Historic Places. The designation will help officials preserve the ranch's structures and open spaces.

McCrea took the advice of good friend Will Rogers in 1932 and invested in land—around 4,000 acres of it in the Conejo Valley for which he had to borrow $4,600. Over the years, McCrea sold much of the land (2,500 acres went to build the Sunset Hills development) and donated other parcels to the YMCA, a Boys and Girls Club and the Conejo Open Space Conservation Agency to create the McCrea Wildlife Refuge in 1981, the 75 acre centerpiece of the 148 acre McCrea Open Space area. Under terms of the agreement with the family, public access to the preserve is limited to protect sensitive resources. In '95, the McCrea family sold a remaining 220 acres to the Conejo Park District for nearly $2 million. Under the deal, family members kept 80 acres and the right to live on the ranch.

★★★

Janss Conejo Ranch

In 1910 Edwin and Harold Janss purchased about 10,000 acres of land in what is now Thousand Oaks. The land was originally a portion of the Rancho Conejo land grant. The ranch, called the Janss Conejo Ranch, was used primarily as a farm and to raise thoroughbred race horses. In the '50s, the brothers bought additional land for investment.

With cactus, sagebrush, sweeping plains, low hills and two waterfalls, Hollywood found the northwest area of the property, now known as the Wildwood Regional Park, perfect for such TV series as "Rawhide". The "Rifleman" cabin was located in this area. "Welcome to Hard Times" ('67) used a six building set on the sloping ground on the eastern edge of the ridge. It's believed a townset was in evidence before 1947 at the southwest edge of Wildwood Park where the sewage disposal plant now stands. The airfield used in Roy Rogers' "Gay Ranchero" ('48) and Gene Autry's "Riders of the Whistling Pines" ('49) was part of the Janss Ranch. Even in filming days, the airfield was adjacent to Ventura Blvd. and a business district.

Essentially, over time, the Janss Ranch became the heart of Thousand Oaks. But there's still a hint of our western heroes in Wildwood Regional Park.

 Sampling of Westerns Filmed at JANSS CONEJO RANCH

- Gay Ranchero ('48)—Roy Rogers
- Riders of the Whistling Pines ('49)—Gene Autry
- Davy Crockett, King of the Wild Frontier ('55)—
  Fess Parker
- Gunsmoke (TV): various episodes ('55-'75)
- Wagon Train (TV): various episodes ('57-'65)
- Westward Ho the Wagons ('57)—Fess Parker
- Gunsight Ridge ('57)—Joel McCrea

- Wild Heritage ('58)—Will Rogers Jr.
- Rifleman (TV): series ('58-'63)
- Rawhide (TV): various episodes ('59-'65)
- Flaming Star ('60)—Elvis Presley
- Man Who Shot Liberty Valance ('62)—John Wayne
- Stage To Thunder Rock ('64)—Barry Sullivan
- Shenandoah ('65)— James Stewart
- Welcome To Hard Times ('67)—Henry Fonda

★★★

Paramount Ranch

The Paramount Ranch in Agoura Hills, about a 40 minute drive on the Ventura Freeway from Los Angeles, was home for several years to the CBS hit, "Dr. Quinn, Medicine Woman".

Although out of Paramount's hands since 1946, in the heyday of westerns the studio used its Agoura western street for a few of its Hopalong Cassidy entries, leased the set to Columbia for Buck Jones and Tim McCoy Bs and a host of independent cheapies. Featured prominently in Gary Cooper's "The Virginian" ('29), Paramount's Agoura western town had one feature which distinguished it from the sets of other studios and location ranches—a church with a high peaked roof and steeple at the end of one street and, camera right of the church, a similar smaller building with peaked roof but no steeple.

When Jesse Lasky and New York theater owner and film distributor W. W. Hawkinson first formed Paramount Pictures, Lasky bought 2,000 acres of land in Burbank on which the studio built standing sets. By 1921, the Burbank sets had become unduly familiar to moviegoers and Paramount acquired its Agoura property.

"Rancho Paramount," as it was called, was situated in the Santa Monica Mountains along Cornell Road and what is now Kanan Road, just south of where the Ventura Freeway currently passes through the Agoura area. The ranch was a huge operation that included not only the western streets but other sets as well, such as a colonial New England town built for Claudette Colbert's "Maid of Salem" ('37) and a massive fortress seen in Gary Cooper's "Adventures of Marco Polo" ('37). A sturdy looking stockade was built the in '31 for Gary Cooper's "Fighting Caravans". The ranch also boasted an entire supporting community of barns, stables, production craft shops and a large commissary.

The original western set, located at what is now the intersection of Cornell and Sierra Creek roads (and much closer to the freeway than the set now seen in "Dr. Quinn" episodes), also saw service in non-western rustics such as "Huckleberry Finn" ('31), for which Paramount converted a portion of Medea Creek into the Mississippi River. Buck Jones' "The Avenger" ('31) gives prominent play to the picket fences and residences built for the "Huck" flick.

The ranch was auctioned in 1943 to a contractor with no immediate plans for the site. The sale left the studio with only its Hollywood western street (seen in "Bonanza" episodes) and a set in Las Vegas until their dismantling in the '80s.

 Sampling of Westerns Filmed at PARAMOUNT RANCH

- The Virginian ('29)—Gary Cooper
- Light of Western Stars ('30)—Richard Arlen
- Santa Fe Trail ('30)—Richard Arlen
- The Avenger ('31)—Buck Jones
- Deadline ('31)—Buck Jones
- Fighting Caravans ('31)—Gary Cooper
- Ghost Valley ('32)—Tom Keene
- Ridin' For Justice ('32)—Buck Jones

- Local Bad Man ('32)—Hoot Gibson
- Phantom Thunderbolt ('33)—Ken Maynard
- Wagon Wheels ('34)—Randolph Scott
- Prescott Kid ('34)—Tim McCoy
- Rose of the Rancho ('36)—John Boles
- Cassidy of Bar 20 ('38)—William Boyd
- Bar 20 Justice ('38)—William Boyd
- Pride of the West ('38)—William Boyd

★★★

Hertz Paramount Ranch

In 1952 a 326-acre parcel of the southern portion of the old Paramount property in Agoura Hills was purchased by businessman William B. Hertz. The original ranch sets, which were a considerable distance north of the Hertz parcel, had been dismantled, but several large, corrugated metal buildings remained on the Hertz property. Hertz and his teenage son, Robert, set to work facing the buildings with western facades. He offered the property for rental to film companies. Soon, "Have Gun, Will Travel", "Cisco Kid", "Gunsmoke", "Bat Masterson", "Zane Grey Theater", and other TV series were filming at the ranch.

As business grew, Bill Hertz added buckboards and other rolling stock, built a fort set on the site where the church often seen in "Dr. Quinn" episodes now stands, and acquired western buildings and props from RKO's Encino ranch, which had been in operation since 1929-'30 but was dismantled following its 1953 sale to developers.

Ill health obliged him to sell the parcel for $200,000 in the late '50s. The property next became the Paramount Sportsman's Ranch, offering a variety of recreational opportunities and a midget-auto race track.

In 1962, Dee Cooper—slit-eyed veteran of Lash LaRue, Whip Wilson, Eddie Dean, Johnny Mack Brown and other latter-day B-western epics—began leasing the property from its current owners for rental to movie and television companies as well as producers of TV commercials.

By the late '70s, the area seemed doomed to the developers' bulldozers. But, in 1980 the National Park Service rode to the rescue, taking permanent possession of the property but also continuing the ranch's long tradition as a filming site. The sets left from the Hertz and Cooper days, refurbished and augmented with new studio-constructed sets, soon attracted a brisk business, including the long-running "Dr. Quinn" series.

It's the only working movie ranch open free to the public (closes at sunset daily). Every first and third weekend there are park ranger guided tours of the western town beginning at 9:30am. (805) 370-2301.

To reach this truly historic filming site, take the Ventura Freeway west from Los Angeles to Agoura Hills' Kanan Road exit, Kanan Road south to Cornell Way, left on Cornell Way to Cornell Road, right on Cornell to the ranch entrance on the right.

The Paramount Ranch western street recently saw duty on "Dr. Quinn Medicine Woman."

Sampling of Westerns Filmed at HERTZ PARAMOUNT RANCH

- Cisco Kid (TV): various episodes ('50-'56)
- Gunsmoke (TV): various episodes ('55-mid '60s)
- Have Gun Will Travel (TV): various episodes ('57-'63)
- Bat Masterson (TV): various episodes ('58-'61)

- Zane Grey Theatre (TV): various episodes ('56-'61)
- Fall Guy (TV): various episodes ('81-'86)
- Shame, Shame On the Bixby Boys ('78)—Monte Markham
- Dr. Quinn, Medicine Woman (TV): series ('93-'96)

★★★

Ingram/4 Star/Hertz Topanga Ranch

PRC cowboy stars James Newill and Dave O'Brien bought a goat ranch off Topanga Canyon Road in Woodland Hills, a few miles west of Los Angeles as a ploy to avoid the WWII draft. The two stars apparently found getting up at 3am daily to tend nearly a hundred goats even less inviting than working for PRC, for when both were classified 4-F, they sold the 200 acre ranch in 1944 to B-western/serial heavy Jack Ingram, who often appeared in Texas Rangers features.

Later, Ingram purchased an old bulldozer and, with the help of Pierce Lyden, Kenne Duncan, Lane Bradford and other B-western veterans, built western sets on the ranch. Once part of the Charlie Chaplin estate, the property included a well landscaped house that became Ingram's home and can be seen in the background of a few scenes in Lash LaRue's "Mark of the Lash," with a white rail fence separating it from the ranch's western street sets.

The Ingram Ranch served as the filming site not only for several of Lash LaRue's titles, but also for such Monogram/Allied Artists stars as Bill Elliott and Wayne Morris, as well as entries for several western TV series, including "Lone Ranger," "Roy Rogers" and "Cisco Kid."

Ingram's home faced west, and the ranch included three streets arranged roughly in a triangle. One street ran northwest down a hill from the Chaplin/Ingram house. A second street began north of the house as a curving entrance road into the town and ran south (and slightly west) by the house to connect with the first street at its southeast end. That street had buildings on one side and a tree with a surrounding bench could often be seen in the middle of the street. A third street intersected with the first and

Badman Jack Ingram lived in this house when he owned the location ranch on Mulholland Drive.

second streets at their northwest and northeast ends, respectively, completing the triangle formed by the three streets.

A livery barn/corral was located camera left in the curve of the entrance road that became the second street and, in later years, a saloon/general store and other buildings were situated camera right of the entrance road. That area sometimes served as yet another street set for the ranch, while a large building with a porch on at least two sides, situated south of the stable, sometimes served as a stagecoach relay station or ranch.

A number of shacks and a large horse stable with doors to each stall rounded out the sets.

Failing health obliged Jack to sell the ranch in the mid-'50s to Four Star Productions, which used the site a number of years in association with ranch owner Bill Hertz for various Four Star series.

The sets were eventually destroyed, but one small, western-style building remains, as do the Chaplin/Ingram house and its white rail fence. During the filming days, the ranch entrance was reached from a side road off Topanga Canyon Road. In fact, the spread was often referred to as the Topanga Ranch.

Easiest way to reach it now is to take the Ventura Freeway west from Los Angeles to Topanga Canyon Blvd., Topanga south to Mullholland Drive, and Mullholland west about a half mile to the ranch site (now a field) on the right, just beyond the side driveway entrance to the Chaplin/Ingram house.

Sampling of Westerns Filmed at
INGRAM /4-STAR / HERTZ TOPANGA RANCH

- Dead Man's Gold ('48)—Lash LaRue
- Mark of the Lash ('48)—Lash LaRue
- Son of Billy the Kid ('49)—Lash LaRue
- Son of a Bad Man ('49)—Lash LaRue
- Lone Ranger (TV) High Heels ('49)
- Curley Bradley, The Singing Marshal (TV): unsold pilot ('50s)
- Quincannon, Frontier Scout ('56)—Tony Martin
- Kansas Territory ('52)—Bill Elliott
- Cowboy G-Men (TV): Gunslingers ('52)
- Cowboy G-Men (TV): Empty Mailbags ('52)
- Gene Autry (TV): Border Justice ('53)
- Crossroad Avenger (TV): unsold pilot ('53)
- Gene Autry (TV): Outlaw Stage ('53)
- Desperado ('54)—Wayne Morris
- Lawless Rider ('54)—Johnny Carpenter
- Cisco Kid (TV): Jumping Beans ('54)
- Cisco Kid (TV): Bounty Men ('54)
- Top Gun ('55)—Sterling Hayden
- Five Guns West ('55)—John Lund
- Last of the Desperadoes ('55)—James Craig
- At Gunpoint ('55)–Fred MacMurray
- The Desperadoes Are in Town ('56)—Robert Arthur
- Lone Ranger (TV): Counterfeit Mask ('56)
- Gunslinger ('56)—Beverly Garland
- Trackdown (TV): various episodes ('57-'59)
- Zane Grey Theatre (TV): 3 Graves ('57)
- Tombstone Territory (TV): Lady Gambler ('58)
- Black Saddle (TV): Burden of Guilt ('60)
- The Plunderers ('60)—Jeff Chandler

Motion Picture and TV Fund Retirement Home

The Motion Picture and TV Fund Retirement Home is at 23388 Mulholland Dr. in Woodland Hills. An approximately 7 ft. bronze statue sculpted by George Montgomery entitled "Hollywood Hero" stands in the garden area of the new Fran and Ray Stark Villa, to the left as you enter the Mulholland property. The bronze was donated by The

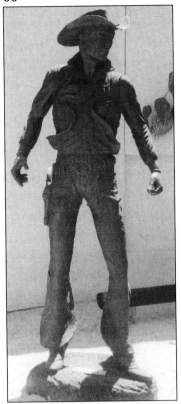

George Montgomery "Hollywood Hero" bronze in Motion Picture Home Villa area.

George Montgomery Foundation for the Arts. The small John Ford chapel, so named in his memory, is a replica of the original on the famed director's ranch. It's on the main grounds of the Motion Picture Home as you enter. The computerized carillon chapel bells were donated by western leading lady Adrian Booth in memory of her husband, actor David Brian.

★★

Agoura/Albertson Ranch

In Agoura Hills, west of Los Angeles along Ventura Freeway, we find the remains of the Agoura Ranch (also known as the Albertson Ranch), site for what once was a 14,000 acre working spread that also played host to many B-westerns.

The Agoura was "Radio Ranch" in Gene Autry's "Phantom Empire" serial as well as a setting for several of the star's later features, including "Home in Wyomin'," "Sons of New Mexico" (as heavy Robert Armstrong's gambling den), and "Hills of Utah" (as Denver Pyle's spread).

Tim Holt saw duty there in several of his post-war entries such as "Target." It served as the Duchess' ranch in two of the Jim Bannon Red Ryders, as Kenneth McDonald's lair in "The Durango Kid", as Iris Meredith's ranch in the 1938 Charles Starrett starrer "West of Cheyenne" and as Wild Bill Elliott's mother's spread in "Bullets for Bandits." The ranch and/or surrounding countryside also hosted several 3 Mesquiteers entries such as "Heroes of the Saddle".

Some Johnny Mack Brown Universals and several Don Barry Republics utilized the Agoura countryside but not ranch house, often settling on the Morrison Ranch house instead. A-movie fans would recognize it as the ranch in the Burgess Meredith/Lon Chaney, Jr. "Of Mice and Men" classic film.

The Agoura Ranch featured a large, two-story main house framed by oak trees, two giant oaks in its front yard, a bunkhouse situated at an angle some distance camera right from the front of the main house, a huge barn located at a greater distance camera right from the front of the house and rolling hills with scattered trees and chase roads. The main house was a movie set which, over time, had at least two front facades—one seen most clearly in "The Durango Kid" and a later one best pictured perhaps in the post-war Columbia Autry and RKO Holt features.

Remnants of the Agoura Ranch.

To reach the spread, take the Chesebro Road exit north off the Ventura Freeway, go about half a mile up Chesebro (itself used for chases in filming days) to the Chesebro Park entrance on the right, walk east from the parking area up the hiking trail about half a mile to a locked, posted, but unmarked entrance gate on the right and walk down the entrance road, now overgrown with weeds, about a half mile to the ranch house area. The main entrance road to the ranch is about a quarter mile up Chesebro from the freeway on the right but is now closed to traffic. Gene rode up that road to the main house from camera left in "Sons of New Mexico" and serenaded Fay McKenzie on it at the end of "Home in Wyomin'."

The main house and barn (except for part of the weed-covered foundation) are gone, but the now ramshackle bunkhouse (slightly altered in appearance from the filming days) is still there. A trailer occupies the spot on which the main house once stood. Visitors can also walk up a hill southeast of the parking area and look down on the rear of the ranch from above.

Sampling of Westerns Filmed at
AGOURA / ALBERTSON RANCH

- The Lash ('31)—Richard Barthlemess
- Guns For Hire ('32)—Lane Chandler
- Phantom Empire ('35)—Gene Autry
- West of Cheyenne ('38)—Charles Starrett
- Heroes of the Saddle ('40)—3 Mesquiteers
- Durango Kid ('40)—Charles Starrett
- Wyoming Wildcat ('41)—Don Barry
- Man From Montana ('41)—Johnny Mack Brown
- Jesse James Jr. ('42)—Don Barry
- Bullets For Bandits ('42)—Bill Elliott/Tex Ritter
- Home In Wyomin' ('42)—Gene Autry

- Red Pony ('49)—Robert Mitchum
- Ride, Ryder, Ride ('49)—Jim Bannon
- Sons of New Mexico ('50)—Gene Autry
- Twilight In the Sierras ('50)—Roy Rogers
- Al Jennings of Oklahoma ('51)—Dan Duryea
- Hills of Utah ('51)—Gene Autry
- Law of the Badlands ('51)—Tim Holt
- Desert Passage ('52)—Tim Holt
- Target ('52)—Tim Holt
- Texas John Slaughter (TV): various episodes ('58-'61)

★★

Joel McCrea and Walter Brennan— in Bronze

Bronze statues of Joel McCrea and Walter Brennan are in Camarillo, part of $7 million in street improvements. The statues cost roughly $150,000 total and stand without pedestals, Brennan's feet planted directly on the street and McCrea's lanky frame permanently sprawled across a bench. Brennan was frequently grand marshal of Camarillo's Christmas Parade. McCrea donated thousands to the town's youth organizations. Both lived in nearby Moorpark.

Camarillo is on Hwy. 101 (west of Los Angeles) between Thousand Oaks and Ventura.

★★★★★★★★★★★★★★★★★★★★★★★★★★★★

Bronze of Joel McCrea in Camarillo.

Ray "Crash" Corrigan's hat and gun are now at his son's bar and grill in Thousand Oaks.

Corrigan's Grill

Ray "Crash" Corrigan's son, Tom, maintains a bar and grill in Thousand Oaks in which many of his father's hats, guns, spurs and other personal items are displayed. "Crash" Corrigan was one of the first group of 3 Mesquiteers (with Robert Livingston and Max Terhune) until he left Republic to start his own trio-series at Monogram, The Range Busters (with John "Dusty" King and—again—Max Terhune).

Established in 1982, Corrigan's is at 556 E. Thousand Oaks Blvd. (805) 495-5234.

★★★

Lake Sherwood

First formed with the completion of the dam in 1904 or 1905, Lake Sherwood and the surrounding countryside have been the site for many B-westerns and serials, as well as numerous A-movies and TVers.

The lake got its name when the Douglas Fairbanks Sr. silent Robin Hood film utilized the oak-studded woods at the base of the dam—the same forest through which heroine Louise Currie was pursued in the "Adventures of Captain Marvel" several years later, with the base of the dam clearly visible in the scene's background.

Originally constructed for the filming of a Mary Pickford silent, the partially fake cliff near the far end of the dam from the entrance road quickly became a favorite spot in films. On rare occasions the camera would be directed toward the dam for dives or falls from the cliff with the tip of the dam visible above the waterline. See, for example, the climax to Chapter 1 of Harry Carey's Mascot serial, "Last of the Mohicans" ('32), one of the earliest films of the sound era to utilize the Lake Sherwood area.

But for most cliff shots the camera was directed away from the dam with part of the cliff serving as a backdrop for the scene. Woods recently stripped for development at the opposite end of the lake from the dam played host to Errol Flynn's "Robin Hood" and the Republic serial "Tiger Woman" (although motorboat chases for that great cliffhanger were shot at Lake Elsinore southeast of Los Angeles). The lake itself was featured in Roy Rogers' "Susanna Pass" among others.

Go south on Westlake Blvd. to Potrero Rd., right on Potrero to the lake, about a mile up Potrero on the left.

Lake Sherwood.

Sampling of Westerns Filmed at LAKE SHERWOOD

- Desperate Trails ('39)—Johnny Mack Brown
- Dark Command ('40)—John Wayne
- Adventures of Captain Marvel ('41)—Tom Tyler (serial)
- King of the Texas Rangers ('41)—Sammy Baugh (serial)
- Jungle Girl ('41)—Frances Gifford (serial)

- Romance On the Range ('42)—Roy Rogers
- Wagon Tracks West ('43)—Bill Elliott
- Silver Spurs ('43)—Roy Rogers
- Haunted Harbor ('44)—Kane Richmond (serial)
- Out California Way ('46)—Monte Hale

★★★

Kentucky Park Farm

Kentucky Park Farm was the principal lensing site for "My Pal Trigger", Roy Rogers' favorite film. Remember the paddock where Dale put Golden Sovereign through his paces, the large brick stable where Trigger's colts were born and the track where Roy trained Trigger for the picture's finale race? The track has been torn down but the stable and paddock are still there along with other filming sites.

In 1923, F. W. Matthiessen, one of the pioneers of the Lake Sherwood area, completed plans for a thoroughbred ranch located in Hidden Valley to be named Kentucky Park because its long rows of white fencing and stable designs resembled the stud farms of the Bluegrass state.

"My Pal Trigger" was lensed at Kentucky Park Farms.

Now called Ventura Farms, it's still devoted to raising thoroughbreds. The ranch—within the 30 mile zone from Los Angeles (see explanation in foreword), thus excellent for one-day filming trips—is also a frequent setting for current theatrical releases.

In the golden era the spread was not only the setting for "My Pal Trigger" but the main house and its swimming pool (although now more luxurious than in their B-western days), as well as the racetrack and rolling hills, were featured in Roy's "San Fernando Valley". A stable scene for "Rainbow Over Texas" was shot there or at a neighboring ranch.

Although *not* open to tourists, you may reach its main gate and gate phone by taking the Ventura Freeway west from Los Angeles to Westlake Blvd. exit, boulevard south to Potrero Road, right on Potrero past Lake Sherwood and into Hidden Valley. It's the first ranch on the right upon entering the valley.

★★★

San Fernando Mission

Bill Elliott's "Frontiers of '49" was partially lensed at the San Fernando Mission as well as Tim Holt's "Mysterious Desperado" ('49) and "Border Treasure" ('50).

The Mission, established in 1797 can be reached by taking I-5 north. Exit at San

Fernando Mission Blvd. and turn left. 15151 San Fernando Mission Blvd. in Mission Hills.

★★★

Pacoima Dam

Overlooking the San Fernando Valley in the hills northeast of Los Angeles, we find the great Pacoima Dam at the southwest end of Pacoima Canyon. Completed in 1929, 372 feet high and 640 feet wide, Pacoima was the setting for an exciting chapter ending in the serial "Zorro Rides Again" as well as action shots for the 1936 Jack Perrin cheapie "Desert Justice" and a 1934 William Berke featurette, "Wild Waters" with Dave Sharpe and the dog, Flash. The steep climb to the top of the dam is via an enclosed tram and a visit requires payment of a $50 fee.

Take I-5 north to Hwy. 118, then northeast on 118 to 210 north (or west). Exit at Hubbard St. and turn right (north). Follow Hubbard until it curves into Gavina Ave. Follow Gavina to Pacoima Canyon Rd. where you turn left and head into the canyon for a short distance.

★★★

Beale's Cut

The establishing scene for the chase across the salt flats in John Wayne's classic "Stagecoach" ('39) lensed at Beale's Cut a few miles north of Los Angeles. The chase itself was filmed on the Lucerne dry lake near Victorville, but the first establishing quick shot of the stagecoach rolling through a deep, narrow pass is Beale's Cut.

First chiseled through the Santa Susanna mountains by General Phineas Banning in 1854, the cut was initially only 30 ft. deep. Used mainly for carrying supplies through the mountains to Fort Tejon, northwest of what is now Newhall, the cut was first known as Fremont Pass and Newhall Pass. But in 1863-'64, it began to acquire its current name when General Edward Fitzgerald Beale, a veteran of California's Mexican-American war and surveyor-general of California and Nevada, led a crew of workers from Fort Tejon in enlarging the pass to a depth of 90 feet.

Soon, Beale began charging fees for the cut's use. In 1910, Los Angeles County bored a narrow tunnel through the mountains, eliminating the need for the cut as a passage to the San Fernando Valley, and in '38-'39, the Sierra Hwy, connecting Los Angeles and the Newhall area north, was completed.

By that point, however, Beale's Cut had also long been a filming site. More than two decades before "Stagecoach," John Ford became one of the first directors to feature the cut—first in "Straight Shooting" ('17) with Harry Carey Sr.

The famous Tom Mix leap across Beale's Cut in "Three Jumps Ahead" (1923).

and later in Tom Mix's "Three Jumps Ahead" ('23), in which the star and his Wonder Horse Tony appear to jump across the cut. Stunt ace Richard Talmadge took credit for the feat, while one Mix chronicler credits Nevada horse trainer and stuntman Earl Simpson, aided considerably by a wooden ramp. Others suspect "camera magic," especially since the whole scene has an unreal look to it and horse and rider appear smaller in scale than surrounding objects. Whatever the truth about "Three Jumps Ahead," a scene of Frankie Darro jumping Rex across the cut in Ep. 2 of "The Devil Horse" ('32) appears clearly to have been a process shot.

For years, an historic marker along the Sierra Highway directed tourists to the cut. But our reel west is fast disappearing. A rockslide in the spring of 1998 filled the cut to half its depth, making the area hazardous for hikers.

Sampling of Westerns Filmed at BEALE'S CUT

- Straight Shooting ('17)—Harry Carey
- Three Jumps Ahead ('23)—Tom Mix
- Iron Horse ('24)—George O'Brien
- Via Pony Express ('33)—Jack Hoxie
- Last Stand ('38)—Bob Baker
- The Phantom ('43)—Tom Tyler (serial)

★★★

William S. Hart Home/ Museum/Park

William S. Hart Park, dedicated in 1958, has to be at the top of any California visit. It's a delightful journey back to the early days of Hollywood and the final days of the Old West.

The beautiful 22 room Spanish style home which cost $100,000 to build (from 1926-1928) is where Hart lived and is almost exactly as he left it in 1946. The 265 acre ranch and home were donated by Hart upon his death to be operated as a free museum. He said, "While I was making pictures, the people gave me their nickels, dimes and quarters. When I am gone, I want them to have my home."

Guided tours every half hour of the home which is filled with a 2,000 volume library, guns belonging to Wyatt Earp, Hart movie memorabilia, bronze sculptures, paintings by Frederic Remington, James Montgomery Flagg, Charles Russell and others, period furniture and much more. Walk the tree-studded yet manicured grounds and you'll feel "The thrill of it all" once again.

Donna Magers outside William S. Hart's former home in Newhall.

Headstone For William S. Hart's famous pony, Fritz, who is buried at William S. Hart Park.

Adjacent to the home is where Bill's beloved horse, Fritz, is buried. At street level is a gift shop and Hart movie memorabilia museum.

Tom Mix used the southwest corner of the town of Newhall as a location site touching on the edge of the Hart ranch along Market Street. It included the lower couple of blocks of Walnut St. In the early '20s Hart utilized a townset built there.

24151 San Fernando Rd., Newhall. Open Wednesday-Friday 10-3, Saturday 10-5. Closed on major holidays. (661) 259-0855.

★★★★★★★★★★★★★★★★★★★★★★★★★★★★★

Newhall Western Walk of Stars

The Western Walk of Stars in Newhall (an area in the Santa Clarita Valley where so many westerns were lensed) begins at the entrance of William S. Hart Park and extends along both sides of San Fernando Rd. for six blocks. Since 1981, around 43 western stars have been inducted with bronze saddles inlaid in terrazzo tile sections of the sidewalk, ranging from the early days to present. Among those included: Hoot Gibson, Gene Autry, Tom Mix, Monte Hale, Tex Ritter, Roy Rogers, Dale Evans, Eddie Dean, Morgan Woodward, Doug McClure, William S. Hart, Rex Allen, Tex Williams, Pat Buttram, Herb Jeffries, Claude Akins, Andy Jauregui, Robert Conrad, Dennis Weaver, John Wayne, Clayton Moore, Clint Walker, Chuck Connors, Iron Eyes Cody, Harry Carey Sr., Ben Johnson, Amanda Blake, Dale Robertson, Jack Palance, Sam Elliott, George Montgomery, Jane Russell, Stuart Whitman, Peter Brown, Richard Farnsworth, Montie Montana, Woody Strode, Hugh O'Brian and Denver Pyle. Some of the names are on side streets off San Fernando Rd., such as Newhall Ave., Market St. and 8th Ave.

Ben Johnson's plaque on the Newhall Walk of Stars.

★★

Monogram/Melody Ranch

The Newhall/Saugus area in the Santa Clarita Valley 40 minutes north of Los Angeles has been a favorite filming site since the earliest days of motion pictures. William S. Hart began using Newhall streets and Placerita Canyon locations for filming as early as 1914. Tom Mix often filmed in the area as did Harry Carey and Hoot Gibson, who, like Hart, were local ranchers as well. Newhall's picturesque Presbyterian church and other landmarks regularly appeared in silent films. A stretch of railroad northeast of Saugus along Soledad Canyon Road was a frequent site for filming (Roy Rogers' "Nevada City" '41), as was the Saugus train depot, now on display near the William S. Hart ranch/park. A Southern Pacific 1629 steam engine donated by Gene Autry is situated on track in

Melody Ranch today.

front of the station. This engine appeared in many films made at Melody Ranch.

But the most famous Newhall/Saugus location of them all was the Monogram/Melody Ranch, now located at 24715 Oak Creek Avenue, near the intersection of Oak Creek and Placerita Canyon Road. Ernest (Ernie) Hickson, often listed as technical or art director in the credits for Monogram titles shot at the ranch, apparently owned the property from 1910 until his death in 1952. By some accounts, Hickson built all the original sets on the property and Hart's "The Disciple" ('15) was the first title lensed there. Others have written that Hickson, an inveterate collector of western Americana, imported some of the sets from Nevada and built others, placing them originally on the Rancho Placeritas, owned by producer Trem Carr, with whom Hickson was associated as a technical director, and situated on the current site of the Disney Studio's Golden Oak Ranch, about a mile east of Hwy. 14 along Placerita Canyon Road.

When Carr later sold his ranch, Hickson moved the sets to the current ranch site. Early sound westerns shot in part at the ranch included most of John Wayne's Lone Star Monogram titles and early Republics (e.g. Gene Autry's "Tumbling Tumbleweeds" '35) lensed during the brief period ('35-'37) that Carr's Monogram studio and others were combined under Herbert Yates' new Republic banner.

The pace of ranch operations really began to accelerate when Monogram separated from Republic in '37 and signed a long-term lease with Hickson, including a stipulation the ranch would bear the studio's name.

Sporting an enlarged and rearranged western street set first seen in, among other titles, Tom Keene's "Where Trails Divide" ('37), Jack Randall's "Danger Valley" ('37) and Tex Ritter's "Starlight Over Texas" ('38) (which not only included the street set but a hacienda and adobe village set as well), the "new" Monogram Ranch quickly became a familiar setting for such studio oater stars as the Rough Riders, the Trail Blazers, Johnny Mack Brown, Jimmy Wakely, the Cisco Kid and Whip Wilson. Also the first Bill Elliott Columbia series ("In Early Arizona" '38); several western serials ("Deadwood Dick" '40;

"Valley of Vanishing Men" '42); a large number of PRC features, including "Song of Old Wyoming" ('45) and other Eddie Dean color titles; and numerous Hoppy entries ("Santa Fe Marshal" '40) were shot there. Following a 1940 fire on its own western street, Republic also used the ranch for a number of titles ("Gangs of Sonora" '41).

Monogram Ranch sets were almost as familiar as the stars shooting there. The oldest structure on the property was a walled adobe ranch seen in Wayne's "Blue Steel" ('34) and "Desert Trail" ('35), among many other titles, and still standing on the northeast corner of the current ranch property. A hotel backdrop was situated at the west end of the main street in the early Monogram days. But by the '48-'49 film season (Johnny Mack Brown's "Hidden Danger" '48; Jimmy Wakely's "Brand of Fear" '49), the hotel had been moved to the south side of the main street at a slight angle, creating an open west end for the main street. A Mexican-style church set stood on a road intersecting a side street that ran north off main street at its north end. East along that road and north of the main street set was an impressive hacienda/mission set seen in Monogram's Cisco Kid entries (Gilbert Roland's "Beauty and the Bandit" '46) but put to best use in Gene Autry's "Big Sombrero" ('49) and "The Lone Ranger" ('56). Beyond the east end of main street was a walled adobe village which can be seen in "Colorado Serenade" ('46) and the Trail Blazers' "Arizona Whirlwind" ('44), among others. The east end of main street, left open dur-

ing the Monogram days, would later feature a small church visible in the opening credit gunfight scene of early "Gunsmoke" episodes and probably put there to block from view the adobe village, an incongruous set even for a TV version of Dodge City, Kansas.

The most frequently used ranch set on the property was situated about 50 yards north of the side street that ran north off main street. That set consisted of a main house with picket fence, a barn and corral located slightly northwest of the main house, a large bunkhouse that sometimes served as a small ranch or relay station and a small bunkhouse. At times, all those sets were used for a title, or sometimes individually without reference to the others. Johnny Mack Brown's "Raiders of the South" ('47) provides a useful view of the main house in relation to the other outbuildings. The barn ("Wild West" '46) and bunkhouses were seen in many titles.

Another elaborate ranch set featuring a large main house with porch, extensive rail fencing, a barn and

Rope stands and training ring for Champion and Little Champ that survived the disastrous 1962 fire are now in the Melody Ranch museum. The inset photo shows Gene training his horses with the very same training ring and rope stands.

other out-buildings was also occasionally used for later titles, including Johnny Mack Brown's "Sheriff of Medicine Bow" ('48). The relatively flat surrounding countryside with scattered trees and bushes was regularly used for filming too. The property also included other houses and cabins, enabling the ranch sometimes to play a rustic community in non-western Monogram titles such as Boris Karloff's "The Ape" ('40). Most of the sets were full structures rather than facades.

Shortly after Ernie Hickson's death on January 22, 1952, Gene Autry, who'd shot parts of his first starring feature there, bought the ranch, renamed it Melody Ranch and converted it into a thriving TV factory not only for such Autry Flying A series as "Annie Oakley," "Range Rider", "Adventures of Champion", "Buffalo Bill, Jr." and his own "Gene Autry Show", but also for segments of Hoppy's TV series, "Wild Bill Hickok," "Wyatt Earp," "Cisco Kid," "Sheriff of Cochise" and of course "Gunsmoke," among many others. The ranch also hosted a number of B-plus and A-westerns, including Fred MacMurray's fine "At Gunpoint" ('55).

In 1958, the NBC series "Wide, Wide World" hosted a 90-minute western special at the ranch, featuring not only Autry, but 'Duke' Wayne, Jim Arness and dozens of other cowboy players. Then, tragedy struck. On August 28, 1962, a massive firestorm roared through the valley, destroying virtually all the structures on the property except the adobe house, another house, the adobe village, schoolhouse, a cabin and the spread's Melody Ranch entrance. 54 structures were burned on the 110-acre ranch, as well as Gene's extensive collection of western Americana and 17,000 recordings, with losses set at $1 million. Autry gave up plans to establish a western museum at the ranch and, over the next three decades, gradually sold all but twelve acres of the property to developers.

Scenes for "Roots II" lensed at the ranch's train depot set which once included four trains running on 1.8 miles of track. Otherwise, the ranch's filming days seemed clearly a thing of the past.

Then, in 1991, after the death of Champion who had been pastured there until his death May 9, 1990 at age 41, Gene sold Melody Ranch, for a reported $975,000, to Renaud and Andre Veluzat, Santa Clarita Valley natives whose family has operated a film ranch in Saugus since the early '50s and who decided to restore the ranch to its former glory. The brothers painstakingly drew on photographs and videotapes in restoring the western street and church sets largely to their appearance during the early television era, with their only sacrifice of historical accuracy a slight elevation of the street sets beyond their original height to eliminate from camera view the blight of condos perched on the hill north of the ranch. Although obliged to modify the sets temporarily for Jeff Bridges' "Wild Bill" ('95) and other features lensing there, the Veluzat brothers have faithfully maintained the permanent sets' Melody Ranch appearance.

The rebuilt ranch is now open for tours Wednesday, Thursday and Fridays from 10am-4pm. Tours last 2 hours and are $25 per person. Special group rates are available. A tour the Veluzat brothers inaugurated in 2001 also includes a newly established museum with items from Gene himself, "Bonanza", "Maverick", "Bronco Billy" and Autry's own guest house which was saved from the devastating fire of '62. Call to arrange a tour (661) 286-1188.

Take Fwy. 170 north from Los Angeles to I-5, I-5 north to Hwy. 14, Hwy. 14 north to the Fernando Rd. exit, Fernando Rd. west past Lyons Avenue to a street on the right that becomes Placerita Canyon Rd. and east on Placerita to the Melody Ranch sign.

Sampling of Westerns Filmed on
MONOGRAM / MELODY RANCH

- Randy Rides Alone ('34)—John Wayne
- Down Mexico Way ('41)—Gene Autry
- Billy the Kid Wanted ('41)—Buster Crabbe
- Billy the Kid's Fighting Pals ('41)—Bob Steele
- Ghost Town Law ('42)—Rough Riders
- Billy the Kid Trapped ('42)—Buster Crabbe
- Wild Horse Stampede ('43)—Trail Blazers
- Wolves of the Range ('43)—Bob Livingston
- Blazing Guns ('43)—Trail Blazers
- Land of the Outlaws ('44)—Johnny Mack Brown
- Springtime in Texas ('45)—Jimmy Wakely
- Code of the Saddle ('47)—Johnny Mack Brown
- Valley of Fear ('47)—Johnny Mack Brown
- King of the Bandits ('47)—Gilbert Roland
- Partners of the Sunset ('48)—Jimmy Wakely
- Frontier Agent ('48)—Johnny Mack Brown
- Fighting Redhead ('49)—Jim Bannon
- Gunslingers ('50)—Whip Wilson
- Fence Riders ('50)—Whip Wilson
- Wichita ('55)—Joel McCrea
- Oklahoman ('57)—Joel McCrea
- Man of the West ('57)—Gary Cooper
- Tombstone Territory (TV): series ('57-'60)
- Gunsmoke in Tucson ('58)—Mark Stevens
- Terror in a Texas Town ('58)—Sterling Hayden
- Oklahoma Territory ('60)—Bill Williams

★★★

Saugus Speedway

In April 1930 Hoot Gibson bought the Roy Baker Ranch and Rodeo in Saugus for $250,000. Baker bought the property in 1923 and built the rodeo arena the next year. Hoot renamed it the Golden State Ranch. Hoot said, "I had the biggest rodeos in the country. It seated 22,000. We put on one show, one day per year. All the big celebrities in the picture business never failed to come to that show. Afterwards, I'd always give a big party at the big ranch house on the estate. We had as high as 400-500 people at the party. I owned some of the finest bucking horses in the world."

By the mid-'30s, depression years, the bank was foreclosing on the property and Hoot sold it to Paul Hill in '34 who in turn sold it to William Bonelli by 1939 when auto races were held in the arena. Some TV westerns were lensed in the area under Bonelli's ownership. It's now called Saugus Speedway and Swapmeet.

Take I-5 north to Valencia Blvd., turn right and follow Valencia which turns into Soledad Canyon Rd. (22500 Soledad Canyon Rd. in Saugus.)

★★★

Jauregui Ranch

Newhall, about a 40 minute drive north from Los Angeles along Highway 14, was home to several prominent B-western locations including the oft-used Jauregui Ranch, the first spread on the left east of Highway 14 along Placerita Road.

The Jauregui's main house and front porch, picket or rail fence (depending on the period or movie company wishes), and large oak tree in the front yard were familiar locales for countless B and A westerns and TV series as well as portions of some serials, including Ralph Byrd's "The Vigilante." Perhaps even more familiar was the ranch's large barnyard, located on the west side of the main house and bordered initially on one side and later on two sides by barns, a stable and corral, a blacksmith shop and other buildings.

View of the Jauregui Ranch house today. This is the original front of the house which, over the years as the road changed, became the rear of the now very much in disrepair home.

Andy Jauregui first leased the land on which the ranch stands from Standard Oil (now Chevron) in 1928. At first, "Fat" Jones, who was to develop one of moviedom's major rental stables, worked the ranch with Jauregui, living with his own family in a bunkhouse behind the main house. Jauregui soon bought Jones' interest in the ranch.

"Texas Cowboy" ('29), a Bob Steele silent, was one of the first westerns filmed there although the spread received perhaps its best display in Gene Autry's "Strawberry Roan," Roy Rogers' "Southward Ho," and a number of Tim Holt features, especially "Arizona Ranger" and "Pistol Harvest."

Over the years, the Jaureguis hosted nearly every cowboy star in the industry, from Fred Scott to Ken Maynard and Bob Steele to Eddie Dean and Lash LaRue (in their "Song of Old Wyoming"), to Buck Jones, Dick Foran, Johnny Mack Brown and Charles Starrett, to Joel McCrea, Randy Scott and the Duke. Non-western A-features lensing at the Jauregui included the Claudette Colbert/Fred MacMurray hit, "The Egg and I," which launched the careers of "Ma and Pa Kettle." Among TV series shooting there were "Stoney Burke," "Scarecrow and Mrs. King," "The Fall Guy," Dennis Weaver's short-lived '87-'88 medical series "Buck James" and "Gunsmoke".

Film companies occasionally made changes to the ranch's appearance. The crew for "Strawberry Roan" added, for example, a large back porch to the main house. For a pre-back porch view of the main house's rear see Fred Scott's "In Old Montana." But the Jauregui appeared on film exactly as it was, a working ranch rather than a movie set; even the rooster (a critic perhaps) crowing in the background of scenes filmed there was authentic, not the product of a special effects department. Jauregui films thus had a realistic quality about them, even if most of their plotlines were pure fantasy.

Advancing civilization brought much change to the spread. Originally, the Placerita road had a dirt surface and actually ran through the ranch's barnyard by the front of the main house and east toward the Walker Ranch, with riders and buckboards often filmed riding to or away from the main house on that road. Now, a two-lane, paved Placerita road runs about 300 yards south of the ranch and an entrance road approaches the rear of the main house and bunkhouse area, leading some to confuse the back porch to the main house with its front porch. Highway 14 cuts through much of the Jauregui meadowland once used for filming.

When daughter Noureen Jauregui moved her then 93 year old mother, Camille, off of the ranch in '96, property owner Chevron wasted no time leveling remaining barns, fencing and outbuildings. The oft-seen large barn had actually been razed a year earlier. The main house still stands as well as a couple of smaller buildings. Chevron promptly sold the land to a developer who, in turn, sold the ranch to the Walt Disney Co. in June '98. The Jauregui is adjacent to Disney's Golden Oak Ranch (which is inaccessible without special permission).

At this time a "No Trespassing" sign and gate block the entranceway to the historic Jauregui at 20165 Placerita Canyon Rd. Permission to enter may be obtained through the Disney Corporation.

 Sampling of Westerns Filmed on the JAUREGUI RANCH

- Texas Cowboy ('29)—Bob Steele
- Border Law ('31)—Buck Jones
- Texas Cyclone ('32)—Tim McCoy
- Two Fisted Law ('32)—Tim McCoy
- Texan ('32)—Buffalo Bill Jr.
- A Man's Land ('32)—Hoot Gibson
- The Fugitive ('33)—Rex Bell
- Fighting Through ('34)—Reb Russell
- Cowboy and the Bandit ('35)—Rex Lease
- Western Frontier ('35)—Ken Maynard
- Wild Mustang ('35)—Harry Carey
- Square Shooter ('35)—Tim McCoy
- Big Boy Rides Again ('35)—Big Boy Williams
- Romance Rides the Range ('36)—Fred Scott
- Guns of the Pecos ('37)—Dick Foran
- Reckless Ranger ('37)—Bob Allen
- Colorado Kid ('37)—Bob Steele
- Fighting Texan ('37)—Kermit Maynard
- Guilty Trails ('38)—Bob Baker
- Durango Valley Raiders ('38)—Bob Steele
- Man From Music Mountain ('38)—Gene Autry
- Prairie Justice ('38)—Bob Baker
- Cattle Raiders ('38)—Charles Starrett
- Last Stand ('38)—Bob Baker
- Flaming Lead ('39)—Ken Maynard
- Desperate Trails ('39)—Johnny Mack Brown
- Southward Ho ('39)—Roy Rogers
- In Old Montana ('39)—Fred Scott

- Billy the Kid Outlawed ('40)—Bob Steele
- Texas Marshal ('41)—Tim McCoy
- Gunman From Bodie ('41)—Rough Riders
- Along the Rio Grande ('41)—Tim Holt
- Lone Rider Fights Back ('41)—George Houston
- Billy the Kid In Santa Fe ('41)—Bob Steele
- Rock River Renegades ('42)—Range Busters
- Lone Rider and the Bandit ('42)—George Houston
- Pirates of the Prairie ('42)—Tim Holt
- Thundering Hoofs ('42)—Tim Holt
- South of Santa Fe ('42)—Roy Rogers
- Man From Cheyenne ('42)—Roy Rogers
- Blazing Guns ('43)—Trail Blazers
- Saddles and Sagebrush ('43)—Russell Hayden
- Black Market Rustlers ('43)—Range Busters
- Lumberjack ('44)—Hopalong Cassidy
- Song of Old Wyoming ('45)—Eddie Dean
- The Vigilante ('47)—Ralph Byrd (serial)
- Smoky River Serenade ('47)—Hoosier Hot Shots
- Arizona Ranger ('48)—Tim Holt
- Return of the Badmen ('48)—Randolph Scott
- Strawberry Roan ('48)—Gene Autry
- Gun Play ('51)—Tim Holt
- Hot Lead ('51)—Tim Holt
- Overland Telegraph ('51)—Tim Holt
- Pistol Harvest ('51)—Tim Holt
- Road Agent ('52)—Tim Holt
- Trail Guide ('52)—Tim Holt

★★★

Walker Ranch

One of the smallest, yet most scenic western film sites, was on the Walker Ranch east of Newhall along Placerita Canyon Road. Frank Evans Walker, owner of the ranch during its filming years, inherited the spread from his mother in the 1890s. The main ranch house, only two stone pillars of which are still standing, was situated in a cove on the right about two miles east up the Placerita road from the area primarily used for filming

Front and chimney-side view today of the historic Walker Cabin seen in dozens of westerns.

and now occupied by a state park. Members of the Walker family occupied a small wooden cabin with cut stone chimney situated in the main filming area that was used as a hide-out shack in many films and still stands today.

Films were shot on the spread in the silent era, but Walker Ranch was home mainly to B-westerns. Although the entire ranch comprised well over 300 acres, the area used primarily for filming was quite small, not much larger than a couple of football fields. Prominent features included white-barked sycamore trees and a creek running east-west across the property, sometimes filmed in the rainy season with a small stream running through its bed (Johnny Mack Brown's "Law Comes to Gunsight" '47) but more often lensed dry and dusty.

The only structure used for filming on that portion of the ranch was the tiny Walker cabin. The rear entrance to the cabin also appeared in several titles, sometimes as a separate ranch or hideout shack. Both entrances were seen in the Trail Blazers' "Blazing Guns" ('43), in which chubby Hoot Gibson climbed up the cabin's stone chimney Santa-style to elude the heavies. At an angle behind the cabin, embedded in a hill, was a small mine entrance seen in Jimmy Wakely's "Across the Rio Grande" ('49) and a few other titles.

A ranch insert road about 150 yards long ran east-west by the cabin, which was often seen in chase scenes shot on the road—in fact, frequently, several times in the same chase.

In the trees across the creek bed from the insert road and cabin was another east-west road sometimes used for filming. At a point near the east end of the main filming area, that road curved north across the creek bed to connect with the insert road. A bridge across the creek bed could also sometimes be seen in the background of Walker Ranch scenes ("Under California Stars" '48). Wooded hills surrounded the filming area.

Although most studios utilized Walker Ranch, it was mainly home to Monogram cowboy heroes such as Jack Randall, Tom Keene, Johnny Mack Brown, Jimmy Wakely, Whip Wilson, Rough Riders and others.

In addition to these main filming sites, there was a natural bridge that created a doorway through an earthen embankment. It's used in both "Gunslingers" ('50) and "Rangeland" ('49) with Whip Wilson as well as "Western Renegades" ('49) with Johnny Mack Brown. Jack Randall made regular use of the site which served as the entrance to Iron Eyes Cody's Indian encampment in Randall's "Overland Mail" ('39) and as a hideout for horse thieves in "Wild Horse Canyon" ('38) and "Wild Horse Range" ('40). The top of the natural bridge, which also appeared in Bob Steele's "Wild Horse Valley" ('40) and had a cameo in Hoppy's "Texas Trail" ('37), has collapsed over time. But its remains, now hidden by foliage, are situated next to the south side of the Placerita road about a mile east of the main filming area.

Another cabin, which no longer stands, was located in trees on the edge of the clearing south of Placerita road, about a mile east of the main filming area. Accessible only in the dry season in the early days, the family called this structure the summer cabin, while the cabin on the part of the ranch most used for films was home to the Walkers in the winter until 1938 when the family began occupying the summer cabin year-round. The two structures were similar in appearance, but the summer cabin was wider and had a step leading up to the front porch, while the winter cabin's porch is flush with the ground. Adjacent to the summer cabin were three small bunkhouses and a separate garage, which resembled a cabin and also made some film appearances. The summer cabin is noted in Whip Wilson's "Range Land," and Bob Steele's "Ridin' the Lone Trail" and "Thunder in the Desert."

Between 1949 and 1959, Frank Walker sold the state the property, which is now the 350 acre Placerita Canyon County and State Park.

To reach Walker Ranch from L.A., take Fwy. 170 north to I-5, I-5 north to Hwy. 14, Hwy. 14 to the Placerita Canyon Road exit and the Placerita road several miles to the park entrance on the right. (19152 W. Placerita Canyon Rd.)

Rear view of the Walker Cabin which was also used as a front entranceway in westerns for variety.

Sampling of Westerns Filmed at WALKER RANCH

- Hard Hombre ('31)—Hoot Gibson
- Diamond Trail ('32)—Rex Bell
- Come On Danger ('32)—Tom Keene
- The Fugitive ('33)—Rex Bell
- Wild Mustang ('35)—Harry Carey
- Big Boy Rides Again ('35)—Big Boy Williams
- Roaming Cowboy ('37)—Fred Scott
- Moonlight On the Range ('37)—Fred Scott
- Rough Ridin' Rhythm ('37)—Kermit Maynard
- Where Trails Divide ('37)—Tom Keene
- Ridin' the Lone Trail ('37)—Bob Steele
- Code of the Rangers ('38)—Tim McCoy
- Durango Valley Raiders ('38)—Bob Steele
- Flaming Lead ('39)—Ken Maynard
- Six Gun Rhythm ('39)—Tex Fletcher
- In Old Montana ('39)—Fred Scott
- Young Bill Hickok ('40)—Roy Rogers
- Kid From Santa Fe ('40)—Jack Randall
- Wild Horse Range ('40)—Jack Randall
- Billy the Kid's Roundup ('41)—Buster Crabbe
- Lone Star Lawmen ('41)—Tom Keene
- Forbidden Trails ('41)—Rough Riders
- Lone Rider Ambushed ('41)—George Houston
- Desert Bandit ('41)—Don Barry
- Outlaws of Cherokee Trail ('41)—3 Mesquiteers
- Kid's Last Ride ('41)—Range Busters
- Rock River Renegades ('42)—Range Busters
- West of the Law ('42)—Rough Riders
- Sunset On the Desert ('42)—Roy Rogers
- Ghost Rider ('43)—Johnny Mack Brown
- Blazing Guns ('43)—Trail Blazers
- Bordertown Gunfighters ('43)—Bill Elliott

- Law of the Valley ('44)—Johnny Mack Brown
- Springtime In Texas ('45)—Jimmy Wakely
- Lawless Empire ('45)—Charles Starrett
- Ghost of Hidden Valley ('46)—Buster Crabbe
- Colorado Serenade ('46)—Eddie Dean
- Springtime In the Sierras ('47)—Roy Rogers
- On the Old Spanish Trail ('47)—Roy Rogers
- Oregon Trail Scouts ('47)—Allan Lane
- Law Comes To Gunsight ('47)—Johnny Mack Brown
- Gay Ranchero ('48)—Roy Rogers
- Under California Stars ('48)—Roy Rogers
- Oklahoma Blues ('48)—Jimmy Wakely
- Eyes of Texas ('48)—Roy Rogers
- Shadows of the West ('49)—Whip Wilson
- Lawless Code ('49)—Jimmy Wakely
- Far Frontier ('49)—Roy Rogers
- Fighting Redhead ('49)—Jim Bannon
- Western Renegades ('49)—Johnny Mack Brown
- Sunset In the West ('50)—Roy Rogers
- Pistol Harvest ('51)—Tim Holt
- Silver City Bonanza ('51)—Rex Allen
- Hot Lead ('51)—Tim Holt
- Overland Telegraph ('51)—Tim Holt
- Roy Rogers (TV): Treasure of Howling Dog Canyon ('52)
- Road Agent ('52)—Tim Holt
- Saginaw Trail ('53)—Gene Autry
- Hopalong Cassidy (TV): Outlaw's Reward ('54)
- Law vs. Billy the Kid ('54)—Scott Brady
- Gunsmoke (TV): Bloody Hands ('57)
- Gunsmoke (TV): Twelfth Night ('57)
- U.S. Marshal (TV): The Promise ('58)
- Bat Masterson (TV): Incident at Leadville ('59)

★★★

Vasquez Rocks

Although the filming days of many of our favorite locations are long past, one impressive natural setting seems almost as busy today as it ever was in the golden era. Geologists tell us the huge Vasquez Rocks along Hwy. 14, about a 50 minute drive north of Los Angeles, rested on the floor of a prehistoric ocean over 20 million years ago. As the salt water receded, repeated floods washed away the soil around the sandstone and violent earthquakes tilted the rocks upward into the sky at a sixty-degree angle like giant rockets poised for firing.

The rocks derived their popular name from the notorious bandit Tiburcio Vasquez, who hid with his gang there until he was captured and hanged for murder in 1875.

The first film may have been shot at Vasquez Rocks as early as 1905 but we know the area best as the setting for numerous westerns, serials, non-western actioners and science fiction/horror titles.

Some B-western heroes never made it to the rocks. Rocky Lane's titles were there, for example, only in stock footage ("Bandits of Dark Canyon" '47), PRC's not at all and Monogram's rarely (Jack Randall's "Trigger Smith" '37; Tex Ritter's "Song of the Buckaroo" '39). The advent of TV brought an onslaught of westerns to the area. Adult TV westerns, from "Wanted Dead or Alive" and "Tall Man" to "Bonanza" and "Hondo," lensed at the rocks, as did big-budget futuristic adventures and non-western TV series. Nor has such demand subsided in recent years. The area played Bedrock in Steven Spielberg's '93 feature version of "The Flintstones." Commercials for Taco Bell, Energizer batteries, MasterCard, Wrigley's gum, Hanes underwear and many other products regularly lense there.

Acquired by L.A. County in the '60s, the 745-acre area became a park in 1970.

To reach the great Vasquez Rocks area, which, despite parking spaces, picnic benches and rest facilities, still looks almost exactly as it did in B-westerns, take Fwy. 170 north from L.A. to I-5, I-5 north to Hwy. 14, Hwy. 14 north to the Agua Dulce exit and the Agua Dulce road left to the entrance road to the rocks, which are also visible from Hwy. 14.

Dramatic Vasquez Rocks loom up off Hwy. 14.

Sampling of Westerns Filmed at VASQUEZ ROCKS

- Walloping Kid ('26)—Kit Carson
- Clearing the Range ('31)—Hoot Gibson
- Branded Men ('31)—Ken Maynard
- Hard Hombre ('31)—Hoot Gibson
- Broadway to Cheyenne ('32)—Rex Bell
- Whistlin' Dan ('32)—Ken Maynard
- Texas Gunfighter ('32)—Ken Maynard
- Son of the Border ('33)—Tom Keene
- Arizona Nights ('34)—Jack Perrin
- Stone of Silver Creek ('35)—Buck Jones
- Tonto Kid ('35)—Rex Bell
- Rustlers of Red Dog ('35)—Johnny Mack Brown (serial)
- Lawless Range ('35)—John Wayne
- Cavalcade of the West ('36)—Hoot Gibson
- Fighting Texan ('37)—Kermit Maynard
- Panamint's Badman ('38)—Smith Ballew
- Song of the Buckaroo ('39)—Tex Ritter
- Golden Trail ('40)—Tex Ritter
- Young Buffalo Bill ('40)—Roy Rogers
- Colorado ('40)—Roy Rogers
- Jesse James At Bay ('41)—Roy Rogers
- Arizona Terror ('42)—Don Barry
- Sunset On the Desert ('42)—Roy Rogers
- Rainbow Over Texas ('46)—Roy Rogers
- Adventures of Don Coyote ('47)—Richard Martin
- Apache Rose ('47)—Roy Rogers
- Along the Oregon Trail ('47)—Monte Hale
- Gallant Legion ('48)—Bill Elliott
- Far Frontier ('49)—Roy Rogers
- I Killed Geronimo ('50)—James Ellison
- Border Rangers ('50)—Don Barry
- Barricade ('50)—Dane Clark
- Sugarfoot ('51)—Randolph Scott
- Last Musketeer ('52)—Rex Allen
- Conquest of Cochise ('53)—Robert Stack
- Massacre Canyon ('54)—Phil Carey
- Stories of the Century (TV): Tiburcio Vasquez ('54)
- Champion (TV): Outlaw's Secret ('55)
- Shotgun ('55)—Sterling Hayden
- Rin Tin Tin (TV): Shifting Sands ('55)
- Cheyenne (TV): Mountain Fortress ('55)
- Buffalo Bill Jr. (TV): Empire Pass ('55)
- White Squaw ('56)—William Bishop
- Champion (TV): Badmen of the Valley ('56)
- Annie Oakley (TV): Tuffy ('57)
- Tombstone Territory (TV): Gatling Gun ('58)
- Broken Arrow (TV): Kingdom of Terror ('58)
- Laramie (TV): opening credits ('59)
- Johnny Ringo (TV): Single Debt ('60)
- Westerner (TV): Ghost of a Chance ('60)
- Overland Trail (TV): opening credits ('60)
- Tall Man (TV): Apache Daughter ('61)
- A Thunder of Drums ('61)—Richard Boone
- Bat Masterson (TV): Dagger Dance ('61)
- Dakotas (TV): A Walk Through the Badlands ('63)
- Wagon Train (TV): Adam MacKenzie Story ('63)
- Wagon Train (TV): Bob Stuart Story ('64)
- Laredo (TV): A Matter of Policy ('65)
- Bonanza (TV): Ride the Wind ('65)
- Bonanza (TV): Last Mission ('66)
- Gunpoint ('66)—Audie Murphy
- Apache Uprising ('66)—Rory Calhoun
- Custer (TV): Dangerous Prey ('67)
- Arizona Bushwackers ('68)—Howard Keel
- Lancer (TV): Splinter Group ('70)
- Bonanza (TV): Gold Mine ('70)
- Bonanza (TV): Shadow of a Hero ('71)

★★

Sable Ranch/Rancho Maria

Along Sand Canyon Road near Newhall, about a 40 minute ride from L.A., are two little-used but interesting locations that continue as filming sites today—Sable Ranch and Rancho Maria.

Area rancher Frank Sentous built the Sable Ranch circa 1920. Later owned by others, the spread received its current name when chickens advertised "smooth as sable" were raised on the ranch. It features a large stone main house with a high front porch and circular stone terrace situated camera right from the front porch of the house.

A stable with individual horse stalls is located camera left down from the front porch. The property also includes other outbuildings. The ranch played a prominent part in "Ride 'Em Cowboy" with Johnny Mack Brown and Dick Foran as straight-men to Abbott & Costello.

Sable received its most impressive B-western display as Roy Rogers' ranch for a brief early scene (with character actors Ed Cobb and John Hamilton on the circular terrace) in "Bells of Coronado", for which most exteriors were shot at nearby Littlerock Dam and other Palmdale-Lancaster area sites.

The Sable Ranch actually has seen more use as a filming location in recent years than during the Golden Age. It was Jim Garner's ranch in "Bret Maverick," the '81-'82 extension of the '50s TV series. A ranch set was constructed in the field between Sand Canyon Road and the main house for Beau Bridges' '93 TVer "Harts of the West" and the main house was also occasionally used in that short-lived series. Other non-western films have lensed there in recent years.

Two hundred yards or so east of Sable Ranch we find Rancho Maria which may have been owned at one time by B-movie producer Philip N. Krasne and known as the Circle-K; at least a 1938 trade item indicates Krasne was then filming "Trigger Pals" ('39) on his Circle-K ranch. The barnyard and stables used in that Lee Powell Grand National closely resemble those at Rancho Maria. It is known that sometime in the '40s movie horse trainer Ralph McCutcheon acquired the 153 acre Rancho Maria property. What is unknown is how long he owned the filming site.

The most interesting feature at this little ranch is not its modest main house, but its patio swimming pool, an excellent site for dude ranch scenes. Rancho Maria and its pool played that part in Jimmy Wakely's first starrer, "Song of the Range", which Krasne produced, and in Gene Autry's big-budget Cinecolor entry, "The Big Sombrero".

Rancho Maria also includes a fence-lined entrance road visible in "Song of the Range," several barns that can be seen (very briefly) in "Big Sombrero" and a small western street, first constructed, according to a caretaker, for the Kenny Rogers TV movie "Gambler III: The Legend Continues".

To reach the ranches, who share a combined 400 acres, take I-170 and I-5 north from Los Angeles to Hwy. 14, Hwy. 14 north to the Placerita Canyon Road exit, right (or northeast) on Placerita to Sand Canyon Road, right on Sand Canyon about 100 yards to the ranch entrances on the right. Both ranches, now owned by an L.A. camera shop operator who prefers to remain anonymous, are accessed by the entrance gate to the Sable Ranch, sometimes locked.

Sable Ranch with its large stone main house still sees use today. It recently saw duty on Fox's serial-like "24" with Keifer Sutherland.

Sampling of Westerns Filmed at SABLE RANCH

- Ride 'Em Cowboy ('40)—Abbott and Costello
- Bells of Coronado ('50)—Roy Rogers
- Bret Maverick (TV): series ('81-'82)—James Garner
- Harts of the West (TV): series ('93)—Beau Bridges

RANCHO MARIA

- Song of the Range ('44)—Jimmy Wakely
- Big Sombrero ('49)—Gene Autry
- Golden Eye ('48)—Roland Winters (Charlie Chan)
- Gambler III ('87)—Kenny Rogers

★★

Lake Los Angeles

Most B-westerns set in an arid area with many rock formations and few, if any, trees were filmed at Lone Pine, Red Rock Canyon or, in later years, Pioneertown. But a number of Republic titles of the later B-western era used an area similar in some respects to those famous sites yet, obviously, a different locale.

The area featured Joshua trees and scattered rock formations similar to those at Pioneertown as well as a large dry lake. In the distance beyond the lake could be seen a large hill and three progressively smaller hills camera right of the largest hill. The rock formations received prominent display in action scenes for "Trigger, Jr." and Roy rode Trigger in the direction of the dry lake and distant hills at the end of the picture. The hills and rock formations are also seen in the exciting horsenapping scene in "South of Caliente" with Roy Rogers as well as for portions of chases in Rex Allen's "The Last Musketeer," although most action scenes for that title were shot at Vasquez Rocks north of Newhall.

Several Jack Randall Monogram titles were shot in part in the same Lake Los Angeles area where the Rogers and Allen titles were filmed.

To reach Lake Los Angeles, about an hour drive from Los Angeles, take Fwy. 170 north to I-5, I-5 north to Hwy. 14, Hwy 14 north to Palmdale and the first Palmdale exit east through town until the road curves sharply to the right (southeast). At that point leave that main road and continue east on a secondary road a few miles to Lake Los Angeles. You'll find residential streets with names such as High Chaparral, Rawhide and MacKenna's Gold even though none of those were lensed there.

Many Jack Randall Monogram Bs were lensed around Lake Los Angeles rock formations.

Sampling of Westerns Filmed at LAKE LOS ANGELES

- Mexicali Kid ('38)—Jack Randall
- Trigger Smith ('39)—Jack Randall
- Overland Mail ('39)—Jack Randall
- Trigger, Jr. ('50)—Roy Rogers

- South of Caliente ('51)—Roy Rogers
- Pals of the Golden West ('51)—Roy Rogers
- Last Musketeer ('52)—Rex Allen

★★★

Littlerock Dam

Action shots for Roy Rogers' "Bells of Coronado" ('50) and "The Far Frontier" ('48) were filmed at Littlerock Dam near Palmdale, about an hour's drive north of Los Angeles. Completed in 1924 to provide water for the area's pear orchards, the 170-foot-tall multi-arch structure is located only a few miles from the San Andreas fault and has been a perennial concern of state bureaucrats—so much so it was briefly drained of water in the '80s. But Littlerock held firm against the torrential rains of the early '90s. Its familiar arched side and impressive downstream view remain today exactly as they appeared in the Rogers films.

Take Palmdale Blvd. through Palmdale. Outside the east end of Palmdale follow the main road as it curves to the right and continue to the community of Little Rock. Ask for directions to the dam.

★★★

Noah Beery Sr. Ranch

The Noah Beery Sr. Ranch near Valyermo, 30 minutes or so southeast of Palmdale, was built in the '20s by brothers Wallace and Noah Beery as a 145 acre playground for their Hollywood friends complete with luxury hotel, huge ballroom, swimming pool and trout ponds.

Sadly, most of the facility burned in 1930 but the stone archway that led to the ballroom in Ken Maynard's "In Old Santa Fe" ('34) can still be seen. The Joshua tree studded countryside was also utilized in that Mascot feature. Bob Custer's "Scarlet Brand" ('32) was also filmed here.

Owned by the Beery family until 1938, the site is now a youth camp.

Leaving Palmdale, go east on Hwy. 138 and exit south at Pearblossom. 5-6 miles to Velyermo.

★★★

Drake Ranch

Prolific director/producer/screenwriter/songwriter Oliver Drake began in the late silent era at FBO working with Tom Tyler and Bob Steele. In the '30s, he rode the low budget range in various capacities with Reb Russell, Jack Hoxie, Bill Cody and Tom Tyler. Moving over to Republic, Ollie supervised/wrote/directed westerns starring Gene Autry and the 3 Mesquiteers. In the '40s Ollie spent time at Universal on the Johnny Mack Brown and Rod Cameron features as well as the Jimmy Wakelys at Monogram.

In the late '40s the ultra lowbudget Sunset Carson pictures were lensed on a ranch Oliver Drake had bought in the early '40s. He and a group of his friends, nicknamed "the Beasties", helped build the ranch house (Ted French, Steve Keyes, Eddie Majors, Lucky Brown etc.). The main house was situated on a bluff overlooking Big Rock Creek near Pearblossom (on desert Hwy. 138 between Palmdale and Apple Valley).

Sampling of Westerns Filmed at DRAKE RANCH

- Fighting Mustang ('48)—Sunset Carson
- Deadline ('48)—Sunset Carson
- Sunset Carson Rides Again ('48)—Sunset Carson
- Battling Marshal ('50)—Sunset Carson
- Adventures of Rick O'Shay (TV): Steve Keyes ('50)
- Kid From Gower Gulch ('50)—Spade Cooley

★★

Chatsworth Depot

The Chatsworth train line from Simi Valley to Chatsworth, including the curve near Iverson's and the nearby underpass, and the Chatsworth Train Depot were often used in westerns and serials. That depot was torn down in 1962. A Metrolink station now stands in the approximate location.

Take the 101 freeway north and exit at Topanga Canyon Rd. Turn right. At Lassen St. turn right, then left at Canoga Ave. and look for the Metrolink station.

The oft-used train tunnel is beneath Topanga Canyon Rd. just south of Santa Susanna Pass Rd. Both sides of the tunnel were used for filming.

Sampling of Westerns Filmed at CHATSWORTH DEPOT

- Local Bad Man ('32)—Hoot Gibson
- Utah Trail ('38)—Tex Ritter
- Mysterious Dr. Satan ('40)—Robert Wilcox (serial)
- King of the Texas Rangers ('41)—Sammy Baugh (serial)
- Heldorado ('46)—Roy Rogers
- Superman ('48)—Kirk Alyn (serial)
- Fancy Pants ('50)—Bob Hope
- Government Agents Vs. Phantom Legion ('51)—Walter Reed (serial)

★★

Chatsworth Lake

Chatsworth Lake, now only a small pond, once played host to Roy Rogers' "Susanna Pass" ('49) and Monte Hale's "Home On the Range" and "Man From Rainbow Valley" (both '46). On Valley Circle Blvd. by Chatsworth Oaks Park in Chatsworth.

★★

Towsley Canyon Road

Winding Towsley Canyon Rd. in the Newhall/Santa Clarita Santa Susanna Mountains area played host to several later westerns including "Last Stagecoach West" ('57) with Jim Davis.

Now part of Davis Park and Nature Trail, it features a terrific narrows with high cliffs and a stream in the canyon. Take I-5 north to Calgrave Blvd. in Santa Clarita, go left under the freeway. Entrance to Towsley Canyon is about a quarter mile.

★★

Bell Ranch

In the mountains separating the famed Iverson location ranch of Chatsworth and Corriganville in the Simi Valley, we find a less well-known filming site, the Bell Ranch. The area was a frequent site for silent flicks; in fact, a 1920s flyer carried real estate advertisements for the Bell Moving Picture Ranch area.

A man named Berry eventually purchased the Bell holdings but later sold his 120 acres to Rosemary Couch and Jean Forsythe who dubbed the area the Berry Ranch when leasing to movie companies. In 1950, Couch and Forsythe sold five acres of the property to a studio location manager who resurrected the Bell Ranch name although location listings for certain films shot there would continue to carry the Berry Ranch location.

In 1955 a western street was built on the Bell Ranch property from the remains of residences then being razed in Los Angeles. Sets constructed for particular productions were also left behind for future use. An adobe cabin on property adjoining the Bell Ranch area became a favorite filming site for Disney's "Zorro" TV series, as did other portions of the ranch.

The western street and the rock formations and chase roads of the area also played host to "Have Gun Will Travel", "Big Valley", "How the West Was Won" and other TVers, as well as such A-westerns as "Outrage" and "Hombre".

The ranch overlooked the San Fernando Valley which was often visible in the background of chase scenes shot there. Its original western street, put to most extensive use perhaps in Audie Murphy's "Quick Gun" ('64), burned in 1965 but was soon rebuilt. The second street was last seen in "Sunset" with Jim Garner and Bruce Willis.

When the county rezoned in 1990, the buildings were donated to the Wilderness Institute of Agoura Hills and moved. Only the adobe structure (which locals fittingly call "Zorro's Cabin") still stands.

To reach the area, take Santa Susanna Pass Rd. west from Chatsworth, left onto Box Canyon Road, turn left at Studio Road (however, it is now prominently labeled "Private Road—No Trespassing"), a half mile or so up Studio Road to the end of the pavement.

Only the adobe "Zorro's cabin" still stands on the Bell Ranch.

Sampling of Westerns Filmed on BELL RANCH

- The Palomino ('50)—Jerome Courtland
- Carson City ('52)—Randolph Scott
- Zorro (TV): various episodes ('57-'61)
- Big Valley (TV): various episodes ('65-'69)
- Quick Gun ('64)—Audie Murphy

- Monroes (TV): Ghosts of Paradox ('67)
- Hombre ('67)—Paul Newman
- Hard On the Trail ('71)—Lash LaRue
- Gunsmoke (TV): Shadler ('73)
- Sunset ('88)—Bruce Willis

★★

Iverson Ranch

One of the most familiar locations of the golden age of westerns is the great Iverson Ranch of Chatsworth, in the northwest corner of the San Fernando Valley, about a forty-minute drive from North Hollywood. For location fans, Iverson's—with its cliffs, chase roads, enormous rock formations and elaborate sets—was the premiere filming site of the western era.

In 1880, Augusta Wagman, a native of Sweden, established a 160-acre homestead on the property that was to become the Iverson Ranch. In 1888 she married Karl Iverson, a native of Norway who had obtained an adjacent 160-acre homestead. Their ranch, eventually to comprise about 500 acres, apparently first played host to a movie company for a 1912 silent "Man, Woman and Marriage."

Later, other silent epics lensed on the Iverson with the ranch reaching its prime in the sound era, ultimately serving as a filming site for more than 2,000 features and TV episodes and at times hosting as many as eight movie crews at once, at fees of $100 per day and up by the mid-forties. Along with B-westerns, many major features lensed at the ranch, including Gary Cooper's "The Plainsman" ('36), Errol Flynn's "They Died with Their Boots On" ('42) and, of course, John Wayne's "Stagecoach" ('39).

In the '30s, when the ranch became a major filming site, a three-way split was arranged, with sons Aaron, Joe, and their parents each receiving a third of the ranch's profits from location rentals. Augusta and Karl Iverson died in the late '40s, and in 1957 the brothers worked out another split, with Joe taking over the portion of the ranch known as the lower Iverson and Aaron assuming control of the upper Iverson, each parcel totaling around 250 acres. In 1958, Aaron had a stroke and his son Edwin took over management of upper Iverson filming sites.

As filming dwindled on the ranch in the early '60s, Joe Iverson sold 16 acres of the lower Iverson in 1963 for construction of Indian Hills trailer park on the site where the ranch's only western street previously stood. Construction of the Simi Valley (now Ronald Reagan) freeway through the property in '65-'67 further diminished the site's value as a filming location and, in 1965, Aaron Iverson sold approximately 90 acres of the upper Iverson. A huge September 25, 1970, fire destroyed most of the movie sets at the ranch and, in later years, Joe sold an additional 200 acres of the lower Iverson, leaving around 22 acres in his hands. In the '80s, Joe sold that parcel to Bob Sherman, a relative of his second wife, whom Joe had married in the late '40s following his first wife's death in an automobile accident. With Sherman living in Joe's house and the elder Iverson occupying the old folk's home overlooking the valley, Sherman attempted to revive the ranch as a motion picture location spread, but with limited success.

90

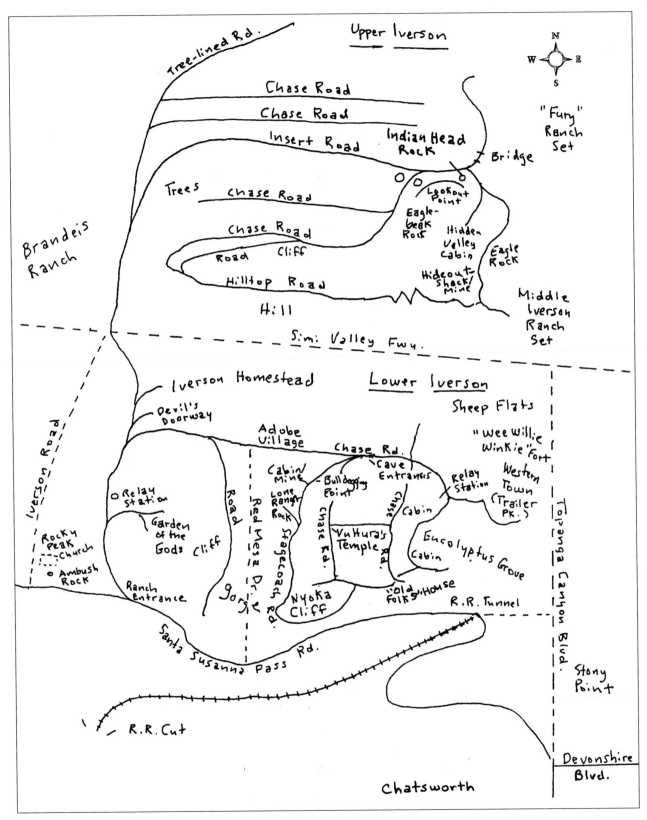

A map of the historic Iverson Ranch filming location as it was circa 1950. *Map designed and drawn by Tinsley Yarbrough.*

By the early '90s, a condo complex covered much of the lower Iverson, huge mansions were desecrating the upper spread, and an apartment complex occupied much of the valley east of the upper spread where the main Iverson ranch set had once been located.

Finally, faced with growing financial difficulties, Sherman, in 1997, sold the six Iverson acres still in his possession to Van Swearingen of North Hills, California, a classic car collector who voiced hopes of constructing a western set, a '50s-era set for display of his autos, a museum of Iverson artifacts and a number of children's attractions on the property before his untimely death.

The most famous site on the ranch, the Garden of the Gods rock formations—so named because of their resemblance to Colorado formations of that name—were donated in the '80s to the Santa Susanna Conservancy for preservation as a nature area.

Edwin Iverson still owns 140 undeveloped acres on the upper Iverson and kept 12 acres of a large hill separating the lower and upper spreads until he sold that parcel about 10 years ago. Much of the remaining property has become a developer's paradise—and a movie fan's nightmare.

Lower Iverson

Although Iverson is now largely finished as a filming site, in its heyday it boasted, by far, the most extensive facilities and sets of all the location ranches, including more than 25 miles of chase roads. The lower Iverson— now bordered on the north by the Simi freeway, on the south by the Santa Susanna Pass Rd., on the east by Topanga Canyon Blvd. and on the west by Iverson Rd.—included numerous separate filming sites such as the famous Garden of the Gods rocks.

West of that area was a field rarely used for filming, which now is the site for the Rocky Peak Church. At the end of the church parking lot, however, you can find one of several ambush rocks ("Out California Way" '46) on the ranch.

A bit north of the Garden of the Gods was a two-story house sometimes used as a stagecoach relay station that, in later years, was moved farther up the road. Its proximity to the Garden of the Gods can be seen in Don Barry's "Stagecoach Express" ('42). It was also used in scenes for Roy Rogers' "Heldorado" ('46).

Farther north on the ranch entrance road one sideroad to the east took riders into a lower Iverson canyon or gorge, another led to the well-known Devil's Doorway rock formation through which Gene Autry rode in "Oh, Susanna" ('36)

Oft seen Devil's Doorway rock formation through which Gene Autry rode in "Oh, Susanna" and Lash LaRue stalked his prey in "King of the Bullwhip".

and Lash LaRue stalked his prey in "King of the Bullwhip" ('51).

In an area east of Devil's Doorway was an adobe Indian village first built for "Last Days of Pompeii" ('35) and later seen in such titles as Eddie Dean's "Romance of the West" ('46) and Lash LaRue's "Outlaw Country" ('49). That village overlooked the Iverson canyon or gorge.

Overlooking the stagecoach road near the south end of the gorge was the famous Nyoka Cliff which not only appeared in that great 1942 William Witney serial, but was also utilized for exciting scenes in "The Crimson Ghost" ('46), "Valley of Vanishing Men" ('42), "Haunted Harbor" and Wild Bill Elliott's "Taming of the West" ('39), among others.

From Nyoka Cliff, up a stagecoach road is the famous Lone Ranger rock before which the Ranger reared Silver at the beginning of each TV episode.

Nestled in large rocks farther up the gorge was a mine entrance, another rock doorway, and a stone cabin which appeared in Bob Livingston's "Pride of the Plains" ('44) and "Adventures of Red Ryder" ('40), among others. That cabin, incidentally, was *moved* to the upper Iverson in later years, where it appeared in several of Lash LaRue's titles.

Can't you just picture the Lone Ranger rearing up on Silver beside this famous Iverson rock location?

The Iverson western street first built by Gary Cooper's production company for his "Along Came Jones" ('45), later appeared in John Payne's "El Paso" ('49) and was often referred to as El Paso street. It was the site for numerous scenes in titles of the later B-western era (e.g. Gene Autry's "Hills of Utah"; Eddie Dean's "Check Your Guns"; Whip Wilson's "Lawless Cowboys" and Columbia's "Vigilante" serial).

The lower Iverson was dotted with chase roads and cabins, now mostly long gone, having given way to the urban sprawl.

Brandeis Ranch

Until the early '40s, film companies sometimes used the neighboring Brandeis Ranch, situated on the western edge of the upper Iverson. At times, in fact, titles utilized both ranches, creating the impression all filming was being done on the same spread.

First homesteaded in the 1870s by Niles and Ann Johnson and known as the Johnson Ranch, the property was later purchased by John Brandeis, scion of the wealthy Omaha, Nebraska, family whose patriarch, Jonas L. Brandeis, founded one of the nation's largest department stores.

The Brandeis Ranch was most frequently home to independent cheapies, such as Tim McCoy's "Lightning Carson Rides Again" ('38) and "Arizona Gangbusters" ('40) and Jack Perrin's "Gun Grit" ('36), but attracted some of the major B-western units as well. Brandeis

The Brandeis Ranch townset was often used as a ghost town in B-westerns. Ghosts of the past on dusty, once-busy chase roads are all that's left today.

sets included a small western street dubbed "Hickyville" by locals, perhaps because of its somewhat ramshackle appearance. It showed up as a ghost town in the 3 Mesquiteers' "Ghost Town Gold" ('36), John Wayne's "Winds of the Wasteland" ('36), Charles Starrett's "Cowboy Star" ('36) and Bob Baker's "Ghost Town Riders" ('38). Lensing at the ranch also featured the surrounding countryside, which included many eucalyptus trees and evergreens as well as rock formations similar to, but less distinctive than, those at Iverson (e.g. Bob Steele's "Sundown Saunders" '36).

The Brandeis caretaker's house, a single-story, white house with slightly pitched roof and a huge boulder visible camera left behind the house, appeared in many titles, including the 3 Mesquiteers' "Heroes of the Hills" ('38), "Cowboy Star" and Johnny Mack Brown's "Law of the Range" ('41)—in which the lower Iverson relay station near the Garden of the Gods served as another ranch.

Near the caretaker's home, against a backdrop of boulders, was a smaller, more modest house often serving as a bunkhouse or hideout shack. That house, which featured an unusual ramp-like structure with crude railing running across its front (camera right), can be seen in Tim McCoy's "Ghost Patrol" ('36) and the 3 Mesquiteers' "Santa Fe Stampede" ('38). The caretaker's home, bunkhouse and several outbuildings were situated about a quarter mile west of the upper Iverson entrance road, while the ghost town was at Hialeah Springs, about a mile and a half west of the caretaker's house near the base of Rocky Peak, an area landmark. A stream from the springs ran beneath a bridge located at one end of the ghost town street.

At some point in the early '40s, John Brandeis ended use of the ranch for filming. Charles Starrett's "West of Tombstone" ('42) was one of the last films to use the caretaker's house; the Range Busters' "Trail of the Silver Spurs" ('41) and "Wells Fargo Days," a Dennis Moore color short filmed in 1940 and released in '44, were among the last titles to feature the ghost town. However, both the bunkhouse and caretaker's house make a several-years-later one-time appearance in Bill Elliott's "Last Bandit" ('49).

Middle Iverson

A valley east of the large hill separating the lower and upper spreads, sometimes referred to as the middle Iverson, hosted the Iverson's ranch set. Termed Halfway House by the Iverson family, the ranch was first constructed in the early '40s, probably as a result of the decision by the owner of the adjacent Brandeis Ranch to no longer permit use of his caretaker's house for filming.

The middle Iverson ranch featured a main house with four front entrances, two of which were frequently used in filming, a large barn (through which a driverless car with Gabby Hayes in the trunk raced in "Bells of Rosarita" '45), and one or two small outbuildings. One of the two frequently used front entrances to the house can be seen in late-'40s PRC/Eagle-Lion films (e.g. "Hawk of Powder River" '48 with Eddie Dean; "Cheyenne Takes Over" '47 with Lash LaRue). The other is observed in Sunset Carson's "Rough Riders of Cheyenne" ('45), one of the relatively few Republic titles to use the ranch set. A full house, the ranch served as the Iverson caretaker's home for years. The barn burned in the mid-forties and was replaced with a long, low, bunkhouse-style building.

In the mid-'50s, the barn seemed to reappear in TVers and B-plus features, but actually the "Fury" TV series company had simply built a very similar ranch set, complete with large barn, about a half mile north of the original ranch set, so the "Fury" set was the one frequently seen in later features and TV entries. The '70 fire destroyed both ranch sets.

Upper Iverson

Although the lower Iverson boasted the best-known filming sites, the upper spread was probably used more frequently for filming, especially in the later B-western era. A field at the north base of the hill, separating the upper and lower Iverson, featured a large rock formation that could be seen in numerous titles jutting through trees at the base of the hill (e.g. "Tiger Woman") and was also sometimes used for cliff fights, as in Allan Lane's "Silver City Kid" ('44).

The upper Iverson was lined with chase roads. Just below a frequently seen eagle-beak rock overlooking the east end of the field was a favorite lookout site for bandit gangs, who would then swoop down onto the upper Iverson's long, wide, east-west insert road for yet another thrilling chase. That insert road was prominent in countless titles, from such cheapies as Buster Crabbe's "Devil Riders" ('43) to Roy Rogers' "Twilight In the Sierras" ('50) and "Spoilers of the Plains" ('51). The lookout spot also served as the site for

some exciting cliff fights, as in Red Ryder's "California Gold Rush" ('46). One chase road curved southward by a section of very unusually shaped rocks, including one resembling an Indian head ("Valley of Hunted Men" '42 w/3 Mesquiteers) and led into a 'Hidden Valley' section of the upper spread where the cabin previously situated in the lower Iverson gorge was placed for later B-western entries.

The upper Iverson is where an often-used hillside hideout shack with stone

A view of Indian Head Rock at Iversons. This famous rock can be seen in literally dozens of B, A and TV westerns.

steps and two fake mine entrances embedded side-by-side in the rock just south of the shack was located. Among countless titles featuring that shack, see the exciting climax to Durango's "Snake River Desperadoes" ('51).

Directions: To get to Iverson, take Fwy. 170 north to I-5, I-5 north to Fwy. 118 (Simi Valley Fwy.), 118 west to Topanga Canyon Blvd. exit, Topanga south to Santa Susanna Pass Rd., Santa Susanna west to Red Mesa Drive and Iverson Rd., the current entrances to the lower and upper Iversons. Unfortunately, the upper and middle Iversons are closed

Sampling of Westerns Filmed on IVERSON / BRANDEIS RANCH

- Cheyenne Kid ('33)—Tom Keene (Lower)
- Singing Cowboy ('36)—Gene Autry (Brandeis)
- Winds of the Wasteland ('36)—John Wayne (Brandeis)
- Ghost Town ('36)—Harry Carey (Brandeis)
- Ghost Patrol ('36)—Tim McCoy (Brandeis)
- Cavalcade Of the West ('36)—Hoot Gibson (Brandeis)
- Blazing Justice ('36)—Bill Cody (Brandeis)
- Oh, Susanna ('36)—Gene Autry (Lower)
- Ghost Town Gold ('36)—3 Mesquiteers (Brandeis)
- Gun Grit (36)—Jack Perrin (Brandeis)
- Feud Of the Trail ('37)—Tom Tyler (Brandeis)
- Cowboy Star ('37)—Charles Starrett (Brandeis)
- Heroes of the Hills ('38)—3 Mesquiteers (Brandeis)
- Prairie Moon ('38)—Gene Autry (Brandeis)
- Santa Fe Stampede ('38)—3 Mesquiteers (Brandeis)
- Whirlwind Horseman ('38)—Ken Maynard (Brandeis)
- Knight Of the Plains ('38)—Fred Scott (Brandeis)
- Gunsmoke Trail ('38)—Jack Randall (Brandeis)
- Ghost Town Riders ('38)—Bob Baker (Brandeis)
- Two Gun Justice ('38)—Tim McCoy (Brandeis)
- Durango Valley Raiders ('38)—Bob Steele (Upper)
- Outlaw's Paradise ('39)—Tim McCoy (Brandeis)
- Taming of the West ('39)—Bill Elliott (Lower)
- Phantom Rancher ('40)—Ken Maynard (Brandeis)
- Trail Of the Silver Spurs ('41)—Range Busters (Brandeis)
- Lone Rider In Ghost Town ('41)—George Houston (Brandeis)
- West of Tombstone ('42)—Charles Starrett/Russell Hayden (Brandeis)
- Valley of Vanishing Men ('42)—Bill Elliott (serial) (Lower)
- Zorro's Black Whip ('44)—Linda Stirling (serial) (Lower)
- Vigilantes of Dodge City ('44)—Bill Elliott (Lower)
- Wells Fargo Days ('44)—Dennis Moore (Brandeis)
- Lone Texas Ranger ('45)—Bill Elliott (Lower)
- Stagecoach to Denver ('46)—Allan Lane (Lower)
- Caravan Trail ('46)—Eddie Dean (Lower)
- Cheyenne Takes Over ('47)—Lash LaRue (Middle)
- Border Feud ('47)—Lash LaRue (Lower)
- Belle Starr's Daughter ('47)—George Montgomery (Middle)
- Dead Man's Gold ('47)—Lash LaRue (Lower, Middle, Upper)
- Fighting Redhead ('49)—Jim Bannon (Middle)
- Saddle Tramp ('50)—Joel McCrea (Upper)
- Arizona Territory ('50)—Whip Wilson (Lower, Upper)
- Gold Strike ('50)—Tex Williams (Brandeis stock footage)
- King of the Bullwhip ('51)—Lash LaRue (Lower)
- Gold Raiders ('51)—George O'Brien (Lower, Upper)
- Blazing Bullets ('51)—Johnny Mack Brown (Lower, Upper)
- Abilene Trail ('51)—Whip Wilson (Lower, Middle, Upper)
- Stage to Blue River ('51)—Whip Wilson (Upper, Lower)
- Overland Telegraph ('51)—Tim Holt (Upper, Lower)
- Leadville Gunslinger ('52)—Rocky Lane (Upper)
- Smoky Canyon ('52)—Charles Starrett (Middle)
- Cisco Kid (TV): Robber Crow ('52) (Upper, Lower)
- Cisco Kid (TV): Pot of Gold ('54) (Upper)
- Stories of the Century (TV): Sam Bass ('54) (Lower)
- Kit Carson (TV): Overland Stage ('54) (Lower, Upper)
- I Killed Wild Bill Hickok ('56)—Johnny Carpenter (Lower)
- Annie Oakley (TV): Annie and the Lacemaker ('56) (Middle)
- Lone Ranger (TV): Outlaw Masquerade ('57) (Lower townset)
- Annie Oakley (TV): Tuffy ('57) (Lower)
- Bonanza (TV): Death On Sun Mountain ('59)
- Rough Riders (TV): A Matter of Instinct ('59) (Middle)
- Tombstone Territory (TV): Innocent Man ('60) (Upper)
- Bonanza (TV): The Savage ('60)
- Bonanza (TV): The Ride ('62)
- Bonanza (TV): The Gamble ('62)
- Bonanza (TV): Walter and the Outlaws ('64)
- Destry (TV): Red Brady's Kid ('64) (Upper)
- Bonanza (TV): Caution: Easter Bunny Crossing ('70)
- Fury (TV): series ('55-'60) (Middle)

Lois Hall, leading lady to Whip Wilson, Jimmy Wakely, Charles Starrett, Johnny Mack Brown, TV's "Range Rider" and others, puts her handprints in wet cement during an Iverson Wild West Days celebration in 1996.

to the public, but the Garden of the Gods area is open. Along Red Mesa Drive, one can see Lone Ranger Rock, Nyoka Cliff and the faint outlines of the stagecoach road.

Once a year in September or October Iverson's stages a Wild West Days Celebration and honors various celebrities with foot printings. Celebrities foot and hand-prints that have been done over the years and can be seen include House Peters Jr., Lois Hall, Dick Jones, Eddie Dean, Lee Aaker, Donna Martell, Kelo Henderson, Elena Verdugo, Bobby ("Fury") Diamond, John Mitchum, Neil Summers, Chris Alcaide, Montie Montana, Tommy Farrell, Jan Merlin, Gloria Henry, Caren Marsh, Ruth Terry and others.

★★

Corriganville

Corriganville in the Simi Valley, second only to the Iverson Ranch as the busiest location site of the golden era, was home to hundreds of western movies, TVers and such non-western fare as several "Jungle Jim" entries and serials. The property once hosted a valley stagecoach stop and was an occasional site for filming in its pre-Corriganville days.

Ray "Crash" Corrigan purchased the 1,740-acre spread, later enlarged to 2,060 acres, in 1937 for $11,354 and lost no time developing the property for film use. Although no footage for Warner Bros.' "Adventures of Robin Hood" was apparently shot at the ranch, the presence of Warner Bros. scouts there at the very time the studio was scouting sites close to Los Angeles for the Errol Flynn hit lends some credence to speculation Corrigan constructed the 372-foot lagoon in an effort to lure that big-budget production to his new

ranch, with the lagoon becoming Robin Hood Lake and the adjoining five-acre oak grove, Sherwood Forest, at that time rather than when Columbia's "Rogues of Sherwood Forest" ('50) lensed there. But those names *may* have originated with the Columbia title.

Western heroes were soon familiar sights at the ranch, with George O'Brien's "Gun Law" ('38) apparently the first film shot there under the Corrigan banner and the 3 Mesquiteers' "Heroes of the

I'm standing on the well-known jump-off rock (part of which is phony) above Robin Hood (or Jungle Jim) Lake.

Hills" ('38) and Tex Ritter's "Starlight Over Texas" ('38) close on O'Brien's heels. By the Trail Blazers' "Blazing Guns" ('43) our heroes were diving or falling off the fake lagoon cliff.

Both Nyoka serials ("Jungle Girl" '41; "Perils of Nyoka" '42) featured the ranch's most prominent cave/mine entrance, and the great Kay Aldridge version put Corriganville's main chase road to thrilling use. Sets also included Corrigan's ranch house, bunkhouse and barn, as well as a couple of hideout shacks.

In 1943, Corrigan began construction of a town adjacent to the ranch. Apparently first used, partially constructed, for Bob Livingston's Lone Rider western "Law of the Saddle" ('43), the completed town appeared initially, most likely, in Buster Crabbe's "Frontier Outlaws" ('44). It quickly became the "official" town set for PRC's Crabbe and James Newill/Dave O'Brien Texas Rangers series as well as the site for several Lash LaRues and other cheapies and for entries in the Bill Elliott and Wayne Morris Monogram/Allied Artists series at the end of the B-western era, with the ranch barn becoming the town's livery stable and, in later years, the ranch house itself often posing as a residence on the edge of town rather than a ranch.

1948 saw the appearance on a plateau above the town of John Wayne's "Fort Apache", later the setting for the "Rin Tin Tin" TV series and many A-westerns.

Especially after Corrigan converted the site into an amusement park in 1949, other sets—most notably a huge stable at the end of the town (now called "Silvertown") and Mexican and Corsican villages—were added to the facility. Several hideout shacks/relay stations, including one constructed for "Fort Apache" which was partially below ground, plus cave/mine entrances and a hideout rock the Durango Kid regularly rode behind for a quick change of costume, also dotted the landscape.

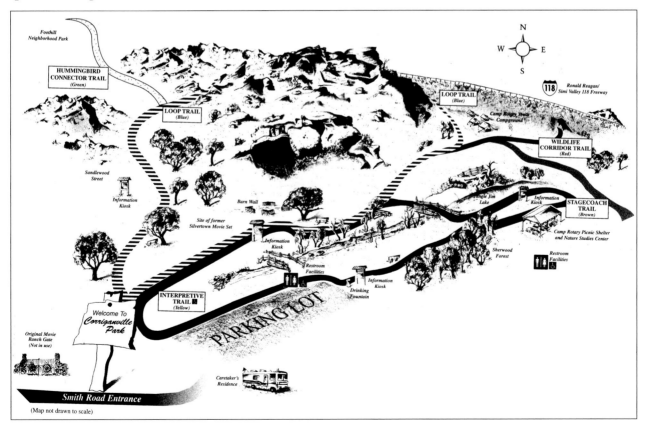

Map of the Corriganville area given out when you visit the area today.

A film crew at Corriganville townset during its heyday.

Corriganville's three insert chase roads were the best in the business. Although Republic, Columbia and Universal film crews probably put Corriganville's chase roads to best use, the cheapie companies also had their moments, most notably in the super horserace scene for "Pinto Bandit" ('44).

Despite Corriganville's large overall size, the principal filming area was very compact; portions of the chase roads, for example, were only a few yards from the town sets. Virtually every western hero, along with not only both Nyoka serials but also other serial figures such as "King of the Texas Rangers," "The Vigilante" and "Sir Galahad", saw duty at Corriganville. But it was home primarily to lowly PRC and Monogram as well as independents, including Ken Maynard's last hurrah "Harmony Trail" ('44), and nearly all the early western TV series. Republic used Corriganville's town only in Gene Autry's "Sioux City Sue" ('47), Roy Rogers' "Down Dakota Way" ('49) and in a very quick clip for Wild Bill Elliott's "Overland Mail Robbery"; Columbia in a few post-war Autrys and Durangos and Universal and RKO never, although those studios used other Corriganville sites extensively, especially before the post-war period.

At its peak, as a tourist attraction, Corriganville reportedly drew as many as 20,000 fans on weekends and was rated as one of the top ten U.S. amusement parks. But as the Simi Valley (now Ronald Reagan) Freeway was being constructed through the area in the mid-'60s, Corrigan sold the ranch in '65 to Bob Hope, presumably for real estate speculation. The next year the facility, renamed Hopetown, was closed to the public.

All that remains of the Corriganville townset area today. Note the corresponding cliffs and trees to the upper left of this photo and the previous photo.

A September 25, 1970, fire gutted most of the sets and left only the chimney standing at the ranch house. Probably the last theatrical western release to feature the location was "Land Raiders," a '69 Telly Savalas epic shot in Europe which included stock footage of an exciting Corriganville stagecoach chase—one originally lensed for Columbia's 1946 feature "The Renegades."

In 1988 the city of Simi Valley purchased the 190 acres that had comprised the ranch's principal filming areas for use as a regional park. In May 1995, final remnants of what was once historic Corriganville were bulldozed to make way for one and two story homes on approximately 217 lots. Over the years, many fans made pilgrimages and visits to Corriganville to relive movie memories...viewing the building remnants, foundations, concrete pads, chase roads, shrubs and small rock formations that remained. Most of that quickly disappeared, pushed aside and plowed under by the heavy equipment of the land developers making way for expensive two story homes. Fortunately, in 1998, a preservation society and the Rancho Simi and Park Recreation District opened a huge section as Corriganville Park. Still to be seen are Robin Hood Lake and the jump-off rock above it (now fenced for safety purposes), the remnants of a cave/mine set beside a primary chase road, foundations of where the townsite and huge barn were, Durango's hideout rock passway and lots of chase roads and trails to explore. A map and brochure are available at strategic spots with some locations having signposts erected to designate filming sites.

To reach Corriganville, take Fwy. 170 north to I-5, I-5 north to Hwy. 118 (Ronald Reagan Freeway), the freeway west to the Kuehner Rd. exit, Kuehner Rd. south to 7001 Smith Rd. and Smith Rd. east a hundred yards or so to the remains of the ranch entrance on the left.

Sampling of Westerns Filmed at CORRIGANVILLE

- Gun Law ('38)—George O'Brien
- Heroes of the Hills ('38)—3 Mesquiteers
- Starlight Over Texas ('38)—Tex Ritter
- Cyclone On Horseback ('41)—Tim Holt
- Jungle Girl ('41)—Frances Gifford (serial)
- Kid's Last Ride ('41)—Range Busters
- Perils of Nyoka ('42)—Kay Aldridge (serial)
- Bullets For Bandits ('42)—Bill Elliott/Tex Ritter
- Texas to Bataan ('42)—Range Busters
- Law of the Saddle ('43)—Bob Livingston
- Border Buckaroos ('43)—Dave O'Brien/ James Newill
- Bullets and Saddles ('43)—Range Busters
- Blazing Guns ('43)—Trail Blazers
- Firebrands of Arizona ('44)—Sunset Carson
- Overland Mail Robbery ('44)—Bill Elliott
- Pinto Bandit ('44)—Dave O'Brien/James Newill
- Arizona Whirlwind ('44)—Trail Blazers
- Harmony Trail ('44)—Ken Maynard
- Frontier Outlaws ('44)—Buster Crabbe
- Whispering Skull ('44)—Tex Ritter/Dave O'Brien
- Navajo Kid ('45)—Bob Steele
- Shadows of Death ('45)—Buster Crabbe
- Along the Navajo Trail ('45)—Roy Rogers
- 'Neath Canadian Skies ('46)—Russell Hayden
- The Renegades ('46)—Willard Parker
- Three Outlaws ('56)—Neville Brand
- Wild West ('46)—Eddie Dean
- Overland Riders ('46)—Buster Crabbe
- Tumbleweed Trail ('46)—Eddie Dean
- Sioux City Sue ('47)—Gene Autry
- Fort Apache ('48)—John Wayne
- Down Dakota Way ('49)—Roy Rogers
- Man From Colorado ('49)—Glenn Ford
- Apache Chief ('49)—Alan Curtis
- Big Sombrero ('49)—Gene Autry
- Beyond the Purple Hills ('50)—Gene Autry
- Border Rangers ('50)—Don Barry
- Rio Grande Patrol ('50)—Tim Holt
- Pecos River ('51)—Charles Starrett
- Hills of Utah ('51)—Gene Autry
- Range Rider (TV): The Hawk ('51)
- Cavalry Scout ('51)—Rod Cameron
- Texas Rangers ('51)—George Montgomery
- Lawless Cowboys ('51)—Whip Wilson
- Passage West ('51)—John Payne
- Kit Carson (TV): Snake River Trapper ('52)
- Fort Osage ('52)—Rod Cameron
- Wagons West ('52)—Rod Cameron
- Indian Uprising ('52)—George Montgomery
- Buffalo Bill In Tomahawk Territory ('52)—Clayton Moore
- Range Rider (TV): Ambush in Coyote Canyon ('52)
- Texas Bad Man ('53)—Wayne Morris
- Nebraskan ('53)—Phil Carey
- Fighting Lawman ('53)—Wayne Morris
- Vigilante Terror ('53)—Bill Elliott
- Topeka ('53)—Bill Elliott
- Fort Vengeance ('53)—James Craig
- Rin Tin Tin (TV): series ('54-'59)
- Annie Oakley (TV): Ambush Canyon ('54)
- Tales of the Texas Rangers (TV): Shooting of Sam Bass ('55)
- Masterson of Kansas ('55)—George Montgomery
- Tales of the Texas Rangers (TV): regular opening ('55)
- Naked Gun ('56)—Willard Parker
- Circus Boy (TV): Little Gypsy ('56)
- Cisco Kid (TV): He Couldn't Quit ('56)
- Roy Rogers (TV): Junior Outlaw ('57)
- Lone Ranger (TV): Courage of Tonto ('57)
- Casey Jones (TV): Gunslinger ('57)
- Roy Rogers (TV): Accessory to Crime ('57)
- Have Gun Will Travel (TV): Great Mojave Chase ('57)
- Return to Warbow ('58)—Phil Carey
- Mackenzie's Raiders (TV): series ('58-'59)
- Bat Masterson (TV): Stage to Nowhere ('60)
- Noose For a Gunman ('60)—Jim Davis
- Buffalo Gun ('61)—Marty Robbins
- Five Guns To Tombstone ('61)—James Brown
- Gambler Wore A Gun ('61)—Jim Davis
- Frontier Circus (TV): Naomi Champagne ('62)

★★

Burro Flats

The late Rex Allen's "Phantom Stallion" ('54) was the last series B-western released by Republic. At the picture's end, Rex (not his stunt double Joe Yrigoyen on that occasion) rode off into the sunset at the site where most, if not all, the original, non-studio exteriors for "Phantom Stallion" lensed. The name and location of that little used but impressive filming locale is Burro Flats.

Dusty chase roads at the oft-used Burro Flats.

It was the setting for the spectacular cliffhanger climaxing Ch. 7 of "Zorro's Fighting Legion" ('39), in which stunt ace Yakima Canutt suffered a seemingly near-fatal mishap executing his famous fall beneath a runaway stagecoach. The riveting stagecoach fight concluding Ch. 1 of "Adventures of Red Ryder" ('40) lensed there also, as did the exciting stagecoach race ending of Ch. 6. So, too, did a number of Roy Rogers, Don "Red" Barry and 3 Mesquiteers Republic features of the late '30s and early '40s. Also, several other early '50s Rex Allen titles, one of the last Allan "Rocky" Lane entries ("Bandits of the West" '53), and even early scenes for Columbia's fine Bill Elliott/Tex Ritter "Lone Star Vigilantes" ('42), as well as a number of A-westerns. Most of the old cowboys called it, "Jackass Flats."

The area is now home to a rocket facility-the Santa Susana Field Laboratory, owned by Rocketdyne Propulsion and Power of Canoga Park, formerly a division of North American Rockwell and currently part of the Boeing Corporation. Over the years, Rocketdyne facilities became the test site for many household names of the space industry. The elaborate rocket facilities scattered over the area where our heroes once roamed gives the site an appearance more suited for sci-fi flicks than our favorite oaters. But much of the area is still readily recognizable to western fans.

Several relatively distinct sections were used for western filming on the flats. The most familiar was a gently sloping grassy plateau with large, unusually shaped boulders scattered mainly along one edge of the plateau. Running inserts of riders, coaches and wagons racing past those boulders at breakneck speed provided front-row kids with truly exhilarating visual delights.

A second, relatively flat plateau bordered on one edge by a sloping hill of solid rock provided another setting for chase scenes. Yak's fall beneath the coach in "Zorro's Fighting Legion" lensed on that part of the flats, as did portions of a race between two stagecoaches in Don Barry's "Frontier Vengeance."

A third filming area featured a road bordered by scattered trees and rocks, while yet another consisted of large boulders overlooking the Simi Valley and mountains in the distance across the valley. Don Barry's confrontation with heavy Arthur Loft in the climax to "Texas Terrors" took place in those rocks, as did portions of "Zorro's Fighting Legion."

Burro Flats appeared fairly regularly in late '30s and early '40s titles, but for some reason, very little filming was done on the flats from the early '40s to the early '50s. But toward the end of the B-western era, Republic returned to the area. As the B-western era came to an end in '54, Burro Flats' contributions to film history largely ended also.

To get to Burro Flats, take Santa Susana Pass Rd. from Chatsworth west toward the Simi Valley, turn left onto Box Canyon Rd. and follow Box Canyon to the Rocketdyne entrance. Or take Topanga Canyon Blvd. to Plummer Road in Chatsworth, turn west onto Plummer and follow Plummer and Valley Circle Blvd. up into the hills to the Rocketdyne entrance. The area is closed to the general public, so be prepared to do some fast talking, perhaps even begging.

Sampling of Westerns Filmed at BURRO FLATS

- Arizona Legion ('39)—George O'Brien
- Kansas Terrors ('39)—3 Mesquiteers
- Zorro's Fighting Legion ('39)—Reed Hadley (serial)
- Adventures of Red Ryder ('40)—Don Barry (serial)
- Frontier Vengeance ('40)—Don Barry
- Covered Wagon Days ('40)—3 Mesquiteers
- Gangs of Sonora ('41)—3 Mesquiteers
- Robin Hood of the Pecos ('41)—Roy Rogers
- Lone Star Vigilantes ('42)—Bill Elliott/Tex Ritter
- Man From Cheyenne ('42)—Roy Rogers
- Land of the Open Range ('42)—Tim Holt
- California ('48)—Ray Milland
- Utah Wagon Train ('51)—Rex Allen

- Wagons West ('52)—Rod Cameron
- Cowboy G-Men (TV): various episodes ('52-'53)
- Iron Mountain Trail ('53)—Rex Allen
- Wings of the Hawk ('53)—Van Heflin
- Shadows of Tombstone ('53)—Rex Allen
- Bandits of the West ('53)—Allan "Rocky" Lane
- Gene Autry (TV): Outlaw Stage ('53)
- Gene Autry (TV): Border Justice ('53)
- Red River Shore ('53)—Rex Allen
- Phantom Stallion ('54)—Rex Allen
- Ride Clear of Diablo ('54)—Audie Murphy
- Drums Across the River ('54)—Audie Murphy
- They Rode West ('54)—Phil Carey

★★

Fess Parker Winery and Vineyard

"Davy Crockett" and "Daniel Boone" star Fess Parker is now "King of the Wine Frontier." After a successful show business career, the 6 ft. 6 in. actor got involved in real estate with his pride and joy being the Fess Parker Winery and Vineyard he started in 1989 on 40 acres of his 700 acre cattle ranch in Los Olivos in the beautiful Santa Ynez Valley. The vineyard now encompasses all 700 acres with his wines being sold in 40 states. To date, Parker wines have won more than 30 medals.

Fess and his wife Marcy also own the elegant, world class Fess Parker Wine Country Inn and Spa in Los Olivos where suites go for $600 a day. He also owns Fess Parker's Doubletree Resort in Santa Barbara.

Fess Parker samples a bit of his own wine for bouquet and taste.

★★

Movieland Wax Museum

Although its origination is uncertain, wax sculpting is considered one of the oldest art forms in history, dating back to ancient Egypt. In the 19th Century, Madame Tussaud, a talented sculptor, gained notoriety with her famous waxworks exhibition in England, laying the groundwork for modern day wax museums. Movieland Wax Museum in Buena Park has life size figures of Tom Mix, Alan Ladd as "Shane", Chuck Connors as "The Rifleman," John Wayne as "Hondo," Clint Eastwood, Gary Cooper and Grace Kelly from "High Noon," Roy Rogers and Trigger, Lorne Greene/Dan Blocker/Michael Landon from "Bonanza," Ward Bond from "Wagon Train" and Will Rogers, as well as Robert Redford and Paul Newman from "Butch Cassidy and the Sundance Kid." All figures are in apropos settings.

John Wayne as "Hondo" is among the large gathering of western stars at Movieland Wax Museum.

Located one block north of Knotts Berry Farm (in Orange County) at 7711 Beach Blvd. in Buena Park. Open 365 days a year, 10-6, Monday-Friday, 9-7 weekends. (714) 522-1154.

★★

Edison International Field

Although 'the cowboy' owned the California Angels for three decades, the baseball franchise never won a pennant. It was the only Champion Gene Autry ever rode that didn't come home a winner. It was always a major disappointment for him. Gene once said, "I've loved baseball all my life. I think what I would have liked most of all was to have been a big league ball player." (The Angels finally won a World Series in 2002.)

In 1960, the Dodgers, wildly successful in a move from Brooklyn to Los Angeles, pulled broadcast of their games off Gene's KMPC-radio and moved to KFI, leaving sports oriented KMPC without a baseball game to air. A group headed by former baseball player Hank Greenberg seemed in line for a new expansion American League franchise, but their bid collapsed. Gene decided to buy the club, if only to protect broadcast rights. Golden West Broadcasters formed Golden West Baseball Co. and on December 5, 1960, Autry (with ex-Stanford football star Bob Reynolds) joined the American League as co-owner of the Los Angeles Angels. They paid $2.5 million. The Angels played one year at the old Wrigley Field in Los Angeles then moved to Dodger Stadium for four seasons and in 1966 went to the new Anaheim Stadium (the Big A) changing their name to the California Angels.

In 1986 the team came within one pitch of reaching the World Series. They became the Anaheim Angels in 1997. Gene sold 25% of the team for $30 million to Walt Disney Corporation in 1996 giving them an option to buy the remaining 75% upon his death, which they did in March of 1999 for an estimated $120 million.

The street that runs into the (now named since 1998) Edison International Field of Anaheim is Gene Autry Way.

On April 1, 1998, a larger than life bronze likeness of Gene Autry was unveiled at the stadium. The statue depicts Gene wearing a smile, western-cut business suit, bolo tie and cowboy boots, holding a Stetson in his left hand while his right reaches out in a handshake gesture. It stands on a round platform (in a courtyard inside the gates to the left of the stadium entrance by the ticket window) surrounded by five stars at the base, repros of his Hollywood Walk of Fame stars. The inscription plate at the base reads, "Gene Autry. Founder of California Angels 1961. His uniform #26 was retired in 1982 by the players. Singing cowboy, actor, composer, airforce pilot, entrepreneur, baseball fan, philanthropist, 33rd degree mason, best friend." The sculptress of the statue, DeL'Esprie, says, "I was trying to capture the feeling of warmth, friendliness and sincerity Gene Autry has, because that is how he truly is. For the stadium piece, she observed actual clothes Autry wore in 1966 (the year he brought the California Angels to the newly built Anaheim Stadium), including a western suit with arrow trimmed pockets and ostrich cowboy boots with alligator wing tips.

A bronze of Gene Autry greets all who enter Edison International Field. This statue is inside the gates to the left of the ticket office.

The Autrys also lent DeL'Esprie jewelry, including a wedding ring with Freemason symbols, jeweled bolo tie and eagle cufflinks. As the plaque states, Uniform #26 was retired in 1982, signifying Autry's presence as an extra player on the club's 25 man roster. The jersey hangs in the Hall of Fame at the stadium.

The new Edison Field also houses Autry's Smokehouse. This sign is the only reference to Gene in the eatery. Today, with Disney assuming ownership, the Owner's Box is now the Autry Box. "No one sits in the Cowboy's seat and his red phone still stands at the ready," states Jackie Autry.

Edison International Field is at 2000 Gene Autry Way. (714) 940-2000.

★★★

Tom Mix Home

A home Tom Mix once owned on Catalina Island has been fully restored under private ownership. The TM brand was custom-made for the home. 110 Marden Lane in Avalon.

★★★

Wild Goose

The Wild Goose, a 136 ft. converted U. S. Navy minesweeper, was John Wayne's favorite retreat and proudest possession. During the last 16 years of his life, the Duke spent much of his leisure time aboard the yacht cruising off Mexico, the Pacific Northwest and Catalina. The Wild Goose came to dominate his life in a way only his family and work had done before. Wayne pur-

The Wild Goose, at harbor in Newport Beach.

chased the ship from a friend in 1962 for $110,000. To maintain the ship cost Wayne approximately $150,000 a year. The week before Wayne died in 1979, the Wild Goose was sold to a Santa Monica lawyer. In 1991 a Newport Beach resident bought the boat and began a major renovation. In 1993, the Wild Goose became one of the few private yachts to ever be fully certified by the Coast Guard for ocean charter service (154 guests). In 1994 Wayne's Wild Goose returned to her old home port of Newport Harbor (in Newport Beach on the Pacific Coast Hwy.) where today she is available for both public and private use as a dinner cruise and charter vessel.

★★

John Wayne's Gravesite

After keeping John Wayne's burial site an unmarked secret for 19 years, in 1998 his family placed an inspiring marker on his gravesite at Pacific View Memorial Park overlooking the scenic harbor at Newport Beach, one of Duke's favorite places. The bronze

marker is of a lone rider and represents, to Wayne devotee John Stovall, Wayne's entrance into an Army camp with flagpole and mission in the background, seen about 25 minutes into "Hondo." The right side of the marker is obviously Monument Valley. The Wayne inscription reads, "Tomorrow is the most important thing in life. Comes into us at midnight very clean. It's perfect when it arrives and it puts itself in our hands. It hopes we've learned something from yesterday."

The Duke rests here.

★★

Candace Cavanaugh of San Francisco (step-daughter of writer Bill Russell) alongside the Duke at John Wayne Airport.

to this day on the 111 acre site.

Located just south of I-210 (Foothill Blvd.) at 301 N. Baldwin Ave. in Arcadia, near the Santa Anita Racetrack. Tram and walking tours. (818) 821-3222.

John Wayne Airport

On June 20, 1979, Orange County Airport was renamed John Wayne Airport by the County Board of Supervisors. In 1982, a $300,000 nine foot tall bronze statue of the western great was installed at the airport. The statue depicts a striding Wayne in western garb. It now occupies a prominent location in the airport's terminal building. The John Wayne Orange County Airport is just off the 405 on McArthur Blvd.

★★★★★★★★★★★★★★★★★★★★★★★★★★★★★★★★★★

Los Angeles Arboretum

Truly not western, but I'm sure you've all seen the many Jungle Jim, Bomba and other jungle films lensed at the Los Angeles Arboretum. Nature and film history come together in a living location at the wildlife refuge and filming property for movies and TV which continues

Many a Tarzan, Jungle Jim and Bomba film lensed in these Arboretum jungles.

 Sampling of Movies Filmed at L. A. ARBORETUM

- Cobra Woman ('43)—Maria Montez
- Tarzan and the Amazons ('44)—Johnny Weissmuller
- Tarzan and the Leopard Woman ('45)—Johnny Weissmuller
- Jungle Jim ('48)—Johnny Weissmuller
- Tarzan and the Slave Girl ('49)—Lex Barker

- Bomba On Panther Island ('49)—Johnny Sheffield
- Lost Volcano ('50)—Johnny Sheffield
- Pygmy Island ('50)—Johnny Weissmuller
- Ramar of the Jungle (TV): series ('52-'53)
- Gambler From Natchez ('54)—Dale Robertson
- Wild Times (TV)—Sam Elliott ('79)

★★★

Gunslinger Gun Shop

The owner of the Gunslinger Gun Shop in Glendora is a huge John Wayne fan with movie posters, paintings and photos of the Duke adorning the walls of his store at 757 E. Arrow Highway. He also sells a Chuck Connors "Rifleman" rifle-replica which is produced by a friend of his. (626) 914-7010.

★★

Movieland Frontier Town

The now abandoned Movieland Frontier Town in Colton is where Sunset Carson filmed portions of his popular "Six Gun Heroes" PBS teleseries, introducing B-westerns. The western theme park was shuttered and fenced off to the public after failing to make a go of it several years ago.

At Valley and Meridian Blvd. in Colton, off I-10 going toward Palm Springs from Los Angeles.

★★

Tommy Ivo

See entry under Florida.

★★

Garner Ranch

Nestled in a beautiful valley across the San Jacinto mountains from Palm Springs is the Garner Cattle Ranch, site for the filming of many B, A and TV westerns. First developed in the 1860s, the ranch was purchased in 1905 by Robert F. Garner Sr. It still remains in the family. Originally 1,500 acres after WWII, it encompassed nearly 10,000 and still runs nearly a thousand head of cattle on 4,000 acres.

The Garner Ranch house seen in so many Tim Holt RKO B-westerns.

The Garner ranch features a white main house with a broad veranda (as well as a modern home), a foreman's house off the left side of the main house, assorted barns and corrals, and huge expanses of pasture land bordered by pine trees and hills scattered with rock formations.

A small movie set remained on the ranch for years, serving as ranch house, bunkhouse, or school (as in Hoppy's "The Frontiersman"). Lake Hemet across from the ranch entrance was also used in films. The ranch was featured most prominently in Gene Autry's "Colorado Sunset", "Springtime In the Rockies" and "Guns and Guitars" as well as in several Hoppys and post-war Tim Holts. The ranch remains today almost exact as it appeared in those great little films.

Take I-10 towards Palm Springs to Banning; Hwy. 243 across the mountains and through Idyllwild to Mountain Center; left on Hwy. 74 for several miles. The ranch entrance is on the left just beyond the Lake Hemet market.

 ## Sampling of Westerns Filmed on GARNER RANCH

- Guns and Guitars ('36)—Gene Autry
- Springtime in the Rockies ('37)—Gene Autry
- The Frontiersman ('38)—Hopalong Cassidy
- Gold Mine In the Sky ('38)—Gene Autry
- Colorado Sunset ('39)—Gene Autry
- Brothers in the Saddle ('49)—Tim Holt
- Rustlers ('49)—Tim Holt
- Masked Raiders ('49)—Tim Holt
- Riders of the Range ('50)—Tim Holt
- Kid From Texas ('50)—Audie Murphy
- Kansas Raiders ('50)—Audie Murphy
- Saddle Legion ('51)—Tim Holt
- Bonanza (TV): several episodes ('59-'73)
- Rawhide (TV): several episodes ('59-'65)

★★

Palm Springs Desert Museum

Western movie fans know George Montgomery (1916-2000) from his roles in westerns or as star of TV's "Cimarron City," but the famous actor had other artistic talents. Sculpture, oil paintings and fine furniture created by George are highlighted at the Palm Springs Desert Museum, 101 Museum Dr. in Palm Springs. Founded in 1938, George donated close to $250,000 to the museum which houses his work. There's also a selection of memorabilia from his movie days on display.

Tuesday-Saturday 1-5, Sunday Noon-5. (760) 325-7186.

The late George Montgomery with one of his many bronzes at the Palm Springs Desert Museum.

★★

Palm Springs Walk of Fame

Not to be out done by Hollywood, Palm Springs has their own Walk of Fame...large terrazzo tile stars with a circular palm tree at the center imbedded in the stone sidewalk of Palm Canyon Dr. (Hwy. 111) in downtown Palm Springs. Over 150 names of celebrities, persons important to the development of Palm Springs, and Medal of Honor winners stretch for about a mile down Palm Canyon Dr., with a few off onto Tahquitz Dr. and clustered around Ruby's Diner.

Many of those honored come from the western field: Buck Jones, Guy Madison, Gene Autry, John Wayne, Monte Hale, Burt Kennedy, Randolph Scott, Gene Barry, George Montgomery, Chris Alcaide, Pierce Lyden, Montie Montana, Ruth Terry, Herb Jeffries, Iron Eyes Cody, Ann Miller, Ronald Reagan, Russell Wade, Ellen Drew, Bill Orr (exec. at Warner Bros.), Ruta Lee, Michael Dante, Ernest Borgnine, Alan Ladd, Howard Keel, Andrew J. Fenady and Sue Ane Langdon.

Veteran badman Chris Alcaide was honored with a star on the Palm Springs Walk of Fame in 1995. (L-R, kneeling) Stumpy Brown, Alcaide, Kelo Henderson, John Mitchum. (standing) Peri Alcaide, Gerhard Frenel, chairman of the Walk of Stars.

★★★

Gene Autry Trail

While you're exploring Palm Springs, keep your eyes out for Gene Autry Trail and the Gene Autry Bridge.

★★★★★★★★★★★★★★★★★★★★★★★★★★★★★★★★★★★★★★

George Montgomery Bronzes

There is a bronze by George Montgomery of his ex-wife Dinah Shore near the 18th hole of the Dinah Shore Tournament Course at Mission Hills Country Club, 34600 Mission Hills Dr. in Rancho Mirage. (760) 324-9400.

There's another bronze by George, this one of "Mr. Palm Springs," actor Charlie Farrell. Farrell's tennis likeness greets visitors at the entrance to the Palm Springs Airport on Tahquitz Canyon Way.

Yet another of George's bronzes, which looks much like

George Montgomery bronze in Cathedral City.

George from his "Cimarron City" TV series, stands in front of the city hall in Cathedral City on Avenida Lalo Guerrero Street. It is a bronze which George donated to Cathedral City (between Palm Springs and Rancho Mirage).

★★★

Eisenhower Medical Center

In 1986 Gene and Jackie Autry made a significant contribution to the Eisenhower Medical Center in Rancho Mirage. The four story Autry Tower was constructed as an addition (east wing) to the hospital as an acute care unit. 39000 Bob Hope Dr. in Rancho Mirage.

★★★

Keen Camp

Keen Camp near Idyllwild, south of Los Angeles and setting for scenes in Gene Autry's "Springtime in the Rockies" ('37) and "Gold Mine In the Sky" ('38), is now the site of an elaborate home for displaced animals.

The Keen Camp lodge and store, seen in Tex Ritter's "Take Me Back to Oklahoma" ('40), burned later in the '40s. The rebuilt store, which closely resembles the original structure, serves as the shelter office.

This is the rebuilt Keen Camp store near Idyllwild.

Two of Republic's Weaver Brothers and Elviry films, "Jeepers Creepers" and "Grand Ole Opry," were partially lensed there. Portions of a couple of Hopalong Cassidy westerns were also shot in the area— "Santa Fe Marshal" ('40) and "The Frontiersman" ('38).

"Heart of the Rockies" ('37) with the 3 Mesquiteers lensed in the nearby Tahquitz mountains and at Lake Hemet.

Idyllwild is south of Palm Springs on Hwy. 243.

★★★

Coachella Valley

One of the most popular and photographically stunning B-westerns of the late '30s is Republic's "Riders of the Whistling Skull" with the 3 Mesquiteers (Bob Livingston, Ray "Crash" Corrigan and Max Terhune).

The filming site is in the Coachaella Valley, southeast of Palm Springs, about a three hour drive from Los Angeles. Specifically, along Box Canyon Road near the village of Mecca, a few miles southeast of Indio. But the desert, cliffs, and hills of the Mecca area are not the only attractions for film companies.

Ray "Crash" Corrigan and Bob Livingston enter Coachella Valley in "Riders of the Whistling Skull."

Extending more than 40 miles along the eastern edge of the valley in a band averaging five miles in width, we also find the Imperial Sand Dunes (Mecca is in Imperial County), host to such modern A-titles as "Star Wars" ('77), "Patriot Games" ('92) and "Dune" ('84), among many others. Veteran director Earl Bellamy remembers working on "Sahara" ('43) and "Ten Tall Men" ('51) in the dunes.

"Riders of the Whistling Skull" was not the only western shot in the Coachella Valley. "The Professionals" with Burt Lancaster was filmed partly in the valley, as was the exciting cattle stampede for Jimmy Stewart's "The Rare Breed", during filming of which ace stuntman Hal Needham and two stuntwomen suffered minor injuries in a scripted Box Canyon buckboard crash gone awry.

Take I-10 southeast from Los Angeles to Indio and Hwy. 111 to Mecca. Box Canyon Road runs east from Mecca and other filming sites cover a large area south of Mecca, bordered by Hwy. 86 on the west, Hwy. 78 to the south and mountains to the east.

Sampling of Westerns Filmed at COACHELLA VALLEY

- Sandflow ('37)—Buck Jones
- Riders of the Whistling Skull ('37)—3 Mesquiteers
- Rare Breed ('66)—James Stewart
- Professionals ('66)—Burt Lancaster

★★★

Joshua Tree

Warner Baxter's Academy Award winning performance in 1929 as the Cisco Kid for "In Old Arizona" was filmed in the Joshua Tree area (Hwy. 62 north of Palm Springs on the way to Twenty-nine Palms). Hopalong Cassidy's "Borderland" ('37) was also shot there.

Director Earl Bellamy took his film crew there in 1966 for Robert Fuller's "Incident At Phantom Hill." Bellamy told me, "It was the most barren area you could find, which lent itself to the story. Those Joshua trees are like sentinels standing by. They're weird at night, weird at day." "The Magnificent Seven Ride" ('72), "Tell Them Willie Boy Is Here" ('70) with an adult Robert Blake and "There Was a Crooked Man" also lensed in this desert area studded with the tall, tree-like desert plants with forking branches that end in a cluster of leaves for which the area is named.

★★★

Pioneertown

Movie badman Dick Curtis spent most of his career menacing the likes of Charles Starrett or Bill Elliott but attempted to supplement his meager movie earnings with real estate investments.

In the mid-'40s, Curtis visited Yucca Valley in California's high desert, a 4,500 ft. elevation 30 miles from Palm Springs and a two and a half hour drive southeast of Los Angeles. Convinced the location would make an excellent site for homes, resorts and dude ranches of the Palm Springs variety, as well as an ideal movie ranch, Curtis soon corralled 17 investors, including Roy Rogers, the Sons of the Pioneers singing group, Russell Hayden, B-western directors Frank McDonald and Tommy Carr, badman Terry Frost and comedian Bud Abbott.

In 1946, each invested $500 in the project, formed a corporation and acquired 32,000 acres, encompassing the entire valley.

Curtis soon left the venture with Russell Hayden replacing him as corporation president. The first building was erected in March of '47. Several restaurants and other businesses, arranged so they could double as a western street set, were established and dubbed "Pioneertown," after the singing group.

But there was one major problem—a water supply entirely inadequate for a desert vacation paradise. For a time, it appeared the venture would be a complete failure. Then, Philip N. Krasne, a Nebraska-born lawyer turned low-budget movie producer, spent a weekend in Pioneertown. Krasne was producing Cisco Kid westerns for United Artists and he and his star, Duncan Renaldo, scouted the area, finding a variety of scenic set-

Rear of a large barn on Pioneertown's Mane Street often used as a soundstage for films made there.

tings. Krasne arranged for production of future series entries in and around Pioneertown. He also built, on the town's "Mane Street", a sound stage that later posed as a livery stable in movies and TVers.

The Pioneertown landscape, with its arid rolling hills, sparse vegetation and distinctive rock formations resembling huge mounds of giant pebbles, was well suited for B-oaters. The road running by the town made an excellent insert stretch for chases.

Although far wider than the typical western street set, "Mane Street," with its Red Dog Saloon and other buildings, had the reel-authentic look of a dusty trail town. Pioneertown became a frequent location, not only for western theatrical releases, but for the "Cisco Kid" TV series and especially such Autry/Flying-A TV productions as "Range Rider," "Annie Oakley," "Buffalo Bill, Jr." and Gene's own show. In fact, Autry spent so much time in Pioneertown his room at the spartan local motel—dubbed Club 9—became a favorite after-hours watering hole for actors and crew. Russell Hayden even settled in Pioneertown.

The original corporation eventually lost the property to the finance company but Hayden was able to purchase acreage for a ranch across the road from the town. He and his wife

Red Dog Saloon in Pioneertown seen in many "Cisco Kid" TVers and Gene Autry westerns.

Mousie built their own modest sets and shot his "Judge Roy Bean" TV series there. After the 1956 auto accident death of his daughter Sandra (from his previous marriage to actress Jan Clayton), Hayden and Mousie moved to Arizona, but returned to Pioneertown in 1966. At his death in 1981, they were living in the building that had served as Judge Roy Bean's general store/court in the TV series amidst the ramshackle sets that comprised the Hayden Ranch and Western Museum. Mousie continued to live there until her death in February of '97.

To get to the high desert area, take I-10 southeast from Los Angeles to Hwy. 62, Hwy. 62 left (northeast) to Yucca Valley, left at the sign onto the road to Pioneertown, which is about nine miles up the road on the right.

 ## Sampling of Westerns Filmed at **PIONEERTOWN**

- Valiant Hombre ('48)—Duncan Renaldo
- Gay Amigo ('49)—Duncan Renaldo
- Daring Caballero ('49)—Duncan Renaldo
- Cowboy and the Indians ('49)—Gene Autry
- Satan's Cradle ('49)—Duncan Renaldo
- Girl From San Lorenzo ('50)—Duncan Renaldo
- Cody of the Pony Express ('50)—Jock Mahoney (serial)
- Annie Oakley (TV): Gunplay ('54)
- The Capture ('50)—Lew Ayres
- Indian Territory ('50)—Gene Autry
- Gene Autry (TV): Devil's Brand ('50)
- Whirlwind ('51)—Gene Autry
- Silver Canyon ('51)—Gene Autry

- Gene Autry (TV): The Raiders ('51)
- Range Rider (TV): Right of Way ('51)
- Range Rider (TV): Bad Medicine ('51)
- Gene Autry (TV): Bullets and Bows ('52)
- Gene Autry (TV): Sheriff Is a Lady ('52)
- Barbed Wire ('52)—Gene Autry
- On Top of Old Smoky ('53)—Gene Autry
- Last of the Pony Riders ('53)—Gene Autry
- Annie Oakley (TV): Trouble Shooter ('55)
- Cisco Kid (TV): many episodes ('50-'56)
- Judge Roy Bean (TV): entire 39 episodes ('55-'56)
- Lust To Kill ('57)—Jim Davis
- Pony Express (TV): The Killer ('60)

★★

Big Bear/Cedar Lake

B-western and serial producers shooting a mountie flick or titles with a far north setting usually headed southeast of Los Angeles about a three-hour drive to Big Bear Lake, originally developed in 1884 from Bear Creek, a tributary of the Santa Ana River. At an elevation of more than 6,000 feet, the lake itself was perfect for motorboat chases in Republic's Allan Lane mountie serials and such later imitations as "King of the Forest

Rangers", "Dangers of the Canadian Mounties" and "Canadian Mounties VS. Atomic Invaders". Neighboring hills, woodlands, grassy plains and chase roads played host to those and other cliffhangers, including Jock Mahoney's "Gunfighters of the Northwest", as well as many westerns and outdoor releases going back to silent days when DeMille's "Call of the North" ('14) lensed at Big Bear. Producers of "The F.B.I.", "Bonanza" and other TV series also made regular use of the site.

Nearly all of the Kirby Grant Monogram Mountie films were lensed at gorgeous Cedar Lake. You can see the mill house in the right rear background.

Big Bear's dam, constructed in 1911 to replace a smaller original dam, appeared only in a chapter of one of the Lane cliffhangers.

Nearby Cedar Lake with its dam (built in 1914), millhouse, water wheel and cabins, was a familiar B-western, serial and TV setting. Constructed initially for Paramount's Technicolor epic "Trail of the Lonesome Pine" ('36) and utilized in such later A-features as John Wayne's "Shepherd of the Hills", Cedar Lake's sets also starred in many B-westerns. In "North of the Great Divide", Roy Rogers battled fur thieves on the lake. Lake cabins served as the hideout of Christmas tree rustlers in "Trail of Robin Hood" and, in the climax to that Rogers color starrer, Roy chased heavy Cliff Young across the dam, then watched him lose his footing and fall from the water wheel to his well-deserved demise. Gene Autry saw post-war service at Cedar Lake in "Riders of the Whistling Pines", "Blue Canadian Rockies" and "Gene Autry and the Mounties". Russell Hayden was there in "Riders of the Northwest Mounted", Hoppy in "Lumberjack" and "Riders of the Timberline" (with Hoppy's stunt double, Gil Perkins, executing a harrowing dive from the top

Donna Magers looks out from the rebuilt mill house on the far end of serene Cedar Lake.

of the dam in the climax to the latter flick), while Rex Allen overcame a heavy on the lake (and in Republic's underwater tank) for "Silver City Bonanza".

Kirby Grant's "Chinook" series, including such titles as "Yukon Vengeance" and "Yukon Gold", was filmed almost entirely on the lake and in the surrounding hills, as were many episodes of "Sergeant Preston of the Yukon", "Gene Autry", "Range Rider" and "Wild Bill Hickok", among other TV series. In fact, with all the movie action that took place there, visitors are surprised to learn Cedar Lake is not much larger than a stock pond and any celluloid trip on that waterway was over almost before it started!

It is truly a beautiful spot, so scenic, in fact, Roy Rogers once considered buying it. The religious organization that beat the King of the Cowboys to the punch razed the dangerously dilapidated millhouse and water wheel in the late '80s but replaced it with a reasonable facsimile. The group still welcomes visitors to the lake by pre-arrangement.

Some filming is done in the Big Bear area even today, easily accessible from Victorville on Highway 18 or from Redlands (situated along I-10 southeast of Los Angeles) on Highway 330. Locals can provide directions to the filming sites.

 Sampling of Westerns Filmed at BIG BEAR / CEDAR LAKE

- The Eagle ('18)—Monroe Salisbury
- Sign of the Wolf ('31)—Rex Lease (serial)
- To the Last Man ('33)—Randolph Scott
- Range Riders ('34)—Buddy Roosevelt
- Rocky Mountain Mystery ('35)—Randolph Scott
  (uses Doble Mine and Stamp Mill on Gold Mtn.)
- Wilderness Mail ('35)—Kermit Maynard
- Daniel Boone ('36)—George O'Brien
- Arizona Mahoney ('36)—Buster Crabbe
- Nevada ('37)—Buster Crabbe
- Renfrew of the Royal Mounted ('37)—James Newill
- Heart of the North ('38)—Dick Foran
- Crashing Thru ('39)—James Newill
- Man From Montreal ('40)—Richard Arlen
- Queen of the Yukon ('40)—Charles Bickford
- Royal Mounted Patrol ('41)—Charles Starrett
- King of the Mounties ('42)—Allan Lane (serial)
- Don't Fence Me In ('45)—Roy Rogers
- Mrs. Mike ('49)—Dick Powell
- Wolf Hunters ('49)—Kirby Grant
- Trail of the Yukon ('49)—Kirby Grant
- Snow Dog ('50)—Kirby Grant
- Call of the Klondike ('50)—Kirby Grant
- Yukon Manhunt ('51)—Kirby Grant
- Roy Rogers (TV): Jailbreak ('51)
- Wild Bill Hickok (TV): Trapper's Story ('52)
- Range Rider (TV): Greed Rides the Range ('52)
- Range Rider (TV): Outlaw's Double ('52)
- Range Rider (TV): Cherokee Roundup ('53)
- Northern Patrol ('53)—Kirby Grant
- Wild Bill Hickok (TV): Avenging Gunman ('53)
- Wild Bill Hickok (TV): Gorilla of Owlhoot Mesa ('54)
- Blazing the Overland Trail ('56) Lee Roberts (serial)
- Bonanza (TV): Newcomers ('59)
- Bonanza (TV): Truckee Strip ('59)
- Bonanza (TV): Other Son ('65)
- Bonanza (TV): The Debt ('65)
- Bonanza (TV): Thornton's Account ('70)

★★

The Captain's Anchorage

The Captain's Anchorage is a landmark restaurant in Big Bear, adding special western history—a well as a ghost story—to every superb dish served.

When it was built in 1946, the restaurant was known as Sportsman's Tavern. In the ensuing 55 years, the establishment has weathered fires, gambling and an innocuous ghost. George, the ghost, was an accountant for Sportsman's Tavern when it was owned by Andy Devine, who purchased the restaurant as a sideline and a place to hang out when he and Guy Madison were filming "Wild Bill Hickok" episodes at nearby Cedar Lake.

The most mysterious aspect about George is the fact no one actually knows how he died. George is said to have committed suicide, but local lore notes he was suspected of having embezzled quite a pocketful of cash before his mysterious death. George was found shot to death upstairs in his office—an office hidden, along with illegal gambling tables, by a false wall. Yep—old "Jingles" operated an illegal gambling den in an upstairs portion of the premises.

According to Lorraine Little, who has worked at the restaurant for over 23 years, Andy's son, Dennis, came in a few years ago and remembered when he was young that the room upstairs was an illegal gambling den. He recalled an incident with the city marshal pounding on the door downstairs while upstairs Dennis and his Mom were hiding gaming tables in the long hall and office covered by a false wall. Where the booths are now upstairs, there used to be slot machines with a false wall that came down to cover them up during such raids by local officials. The current back dining room upstairs used to be offices—the ones where George mysteriously died.

Lorraine Little has many spooky George ghost stories to relate—hair pullings, beer bottles jumping off the ledge of the bar, etc.—so be sure to ask for her.

The present owner bought the restaurant/bar from Andy in the mid '60s. The menu still carries his photo and there are lots of stills and photos of Andy on the walls. Hwy. 18 and Moonridge Rd. (909) 866-3997.

★★

Lake Arrowhead

Near famous Big Bear Lake is Lake Arrowhead. In need of irrigation water for the low lying lands below the mountain, a group of Ohio businessmen surveyed the area in 1891 and decided a reservoir should be built there. After purchasing the land and obtaining water rights, they began construction of the dam in 1893. The Arrowhead Reservoir Company completed construction of the dam, cleared the land, and dug tunnels, all by 1908. It was their idea to harness the water power and generate electricity by sending the water down the San Bernardino side of the mountain. Unfortunately for them, the California Supreme Court ruled in favor of the ranchers on the Mojave side of the mountain and the water could not be diverted to the south side.

With the dam built and water in the process of being collected, the project was abandoned until around 1921-'23 when new owners purchased the property and renamed Little Bear Lake as Lake Arrowhead.

Arrowhead is west of Big Bear, simply follow Hwy. 18.

 Sampling of Westerns Filmed at LAKE ARROWHEAD

• Squaw Man ('14)—Dustin Farnum	• Outpost of the Mounties ('39) Charles Starrett
• Wolf Dog ('33)—Frankie Darro (serial)	• The Yearling ('46)—Gregory Peck
• Fighting Trooper ('34)—Kermit Maynard	

★★

The Raven

In 1919 two ambitious middle-aged sisters moved from the Midwest to Lake Arrowhead to build their dream castle. This resulted in the Raven, a 28 room three-story English Tavern that played host to Hollywood's elite for 34 years...John Wayne, Howard

Hughes, etc. The legendary Raven was sold to the present owners in 1983 at which time they renamed it the Saddleback Inn. A perfect and historic place to stay while in the Lake Arrowhead/Big Bear area. Try to make your accommodations in The Duke, a room where John Wayne slept. 300 S. State Hwy. 173 in Lake Arrowhead. (909) 336-3571.

★★★

Roy Rogers/Dale Evans Museum

The larger-than-life statue of Trigger rearing outside the Roy Rogers/Dale Evans Museum has become a recognizable I-15 landmark in Victorville, but it's due to move in the spring of 2003 to Branson, Mo. Literally thousands of artifacts and collectibles inside this extremely personal museum of Roy and Dale's give you a comprehensive look at two very special people's lives.

Here you'll not only find Trigger and Buttermilk mounted, Pat Brady's jeep Nellybelle, the dog Bullet, Roy's guns and guitars, thousands of toys, but hundreds of intimately personal momentos. In Roy's own words, "We've had a lifetime of Happy Trails full of love, laughter, and sometimes sorrow. Everything we've ever done is right here for everyone to see. I've always liked to save things. No matter what came my way, whether it was a letter from a boy or girl movie fan or from a president, or a nice shotgun or an old-time telephone, I stuck it in the basement, or the garage, or in drawers at home."

"In 1976, we moved from our museum in Apple Valley to the current location in Victorville. Our place isn't really a typical museum—it's personal—things that Dale and I have done and the kids and the family and Trigger. All the stuff I saved—tools my dad had when I was little, some of my mom's scrapbooks, pictures from the early days of the Sons of the Pioneers, all sorts of things that meant something to me and Dale. You know, Trigger is one of our most popular exhibits, mounted like so many people remember him—rearing up on his hind legs."

"As you walk past all the glass cases and displays in the museum you will see the old battered car that took my family out of Ohio to the promised land of California. There's Pat Brady's jeep Nellybelle, and pictures of Gabby Hayes when he was a serious young actor. There's Dale wearing fancy hats for her first recording session, and me in overalls standing next to my first horse, Babe. Roy and Dale's memories of the good times and the bad times and hard times."

"Dale and I like to think it will be a place for people to come have fun and learn about our lives, and also to remember what America was like so many years ago. We're

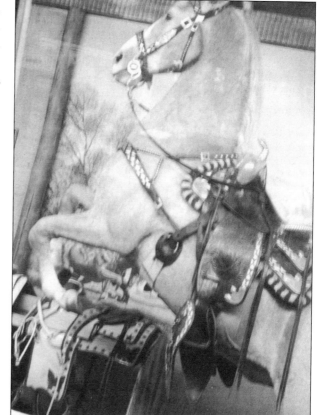

The Smartest Horse in the Movies, Trigger, is mounted and on view at the Roy Rogers/Dale Evans Museum.

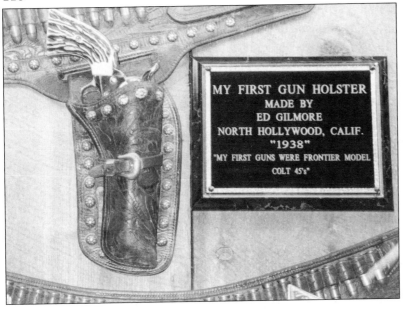

Roy Rogers' first holster set.

happy to share a glimpse of our lives together with you, and we invite you to come on in, take a look, and spend some time."

Going through the museum you'll be reminded of a couple who have devoted their lives to making young and old happy by keeping the spirit of the American West alive. Housed inside the exhibit walls are memories and treasures of two life times and all they love—a permanent reminder of a simple and innocent time when many Americans dreamed of living the King of The Cowboys' exciting adventures.

You'll find family photos dating back to Roy and Dale's childhood, colorful costumes, parade saddles, memorabilia from the silver screen and television, artifacts from Roy's real-life safari adventures, fan mail, comic strips, Roy and Dale's Remington collection, tributes to his friends and sidekicks, and much, much more!

The current museum is located just off Roy Rogers Dr. exiting from I-15. Technically, 15650 Seneca Rd. Open 9-5 through February '03. (760) 243-4548. (760) 243-4547—recorded message. Gift shop: (760) 245-5503.

An all new, much more interactive, Roy Rogers/Dale Evans Museum will open in Branson, Missouri, in April or May, 2003. Hundreds of hours of recorded interviews with Roy and Dale will be utilized in interactive kiosks to tell you about Trigger, Nellybelle, family, sidekicks, God and country. You will see as well as hear Roy

Roy Rogers, Dale Evans, Kelo ("26 Men") Henderson at the grand reopening of the Roy Rogers/Dale Evans Museum on February 3, 1996.

and Dale's lives in their own words. There will be roping steers, stick horses, rubbing stones and other activities for the kids, as well as a state-of-the-art shooting gallery, designed to look like the Sheriff's office in Mineral City, for the big kids. The Happy Trails Gift Shop will double in size at the Branson facility which will be located at 3950 Green Mountain Road. The phone will be (417) 339-1900. "Dusty" Rogers Jr. and his band, the High Riders, will perform twice daily, five days a week, for most of the year. Dusty's nieces, the Rogers Legacy, and Dusty's nephew, Rob Johnson and his band Heritage, will also perform in a family-themed 325 seat theater.

★★

Dale Evans Parkway

When you're in Victorville, watch for Dale Evans Parkway (connecting road from I-15 to Waalew Rd.) and Happy Trails Highway (formerly Hwy. 18).

★★

Rogers' Early Home

An historical-interest marker in Apple Valley designates a home once owned by Roy Rogers and Dale Evans at 19900 Hwy. 18 near Rimrock Rd. The Rogers purchased the home in 1965 and lived there til 1980.

Roy's Apple Valley Inn was also on Hwy. 18 as was their original museum (now Gold Strike Lanes bowling alley.)

Roy and Dale's former Apple Valley home as it appears today.

★★

Roy Rogers and Dale Evans' Home

Roy and Dale outside their home on Tomahawk Avenue in Apple Valley.

The last house in which Roy Rogers and Dale Evans lived in Apple Valley is at 19838 Tomahawk Rd. Look for the double RR on the gate.

The home, located on 1.62 acres backing up to the Apple Valley Country Club and golf course, was designed and built by Roy "Dusty" Rogers Jr. Over 4,900 sq. ft. of living space with four bedrooms and four baths. There is a 725 sq. ft. guest house next to the beautiful in-ground pool.

★★

Roy Rogers and Dale Evans Final Resting Place

Roy Rogers and Dale Evans' final resting place is at Sunset Hills Memorial Park in Apple Valley. The beautiful desert setting features a waterfall which leads to a stream that runs under the road and beside Roy and Dale's gravesites. A stone "Republic eagle" alights nearby. The area is covered with green grass and an abundance of flowers and plants. 24000 Waalew Rd., Apple Valley. (760) 247-0155.

Roy Rogers and Dale Evans gravesites at Sunset Hills.

★★

Peggy Sue's

Hungry on your travels around Southern California? How about a Gary Cooper (ham and cheese sandwich)? A John Wayne (barbecue)? Or a Cisco Kid (chili cheese omelet)?

Check out Peggy Sue's, a '50s roadside diner in Yermo. Autographed photos of Gene Autry, Roy Rogers, John Wayne, R. G. Armstrong and Clayton Moore (among others) adorn the walls. And the food ain't bad either.

There's another Peggy Sue's in Victorville, which I assume is much the same although I've never eaten there.

In Yermo on I-15…or turn off I-40 at Dagget and go 3 miles North.

★★

Red Rock Canyon

Red Rock Canyon, on the edge of California's Mojave desert, was a favorite western filming site. The canyon is located along Hwy. 14, 100 miles north of Los Angeles.

Red Rock Canyon's cathedral cliffs and other sites furnished moviemakers with spectacular backdrops. The canyon is part of the Ricardo Formation, a 6,500 foot thick deposit of white clay, red sandstone, dark brown lava and pink surface volcanic rock from which the area gets its vibrant, contrasting colors. Native Americans inhabited the area long before other settlers, who first arrived in search of gold in the mid-19th century. In 1896, Rudolph Hagen settled there, acquired water rights, and filed for mineral and homestead rights. By 1913, Hagen had obtained nearly complete control of the canyon and some of the surrounding area. His Ricardo Land and Water Company also operated a general store near where the visitors' center for

Cathedral cliffs of Red Rock Canyon.

Red Rock Canyon State Park is now situated. Ricardo camp is featured in Jack Randall's "Danger Valley" '37, among other titles.

By the mid-'20s, at the latest, they were filming in the canyon and elsewhere in the desert, with Hagen charging fees for the use of his property and imposing production guidelines on moviemakers. Following Hagen's death in 1937, his second wife inherited the property. She and her heirs continued the family's arrangements with production companies into the '60s.

 Sampling of Westerns Filmed in RED ROCK CANYON

- Wild Horse Canyon ('25)—Yakima Canutt
- Flaming Guns ('32)—Tom Mix
- Heritage of the Desert ('32)—Randolph Scott
- Tombstone Canyon ('32)—Ken Maynard
- Lawless Frontier ('35)—John Wayne
- Cyclone of the Saddle ('35)—Rex Lease
- For the Service ('36)—Buck Jones
- Danger Valley ('37)—Jack Randall
- Zorro Rides Again ('37)—John Carroll (serial)
- Pals of the Saddle ('38)—3 Mesquiteers
- Colorado ('40)—Roy Rogers
- Young Buffalo Bill ('40)—Roy Rogers
- Great Train Robbery ('41)—Bob Steele
- Badlands of Dakota ('41)—Robert Stack
- Pride of the Plains ('44)—Bob Livingston
- Wanderer of the Wasteland ('45)—James Warren
- Grand Canyon Trail ('48)—Roy Rogers
- Last Bandit ('49)—Bill Elliott
- Big Sombrero ('49)—Gene Autry

- Calamity Jane and Sam Bass ('49)—Howard Duff
- Davy Crockett, Indian Scout ('50)—George Montgomery
- Tumbleweed ('53)—Audie Murphy
- Law and Order ('53)—Ronald Reagan
- Bounty Hunter ('54)—Randolph Scott
- Tension at Table Rock ('56)—Richard Egan
- Have Gun Will Travel (TV): Great Mojave Chase ('57)
- Man of the West ('58)—Gary Cooper
- Apache Territory ('58)—Rory Calhoun
- Big Country ('58)—Gregory Peck
- Bonanza (TV): Dark Gate ('61)
- Bonanza (TV): The Gift ('61)
- Apache Rifles ('64)—Audie Murphy
- Virginian (TV): Beloved Outlaw ('66)
- Bonanza (TV): Ride the Wind ('66)
- Bonanza (TV): Sense of Duty ('67)
- Forty Guns To Apache Pass ('67)—Audie Murphy
- High Chaparral (TV): Survival ('68)

Red Rock Canyon proved a reasonably popular filming site, even for low-budget productions such as Ken Maynard's "Tombstone Canyon," particularly because of its convenient proximity to the highway. Republic ace Bill Witney recalled fondly that a film crew could simply drive into the canyon, "get out and shoot from the road."

Red Rock also stood in for the moon in the Republic cliffhanger "Radar Men From the Moon" ('52) with George ("Commando Cody") Wallace sweating through his scenes in the sweltering heat of the canyon. Universal made effective use of the area in several of its chapterplays, including "Buck Rogers" ('39) and "Riders of Death Valley" ('41).

Although the canyon has long been a state park with parking areas and a campground, Red Rock remains largely unmarred by civilization and has even appeared in a few recent features, including "Jurassic Park" ('93).

★★

Kernville

The Kern River Valley, three hours north of Los Angeles, furnished one of the more scenic and realistic settings for western and serial filming. Film crews may have begun shooting in the area as early as 1916 but Yakima Canutt's "Branded a Bandit" ('24), the climax to which was set at the Kern River lagoon and cliffs, seen in so many later titles, was apparently the first film of record to be shot in the area. Other silents quickly followed and, in 1931, two early Mascot sound serials, "Lightning Warrior" and "Vanishing Legion," lensed there, with the former using an area mine as well as what were to become familiar filming sites of the golden age. Bob Steele's "Man from Hell's Edges" ('32) and several of John Wayne's early Monogram Lone Star productions were among the first sound westerns filmed there. Beginning with "Eagle's Brood" ('35), Hopalong Cassidy shot over 20 films in the Kern Valley.

When Lake Isabella was flooded at Kernville, the Kernville Community Church was moved to a safe location in town. Over the years, it's seen modifications but its familiar steeple is still recognizable.

Although the original village of Isabella (now under Lake Isabella) was specifically referred to in Canutt's "Branded a Bandit", and may have been the community actually seen in that title, most area filming was done in the original Kernville (also now under Lake Isabella); in the hills northwest of Kernville along the raging Kern River (and Hwy. 190); on Kernville ranches; along the river bottom by and south of town and in the lagoon area farther south (now south of the Lake Isabella dam, along Hwy. 155), as well as in the surrounding hills of rocks and scattered pines.

Kernville's street set was

clearly the most enduring and most frequently used. It paralleled Kernville's actual Main Street. At its northwest end was the Kernville Community Church with its stately steeple, which was seen in many titles and played a key role in the plot of Buck Jones' "Boss of Lonely Valley" ('37).

When Lake Isabella was created, flooding Old Kernville and much of the surrounding area, Kernville's famed Wofford Ranch, star of so many oaters, was moved intact to a new location near the local airstrip, where it remains today. Even the old church that once stood at the end of Kernville's western street set was relocated to the town's post-Isabella site. Substantially modified in appearance, any local can direct you to it.

The principal Kernville ranch used for filming was the Wofford Ranch, located about a mile southwest of town and owned by Irven Wofford, a forest ranger turned rancher and then developer, who was principally credited with bringing movie companies to the valley. Portions of Roy Rogers' "Roll On Texas Moon," Hoppy's "The Showdown" ('40) and even Jimmy Wakely's "Rainbow Over the Rockies" ('47) used the Wofford Ranch.

Other area ranches used for filming Roy Rogers' "Roll On, Texas Moon" and other titles included the Doyle spread and Brown Ranch, located about ten miles east of Isabella along Hwy. 178.

 Sampling of Westerns Filmed in KERNVILLE

- Branded A Bandit ('24)—Yakima Canutt
- Lightning Warrior ('31)—George Brent
- Man From Hell's Edges ('32)—Bob Steele
- Border Devils ('32)—Harry Carey
- Last of the Mohicans ('32)—Harry Carey (serial)
- Without Honor ('32)—Harry Carey
- Sagebrush Trail ('33)—John Wayne
- Riders of Destiny ('33)—John Wayne
- Strawberry Roan ('33)—Ken Maynard
- Blue Steel ('34)—John Wayne
- Western Justice ('35)—Bob Steele
- Outlawed Guns ('35)—Buck Jones
- Eagle's Brood ('35)—Hopalong Cassidy
- Lawless Riders ('35)—Ken Maynard
- Undercover Man ('36)—Johnny Mack Brown
- Riding Avenger ('36)—Hoot Gibson
- Cavalry ('36)—Bob Steele
- Yellow Dust ('36)—Richard Dix
- Frontier Justice ('36)—Hoot Gibson
- Heart of the West ('36)—Hopalong Cassidy
- Three Mesquiteers ('36)—3 Mesquiteers
- Forlorn River ('37)—Buster Crabbe
- Gun Packer ('37)—Jack Randall
- Public Cowboy No. 1 ('37)—Gene Autry
- Mystery of the Hooded Horsemen ('37)—Tex Ritter
- Boss of Lonely Valley ('37)—Buck Jones
- Black Aces ('37)—Buck Jones
- Frontier Town ('38)—Tex Ritter
- Trigger Trio ('38)—3 Mesquiteers
- Overland Express ('38)—Buck Jones
- Rolling Caravans ('38)—Jack Luden
- Oregon Trail ('39)—Johnny Mack Brown (serial)
- Phantom Stage ('39)—Bob Baker
- Oklahoma Terror ('39)—Jack Randall
- Cherokee Strip ('40)—Richard Dix
- Showdown ('40)—Hopalong Cassidy
- Stagecoach War ('40)—Hopalong Cassidy
- Riders of Death Valley ('41)—Dick Foran (serial)
- Silver Spurs ('43)—Roy Rogers
- 40 Thieves ('44)—Hopalong Cassidy
- Frontier Gal ('45)—Rod Cameron
- In Old Sacramento ('46)—Bill Elliott
- Roll On Texas Moon ('46)—Roy Rogers
- Fool's Gold ('46)—Hopalong Cassidy
- Wyoming ('47)—Bill Elliott
- Jack Armstrong ('47)—John Hart (serial)
- Rainbow Over the Rockies ('47)—Jimmy Wakely
- Drums Across the River ('53)—Audie Murphy
- Cattle King ('63)—Robert Taylor
- Bonanza (TV): Thanks for Everything Friend ('64)
- Showdown ('73)—Dean Martin

Kernville itself was also sometimes featured in movies shot in the valley. Early in "Roll On Texas Moon," for example, Dale Evans drives a buckboard into Kernville from the south, passes the Kernville Garage (formerly Cook's Livery Stable) and pulls up in front of Andrew Brown's general store.

In the hills 20 miles northwest of Kernville on the road to Johnsondale (Hwy. 190) were a waterfall and the Johnsondale bridge (which now stands next to a more modern bridge), also used for filming. The bridge and surrounding area furnished the setting for an exciting ambush scene between Roy Rogers and heavy Hal Taliaferro in "Silver Spurs." Autos sometimes plunged (in miniature) into the raging river nearer town ("Lights of Old Santa Fe"). South of Kernville was the lagoon area used in many cliff fights and horse falls. Just beyond the lagoon (now southwest of the dam) was a swinging bridge seen in many titles ("Trigger Trio" '38). The rolling hills of the area furnished the setting for countless chases.

But nothing lasts forever. In 1943, the army bought the Movie Street sets from Andrew Brown's son, Sumner, for $1,500 and transported them to Camp Santa Anita for training exercises, but not before the street made one last appearance, as a ghost town in "Silver Spurs."

In the early '50s a dam was constructed, flooding the valley, creating Lake Isabella and requiring the transplanting of the original Kernville and Isabella to their current locations.

Today, the valley is the site for an occasional TVer, commercial or feature, such as "Thelma and Louise" ('91).

To reach the Kern River Valley from Los Angeles, take Fwy. 170 north to I-5, I-5 north to Hwy. 14, Hwy. 14 north past Mojave and Red Rock Canyon to Hwy. 178 and Hwy. 178 west into the valley.

★★★

Kern Valley Museum

Remnants and memories of the dozens of westerns shot in the Kernville area are on display in the Kern Valley Museum in Kernville, a small rustic building next to the post office. Real gold mines, outlaw shootouts, stagecoaches and water wars were plot lines in the exciting past of Kern County—in addition to its movie history which is documented in dozens of photos and artifacts in a special alcove.

Behind the museum sits a mud coach which was reportedly modified in 1938 to a Concord style stagecoach for use in John Ford's "Stagecoach".

The free museum at 49 Big Blue Rd. is open 10-4 Thursday-Sunday. (760) 376-6683.

Mud coach at Kern Valley Museum reportedly modified in 1938 to a Concord style stage for use in "Stagecoach" with John Wayne.

★★★

The gorgeous Alabama Hills of Lone Pine.

Lone Pine

The distinctive rocky hills and sagebrush-covered flats at the base of the Sierras just a few miles west of Lone Pine have a lengthy and illustrious movie history. The unique contours of the odd shaped, bronze-colored rocks known as the Alabama Hills (so named in the mid 1800s after a Confederate battleship) backed by Mt. Whitney in the majestic snow-covered Sierra Nevadas offered filmmakers a spectacular setting for countless westerns as well as other films such as "Gunga Din" ('39), "Charge of the Light Brigade" ('36), "High Sierra" ('41) and "Tarzan's Desert Mystery" ('43)...even serials like "Jungle Raiders" ('45).

The first known movie lensed in Lone Pine was evidently "The Round Up" in 1920 with comedian Fatty Arbuckle.

The maze of roads and trails through the Alabama Hills were carved out by the various movie companies that came there to film in the early days...a necessity so they could get their equipment to their shooting destination.

Lone Pine residents often worked as stuntmen or extras. Industrious rancher Russ Spainhower even built a business around supplying movie companies with horses, cattle, wagons and props. In 1939, a western street and a Spanish mission set were built on his Anchor Ranch on the south end of town on the west side of Hwy. 395. The mission set was surrounded on four sides by gated stucco walls. A western street was added over time opposite the east gate of the hacienda. The town was removed in the early '60s and the hacienda came down in 1975. Very little remains today although the property is still there.

Strict federal requirements about removing all traces of the dozens of cabins and sets built over the years in the Alabama Hills, which is mostly federal land, insured virtually no physical evidence of movie remains in the hills. What is commonly called "the Tim Holt cabin" still stands south and west of town (ask locals for directions). It was used in "Arizona Ranger", "Guns of Hate" and "Indian Agent" all with Tim Holt.

Movie Road, one of the main dirt roads extending north from

The "Tim Holt Cabin" at Lone Pine first seen in "Arizona Ranger."

The Hoppy Cabin at Lone Pine where William Boyd and wife Grace stayed while he was filming there. The cabin was also seen in well over a dozen westerns.

Whitney Portal Rd. was so named because it was used so often for filming chases and stagecoach scenes.

Another prominent building is the "Hoppy cabin" where William Boyd and his wife Grace used to stay while Hopalong Cassidy films were being made in Lone Pine. The cabin, built in 1930, was soon sold to Harry Sherman's film company for use in the Hoppy films. Upon completion of filming, it was a sort of Lone Pine Country Club for several years but is now occupied by a resident who, shall we say, is no movie buff. It's just a house to him. On Tuttle Creek Rd., it can be seen in "Hopalong Rides Again" ('37), "Bar 20 Rides Again" ('35), "Pride of the West" ('38), "Heart of Arizona" ('38), "Renegade Trail" ('39) and "Colt Comrades" ('43) as well as Tim Holt's "Stagecoach Kid" ('49) and "Mysterious Desperado" ('49), Bill Cody's "Frontier Days" ('35), Ken Maynard's "Western Frontier" ('35), "Gunsmoke Ranch" ('37) with 3 Mesquiteers and Randolph Scott's "Seven Men From Now" ('56).

There is rock formation after rock formation (Gene Autry Rock, Pot-sa-ga-wa Gardens, Ruiz Hill, Lone Ranger ambush site, "Mule Train" waterhole, Horseshoe Meadow) you'll recognize. Allow yourself at least a day (if not two) to explore the Alabama Hills and surrounding area.

For an extra feel of "how it was," try to make your accommodations at the old Dow Hotel right in town on Hwy. 395. It's where all the stars and crews stayed when on location in Lone Pine.

Look for Hopalong Cassidy Lane and be sure to visit the Lone Pine train station. This wasn't a set, but a real depot. Watch for it in "Boots and Saddles" and "Blazing Sun" both with Gene Autry, "Bad Day At Black Rock" with Spencer Tracy, "Sinister Journey" with Hoppy and a handful of Gene Autry-produced TV episodes such as "Steel Ribbon" with Gene and "Annie Oakley: Annie and the Brass Collar".

Your guide while in Lone Pine will be Dave Holland's excellent ON LOCATION IN LONE PINE available at several shops around town.

Lone Pine train station.

Sampling of Westerns Filmed in LONE PINE

- Flaming Guns ('32)—Tom Mix
- Blue Steel ('34)—John Wayne
- Between Men ('35)—Johnny Mack Brown
- Hop-A-Long Cassidy ('35)—William Boyd
- Danger Trails ('35)—Big Boy Williams
- Lawless Range ('35)—John Wayne
- Comin' Round the Mountain ('36)—Gene Autry
- Cattle Thief ('36)—Ken Maynard
- Phantom of the Range ('36)—Tom Tyler
- Boots and Saddles ('37)—Gene Autry
- Across the Plains ('39)—Jack Randall
- Cisco Kid and the Lady ('40)—Cesar Romero
- Border Vigilantes ('41)—Hopalong Cassidy
- Nevada ('44)—Robert Mitchum
- Utah ('45)—Roy Rogers
- Trail to San Antone ('46)—Gene Autry
- Wild Horse Mesa ('47)—Tim Holt
- Code of the West ('47)—James Warren
- Yellow Sky ('48)—Gregory Peck
- Arizona Ranger ('48)—Tim Holt
- Borrowed Trouble ('48)—Hopalong Cassidy
- Doolins of Oklahoma ('49)—Randolph Scott
- Loaded Pistols ('49)—Gene Autry
- Blazing Sun ('50)—Gene Autry
- Along the Great Divide ('51)—Kirk Douglas
- Rawhide ('51)—Tyrone Power
- Stage to Tucson ('51)—Rod Cameron
- Hangman's Knot ('52)—Randolph Scott
- Desert Pursuit ('52)—Wayne Morris
- Range Rider (TV): Secret of Superstition Peak ('52)
- Ride Clear of Diablo ('54)—Audie Murphy
- Lone Ranger (TV): Wooden Rifle ('56)
- Tall T ('57)—Randolph Scott
- Comanche Station ('60)—Randolph Scott
- Bonanza (TV): The Pursued (Pt. 1-2) ('66)
- Posse From Hell ('61)—Audie Murphy
- Have Gun Will Travel (TV): Ben Jalisco ('61)
- Have Gun Will Travel (TV): A Knight To Remember ('61)
- Maverick ('94)—James Garner

★★★

Tinemaha Dam

The dam used in Roy Rogers' first starrer, "Under Western Stars", is the Tinemaha Dam, located exactly 33 miles north of Lone Pine (where much of "Under Western Stars" was filmed) on Hwy. 395. As you drive north (of Independence) before the divided highway, you see a sign on the right, "Wildlife View Point". Drive down this unpaved road until you reach a fenced-off area. The property is owned by the Department of Water and Power.

★★★

Mammoth Lakes Area

The picturesque and rugged Mammoth Lakes area of the Sierra Nevada mountain range north of Bishop off Hwy. 395 is where Herman Brix as Tarzan-like Kioga, marooned and raised on a semi-tropical island north of the Arctic Circle, battled evil treasure seekers for 12 chapters of 1938 Republic serial, "Hawk of the Wilderness."

Several Gene Autry titles were filmed in the area also—"Melody Ranch" ('40) and "Sierra Sue" ('41).

June Lake, a little further north, hosted John Wayne and Noah Beery Jr. in 1934 for "The Trail Beyond".

★★★

Hopalong Cassidy Milk

Hopalong Cassidy's name and image still grace Producers Dairy milk cartons in the Fresno area. William Boyd was a guest at the Producers opening in 1959...when over 14,000 people came to see Hoppy.

★★

Hornitos

The ghost town of Hornitos (in the desert southeast of Modesto, but just a few miles west of Mariposa) is where Tom Keene's exciting "Ghost Valley" ('32) was filmed.

Born out of the gold rush of '49, the town is forever associated with Mexican bandit Joaquin Murieta as he was almost captured there in the early 1850s but escaped.

★★

Tuolumne County

Westerns and serials featuring railroad scenes utilized several locations near Los Angeles. The exciting train chases for the William Witney-John English serial hit "Zorro Rides Again" ('37) lensed on track in the San Fernando Valley north of Los Angeles, near the point where I-5 and Hwy. 14 connect. Witney shot railway scenes for Roy Rogers' "Night Time in Nevada" ('48) and "Sunset in the West" ('50) on a stretch of track between Fillmore and Saugus, while rail shots for Roy's "Nevada City" ('41) (reused as the opening to TV's "Stories of the Century") used track in Soledad Canyon northeast of Saugus.

But Tuolumne County near Yosemite in northern California was undoubtedly the most frequently used and scenic setting for such sequences. Tuolumne's film history apparently dates from 1919, when Universal shot the final episodes of its serial "The Red Glove" there. Since that time the county has played in more than 300 films and TV shows, as well as countless commercials and industrial entries. With virtually every type of scenery available, from rolling hills with scattered trees, to expansive plains, woodlands and streams, Tuolumne furnished a superb setting for outdoor epics.

But its Sierra Railway was perhaps its principal attraction for film companies. Built in 1897 to transport lumber from the Tuolumne mountains to major rail connections in Oakdale, the 57-mile-long railroad has appeared in many titles. Even after the company converted to diesel in 1955, it retained several steam locomotives and an assortment of antique passenger and freight cars at its Jamestown yard for studio use.

Over the years, two of the company's locomotives, No. 3 (built in 1891) and No. 18 (built in 1906), became true stars. No. 18, the most popular engine in the '30s and '40s,

Director Earl Bellamy shot many episodes of Dale Robertson's "Tales of Wells Fargo" using this Jamestown railroad station and track.

appeared in "Dodge City" and "Duel in the Sun," among other titles. No. 3 became the 'star' on No. 18's retirement in 1951, appearing in such films as "The Virginian," "High Noon," "Rage At Dawn" and "Unforgiven." First used for a TV series in 1956, when "The Lone Ranger: The Twisted Track" filmed in Tuolumne, No. 3 was a regular cast member in Alan Hale Jr.'s "Casey Jones," Dale Robertson's "Tales of Wells Fargo" and "Iron Horse" and the long-running "Petticoat Junction." No. 3 also appeared in segments of "Big Valley," "Gunsmoke," "Death Valley Days" and "Wild, Wild West," among other TV series. "Petticoat Junction" gave prominent play to the water tower at the Jamestown station, while the Jamestown yard and roundhouse were featured in an exciting shootout for Audie Murphy's "Cimarron Kid" ('52).

The depot and track on the plains of Warnerville, about 20 miles west of Jamestown, saw

service in "High Noon," as did the historic mining community of Columbia a few miles north of Sonora, with a quaint residence with picket fence and shrubbery appearing as the house in which cowardly Henry Morgan lived. It's now the only privately owned home in Columbia. On Main St. a few doors away from the visitor's center. Columbia's streets joined with the famed western street at the Columbia Studio ranch in Burbank for the final shootout in that terrific film. A few miles southeast of Columbia you'll find the church where Gary Cooper pleads for deputies. It's St. Joseph's Catholic Church on Gardner in Tuolumne City just off Route 108.

Donna Magers poses before the house in the historic community of Columbia in which Henry Morgan 'lived' in "High Noon".

Columbia's streets and stores, as well as a picturesque Tuolumne covered bridge and the Sierra Railway, were also featured in Randolph Scott's "Rage at Dawn" ('55).

Murphys, a village about an hour's drive north of Sonora, was given a prominent role in the underrated "Texas Lady" ('55), in which Gregory Walcott stole the picture from stars Claudette Colbert and Barry Sullivan.

In 1989, Universal built its Hill Valley western town in Tuolumne's Red Hills area a few miles southwest of Sonora and Jamestown for Michael J. Fox's "Back to the Future III" ('90), which also featured Locomotive No. 3. Although used in several later productions, that town, then known as Red Hills Ranch, burned in 1996.

Columbia (a state historic park since 1945) features guided tours and looks much as it did in the gold rush days. (209) 532-4301.

In 1979 the Sierra Railway sold the Jamestown yard to the California park system, donating its old-time rolling stock, including No. 3, to the state. In July 1983, the facility was reopened as Railtown 1897 State Historic Park (where #3 now resides), with tours of the facilities and train rides for tourists. Call (209) 984-3953 for roundhouse tour and steam train excursion info. On 5th Ave., just three blocks south of Hwy. 108.

130

Sampling of Westerns Filmed in **TUOLUMNE COUNTY**

- The Terror ('20)—Tom Mix
- Toll Gate ('20)—William S. Hart
- Covered Wagon ('23)—J. Warren Kerrigan
- North of 36 ('24)—Jack Holt
- Galloping Ace ('24)—Jack Hoxie
- Timber Wolf ('25)—Buck Jones
- Virginian ('29)—Gary Cooper
- Fighting Caravans ('31)—Gary Cooper
- Wagon Wheels ('34)—Randolph Scott
- Robin Hood of El Dorado ('36)—Warner Baxter
- Wells Fargo ('36)—Joel McCrea
- Conflict ('37)—John Wayne
- North of the Rio Grande ('37)—William Boyd
- Dodge City ('39)—Errol Flynn
- Timber Stampede ('39)—George O'Brien
- Go West ('40)—Marx Brothers
- My Little Chickadee ('40)—Mae West, W. C. Fields
- When the Daltons Rode ('40)—Randolph Scott
- Duel In the Sun ('46)—Gregory Peck
- Whispering Smith ('49)—Alan Ladd
- Stampede ('49)—Rod Cameron
- Wyoming Mail ('50)—Stephen McNally
- Silver City ('51)—Edmond O'Brien
- Sierra Passage ('51)—Wayne Morris
- Texas Rangers ('51)—George Montgomery
- Painted Hills ('51)—Lassie, Gary Gray
- Great Missouri Raid ('51)—Macdonald Carey
- High Noon ('52)—Gary Cooper
- Kansas Pacific ('52)—Sterling Hayden
- Silver Whip ('53)—Dale Robertson
- Wichita ('55)—Joel McCrea
- Lone Ranger (TV): Twisted Track ('56)
- Big Land ('57)—Alan Ladd
- Tales of Wells Fargo (TV): series ('57-'62)
- Big Country ('58)—Gregory Peck
- Shadow Riders ('82)—Tom Selleck, Sam Elliott
- Paradise (TV): pilot ('88)
- Young Riders (TV): pilot ('89)
- Adv. of Brisco County Jr. (TV): many episodes ('93)
- Bonanza (TV): The Return ('93)
- Unforgiven ('92)—Clint Eastwood
- Bad Girls ('92)—Drew Barrymore

★★★

Mission Ranch Resort

Clint Eastwood not only owns Mission Ranch Resort in Carmel, he's intimately involved. He chose the menu for the restaurant, the music for the piano bar, and worked directly with architects and designers in the renovation and furnishing of the 150 year old former dairy farm which he bought in 1987. Clint spent millions in renovation as he delegated specifics to a contractor. The Ranch is adjacent to San Carlos Borromeo Mission which dates back to 1771. When Eastwood bought the property for $4 million he divided it, keeping 22 acres for the resort and donating the remaining acres that run along the Carmel River, where it empties into the Pacific Ocean, to the city of Carmel as a wildlife preserve.

It's a gorgeous, serene seaside place to spend a few days of your vacation. And Clint often drops

Mission Ranch Resort owned by Clint Eastwood.

into the restaurant in the evening! 26270 Dolores St. in Carmel. (800) 538-8221 for reservations. (831) 625-9040 for the restaurant.

★★★

Pebble Beach

Next time you golf 18 holes (or 9 as it may be) at Pebble Beach (on the California Coast), be it known it's now owned by Clint Eastwood along with a group of owners which includes pro golfer Arnold Palmer and former baseball commissioner Peter Ueberroth. The group purchased Pebble Beach from a Japanese golf resort operation for $820 million in 1999.

★★★

Nickelodeon Theatre

Both Rory Calhoun and Walter Reed are immortalized with their handprints/footprints and signatures in cement in front of the historic Nickelodeon Theatre, 210 Lincoln in Santa Cruz. There's a photo display of both actors inside the theatre. Calhoun was a native son and Reed lived in and had business investments in Santa Cruz for many years of his later life. Santa Cruz is on the ocean south of San Jose.

★★★

Backstage Restaurant and Cabaret

When you're in the Santa Cruz/San Jose area, drop by the Backstage Restaurant and Cabaret. There are many movie photos on the walls—including autographed photos of John Hart as the Lone Ranger, Rory Calhoun, Walter Reed, Clint Eastwood, Ronald Reagan, etc. 230G Mt. Herman Rd., Scotts Valley (off Hwy. 17 north of Santa Cruz).

★★★

Linda Evans Fitness Centers

Linda Evans, Audra Barkley on ABC's "Big Valley" from '65-'69, has endorsed a chain of at least 18 fitness centers in California, most of them in the San Francisco area, although the chain is expanding in the Los Angeles area (Huntington Beach, Garden Grove, San Juan Capistrano, Tustin, Yorba Linda, Fullerton, Fountain Valley).

Around the Frisco area, the workout centers are in Antioch, Alamo, Cupertino, Los Gatos, Martinez, Moraga, Pleasanton, San Jose, Walnut Creek, Union City with headquarters in San Ramon at 2404 San Ramon Blvd. (925) 743-3399.

★★★

Audie Murphy Rose

A vivid, rich, crimson tea rose was first grown and named for Audie Murphy by Roseway Nurseries of Beaverton, Oregon, in 1955 who stated "this brilliant red rose is symbolic of the bravery and valor" of his legendary deeds. The Audie Murphy Rose received a plant patent in 1957 when it was first introduced for sale to the public.

Although Roseway Nurseries are long out of business, you may order the "very popular" Audie Murphy Rose (which come in 3x3x5" pots) for about $11 (plus shipping) from Vintage Gardens, 2833 Old Gravenstein, Sebastopol, CA 95472. <www.vintage-gardens.com> (707) 829-2035.

★★

California State Railroad Museum

Movie studios bought most of their locomotives, rolling stock and other equipment over the years from Nevada's Virginia and Truckee Railroad, a classic short line originally used for ore shipments from Nevada's Comstock Lode. Many of these locomotives are on display at the Nevada State Railroad Museum (see that entry) but V&T's locomotive #21 saw service in "Rock Island Trail" ('50), "Union Pacific" ('39) and the recent debacle, "Wild, Wild West" ('99). This 1875 Baldwin steam locomotive can be seen at the California State Railroad Museum located in Old Sacramento.

The museum is a complex of historic facilities and unique attractions, widely regarded as one of North America's most visited railroad museums. Open daily 10-5 except major holidays. 111 I Street (at 2nd and I St.). (916) 445-7387

★★

Northern Queen Inn

Railroad sequences furnished some of the most thrilling scenes in westerns, both of the B and A variety.

For the historic railroad scenes in "The Spoilers" ('42) with John Wayne and Randolph Scott, Universal purchased a locomotive built by Baldwin in 1875 during Nevada's bonanza days. The Nevada Narrow Gauge Railroad #5 locomotive sat on the backlot for years until about 1950 when it was used in "Winchester '73" ('50), "Dawn At Socorro" ('54), "The Spoilers" ('56) remake, "Rails Into Laramie" ('54) and "Shenandoah" ('65). No. 5 also saw service in "The Virginian" TV series ('62-'70), "Laredo" ('65-'67), "Alias Smith and Jones" ('71-'73) and "Hec Ramsey" ('72-'74). Altogether, #5 was seen in approximately 100 movies and/or TV episodes.

This locomotive is on display at the Nevada County Narrow Gauge Railroad and Transportation Museum which sports over 25 pieces of historical railroad equipment. Located at the Northern Queen Inn in Nevada City, 400 Railroad Ave. (916) 265-3668 or (530) 265-5824 ext. 262. Nevada City is off I-80 on Hwy. 20 between Sacramento and Reno, Nevada.

★★

COLORADO

Fred Harman Art Museum

The Fred Harman Art Museum is two miles west of Pagosa Springs at 2560 W. Hwy. 160. In 1938 Fred created "Red Ryder" for the comic strips, then came a radio show and Republic picked up the lanky redhead as a B-western vehicle for Don Barry, Bill Elliott and Allan Lane. Jim Bannon later made four "Red Ryder" features in color for Equity.

Harman continued to draw "Red Ryder" until 1963. By then he was heavily involved in his oil paintings. In 1965 he helped found the Cowboy Artists of America with four other well-known artists. He died in 1982.

Loads of marvelous original Harman comic strip and oil painting artwork are at the museum which is maintained by Fred's son.

Open 10:30-5 Monday-Saturday. Noon-4 Sunday. Winter hours are 10:30-5 Monday-Friday. (970) 731-5785.

Fred Harman Jr. at his father's museum.

The Red Ryder Rodeo is still held every July in Pagosa Springs.

★★★

Canon City Area

In the 300 block of Main St. in Canon City is where Selig studios set up shop and filmed interiors for Tom Mix westerns and other short features. The old race track and stands on Poplar Street served as rodeo grounds and have changed little since Tom was there in 1912.

Head north out of town on Illinois Ave. and follow the signs on Hwy. 50 to the Royal Gorge where the world's highest suspension bridge stands 1,053 feet above the Arkansas River. Tom Mix's "Great K&A Train Robbery" was lensed here. (719) 275-7507

As you near the gorge, you'll want to visit Buckskin Joe's movie ranch comprised of many authentic buildings, some over 100 years old, moved there from all over Colorado to create the town. Opened in 1958, the Old West theme park features an antique steam train museum, a gold mine, stagecoach rides, gunfights in the street, Royal Gorge train ride as well as a restaurant and gift shop. There are literally dozens of photos and posters from films shot there on display. The Buckskin Joe Western Heritage Roundup is held every September. Music, historical reenactments, gunfights and more. 8 miles west of Canon City out U.S. 50, then follow the signs. Open Memorial Day to Labor Day 9-7:30. (719) 275-5149

Sackett house at Buckskin Joe's used in TV's miniseries "The Sacketts" (1979).

Sampling of Westerns Filmed at BUCKSKIN JOE'S

- Saddle the Wind ('58)—Robert Taylor
- Cat Ballou ('65)—Lee Marvin
- Stagecoach ('66)—Alex Cord
- Barquero ('70)—Lee Van Cleef
- The Cowboys ('72)—John Wayne
- White Buffalo ('76)—Charles Bronson
- Duchess and the Dirtwater Fox ('76)—George Segal
- How the West Was Won (TV): various episodes ('77-'79)
- True Grit ('78) (TV)—Warren Oates
- Sacketts ('79) (TV)—Sam Elliott
- Conagher ('91) (TV)—Sam Elliott
- Lightning Jack ('93)—Paul Hogan

★★

Pro Rodeo Hall of Fame

The Pro Rodeo Hall of Fame in Colorado Springs, at the foot of Pike's Peak, plays home to the best in rodeo including personal memorabilia from Ben Johnson, Yakima Canutt, Casey Tibbs, Rex Allen, Montie Montana and others. Inductees include Gene Autry and Andy Jauregui (as rodeo stock contractors), Glenn Randall (who trained Trigger and other movie horses), Bill Pickett (steer wrestling), Ben Johnson (for team roping) and Montie Montana. The audio-visual presentation mentions Gene, Ben and Slim Pickens.

West of I-25 exit 417 at 101 Rodeo Dr. Look for the huge courtyard sculpture called "Champion" which shows Casey Tibbs aboard a bronc named Necktie. (719) 528-4764. Open year round 9-5.

★★

Pikes Peak or Bust Rodeo Hall of Fame

Although it sounds like it, in Colorado Springs, the Pikes Peak or Bust Rodeo Hall of Fame is *not* a building with displays or plaques. In the center of downtown (Pikes Peak

Ave. and Tejon St.), there is a statue of "Hank," the rodeo's logo cowboy. Just behind the statue is a 9 ft. rock on which are inscribed the names of individuals who have been inducted over the years since the rodeo began in 1939. Included are Rex Allen, Montie Montana, Ken Curtis and Milburn Stone.

Allen first appeared at the rodeo in an old stadium at the famous Broadmoor Hotel in 1958.

★★★

Will Rogers Shrine of the Sun

The Will Rogers Shrine of the Sun is a stone structure on the side of the mountain that reflects the sun. Located in the Cheyenne Mountain Zoo in Colorado Springs, the Shrine was constructed by Penn Rose (who owned the famous Broadmoor Hotel in Colorado Springs) and other friends of Will's in the cowboy's honor. Zoo number is (719) 633-9925.

★★★

Denver Broncos

A 23 ft. white fiberglass horse that has greeted Denver Broncos football fans since 1976 at Mile High Stadium is from the same mold as the Trigger statue in front of the Roy Rogers Museum. When Trigger died in 1965, Roy asked Fiber Glass Menagerie, Alpine, Colorado, to make a larger than life statue of his beloved palomino. Then, when a Chicago concern contacted the company in 1975 after creating a horse for the Broncos scoreboard, they checked and received permission from Roy to use the same mold, turning it into a white horse.

★★★

Glenwood Springs Museum

The local history museum in Glenwood Springs (I-70 west of Denver) has photos of Tom Mix who filmed scenes for "Great K&A Train Robbery" at the Royal Gorge.

★★★

Durango and Silverton Narrow Gauge Railroad

All aboard! For an authentic turn-of-the-century steam-powered, coal-fueled scenic railroad ride through the spectacular San Juan Mountains of southwest Colorado, take a trip on the historic Durango and Silverton Narrow Gauge Railroad. More than a train ride, it's a step back in time and history.

Based in Durango (479 Main Ave.), the Denver and Rio Grande arrived there in 1881 when construction began on the line. Completed to Sliverton in 1882, the line was constructed to primarily haul gold and silver mine ore from the San Juan Mountains. It's estimated over $300 million in precious metals rode this route.

During the late '60s, the D&RG abandoned the tracks from Antonito, Colorado, to Durango, thereby cutting Durango from the balance of the D&RG system. After this, the only narrow gauge trackage remaining was the 45 miles from Durango to Silverton.

Waiting for an "all aboard" from the Durango and Silverton Railroad in Durango.

The D&RG sold the Silverton branch, with all of its rolling stock, station, etc. to the Durango and Silverton Narrow Gauge Railroad Co. in 1981.

The train travels through the remote wilderness area of the San Juan National Forest, following the Animas River to Silverton. The trains serve Tall Timber Resort and stop twice northbound for water and once returning to Durango.

Although earlier westerns utilized the railroad, "A Ticket To Tomahawk" was the first film to use the line's 45 mile beautiful Silverton branch, including the Silverton train depot, still standing.

Sterling Hayden was a ruthless engineer opposing Edmond O'Brien in the classic railroad film, "Denver and Rio Grande," in which producer Nat Holt acquired and permitted director Byron Haskin to wreck and destroy full-size trains in the only train-wreck scene of its kind ever filmed. A co-star in the film, Laura Elliott, was there. "150 members of the press congregated, waiting for these two trains to crash. The sun was out and we all gathered umpteen hundred yards away from the trains because they were rigged with dynamite. Two engineers started the trains from opposite ends, and as they gathered speed, six to ten miles an hour, they jumped with the controls locked down. Stuntmen didn't know how to drive the trains. The special effects people had the trains rigged with dynamite to make it really explode when they crashed. Well, once the trains are put in motion on the track, they're not going anyplace else. When those trains hit, *man*, the smoke went and the fire and everything! Hunks of metal flew as far out as we were, although no one was injured. It was emotional. Those engineers just cried. They'd driven those trains for 50 years. It was very exciting. I'm very lucky. I have one of those gorgeous big, brass and copper original chandeliers from one of the cars. It was filmed outside Durango, Colorado." The ex-Denver and Rio Grande western railroad locomotives #473, #476 and #478 are all still operable and are the locomotives seen in "Maverick Queen" ('56), "Night Passage" ('57), "Run For Cover" ('55), "Butch Cassidy and the Sundance Kid"

('69) and "Support Your Local Gunfighter" ('71).

Dennis Weaver narrates an audio-visual presentation which can be viewed in a railroad car museum in Durango. Trains to Silverton run May-October. Reservations necessary. (970) 247-2733.

Sampling of Westerns Filmed on THE D&RG

- Texas Rangers ('36)—Fred MacMurray
- Colorado Territory ('49)—Joel McCrea
- A Ticket to Tomahawk ('50)—Rory Calhoun
- Across the Wide Missouri ('51)—Clark Gable
- Viva Zapata! ('52)—Marlon Brando
- Denver and Rio Grande ('52)—Edmond O'Brien
- Run For Cover ('55)—James Cagney
- Maverick Queen ('56)—Barbara Stanwyck
- Night Passage ('57)—James Stewart/ Audie Murphy
- How the West Was Won ('63)—George Peppard
- Diamond Jim Brady (TV): unsold pilot with Dale Robertson ('64)
- Butch Cassidy and the Sundance Kid ('69)—Paul Newman/Robert Redford
- Support Your Local Gunfighter ('71)—James Garner
- The Tracker ('88)—Kris Kristofferson

★★★

Rochester Hotel

In Durango, a hotel gem is the beautifully renovated historic Rochester Hotel, built in 1892, where each of 15 rooms is decorated with memorabilia from westerns filmed in the area. Included is the Harry Carey Jr. room.

Even the hallways of the classic hotel feature still photos and one sheet posters from dozens of films made in the area.

The Rochester was designated as the Flagship Hotel of Colorado by Condé Nast in 1996.

The hotel is only a few blocks away from the Durango and Silverton Narrow Gauge Railroad Station. 726 E. Second Ave. (800) 664-1920.

★★★

New Sheridan Hotel

The New Sheridan Hotel, 231 West Colorado Ave. in Telluride, has a bar used in "Butch Cassidy and the Sundance Kid."

Telluride, a skier's paradise, is on Hwy. 145 in the southwest corner of Colorado.

★★★

Dennis Weaver

Dennis Weaver's environmentally friendly, yet beautiful, home is near Ridgway, north of Durango on Hwy. 550. The house uses tires, aluminum cans and other recycled material as part of the structure and is called an Earthship. The house uses solar mass to conserve heat and solar power.

This small town appeared as the frontier town in John Wayne's "True Grit" ('69).

★★★

The late Walter Reed stands beside the remnants of a set used in John Ford's "Cheyenne Autumn" in which Reed had a role.

★★★★★★★★★★★★★★★★★★★★★★★★★★★★★★★★

Buddy Roosevelt

Meeker is the hometown of silent and early talkie B-western star Buddy Roosevelt (1898-1973). Located in the lonely northwestern quadrant of Colorado on Hwy. 64, the White River Museum honors Buddy with his own special section. Several items of his regalia, including a bullwhip he was especially fond of, his wooly chaps, several family items, newspaper clippings and lots of photos. Folks at the museum will also direct you to Buddy's old house in Meeker.

Buddy's career started as a stunt double around 1915. His starring silents ("Rough Ridin'," "Biff-Bang Buddy," "Cyclone Buddy" etc.) were in the mid-'20s. After several support roles, he starred in a short-lived 1934 series for Superior Talking Pictures. That ended his starring career, but not his work in films as he kept on working until 1962 with his last appearance in "Man Who Shot Liberty Valance."

"Cheyenne Autumn"

Remnants of buildings used for "Cheyenne Autumn" ('64) and earlier in portions of "The Searchers" ('56) still remain about ten miles out of Gunnison north on Hwy 135 (left side of road).

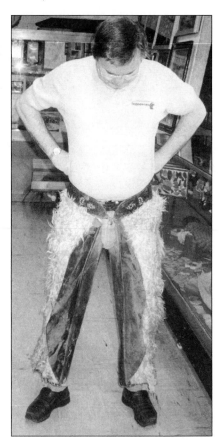

Looks like Buddy Roosevelt and I were about the same size as I try on a pair of his wooly chaps at the White River Museum.

★★

CONNECTICUT

Wesleyan University

The Cinema Archives at Wesleyan University in Middletown houses Clint Eastwood's complete papers. The star of TV's "Rawhide" and several Euro-oaters was awarded an honorary Doctor of Fine Arts degree at Wesleyan in May, 2000.

★★

DISTRICT OF COLUMBIA

Smithsonian

One of Clayton Moore's Lone Ranger masks is enshrined and on permanent display at the Smithsonian Institute in Washington (14th St. and Constitution Ave. N.W.). It can be found by looking for the four cases dedicated to 'Icons of Popular Culture.'

Also in these cases are Dorothy's ruby slippers from "The Wizard of OZ," Sonja Henie's ice skates and other 20th Century sports and pop culture artifacts.

★★★

Pentagon

Audie Murphy's portrait hangs in the Hall of Heroes, a dedicated corridor at the Pentagon in Washington which honors all Medal of Honor holders.

Unfortunately, tours of the Pentagon have been suspended for the time being.

★★★

Roy Rogers Restaurant

Roy Rogers Restaurant still operational (See details under Maryland.) 401 M St. S.W., Washington, D.C.

★★★

FLORIDA

Tommy Ivo

Tommy Ivo went from western movie child star opposite the Durango Kid and others to being TV Tommy Ivo, nationally known drag strip star. He was the first inductee into the International Drag Racing Hall of Fame in Ocala. At Don Garlits Museum of Drag Racing in Ocala (at 13700 SW 16th Ave. off I-75) there is a granite block with Tommy's name inscribed. The museum houses Ivo's dragster with two Buick motors. (352) 245-8661.

Meanwhile, Tommy's "signature car," a dragster powered by four Buick motors and built by Tommy in 1961, is on display at the NHRA Motor Sports Museum at the Los Angeles Fairplex in Pomona off I-10. Tommy's most famous dragster was first known as the Showboat and later as the Wagon Master. This musuem also houses his Ford Model-T Buick-powered roadster which Tom build at 19.

A special exhibit at both locations recognizes his film and TV career starting at age 3 and continuing with film clips from "Treasure of Lost Canyon," his Durango Kid films and others.

TV Tommy Ivo stands in the "Hall of Champions" amidst his movie posters, race cars, photos, helmets, awards and more.

★★

Stars Hall of Fame Wax Museum

The Stars Hall of Fame Wax Museum on I-4 (midstate) has wax figures of Tom Mix, Ken Maynard, William S. Hart.

★★★

Planet Hollywood

Surround yourself with movie memorabilia when you grab a quick bite to eat at any of the over 15 Planet Hollywood restaurants in the U.S., with many more worldwide. Ten of the locations in the states display some western memorabilia. The items listed on this chart are among the more dynamic artifacts. Each of these locations may have other western props as well, especially from more recent westerns such as "Maverick", "Wild Bill", "Geronimo" and "Wyatt Earp." The Orlando Planet Hollywood is at Walt Disney World Resort, 1506 E. Buena Vista Dr. (407) 827-7827. The exact locations for the other eateries in this chart are listed in their respective states in this book.

Location	*Star*	*Item*
Orlando, Florida	Clint Eastwood Lee Van Cleef Robert Vaughn Mel Gibson James Garner	Navy Colt from "The Good, The Bad and the Ugly" Rifle from "For a Few Dollars More" Holster belt from "Magnificent Seven" Playing cards from "Maverick" .45 Colt from "Maverick"
Atlantic City, New Jersey	Richard Harris Phillip Ahn Kevin Costner	Buckskin jacket from "A Man Called Horse" Contact lens from "Kung Fu" Coat from "Wyatt Earp"
St. Louis, Missouri	"Gunsmoke" Val Kilmer	Wooden boat paddles Silver pistol from "Tombstone"
New York, New York	Henry Fonda Kevin Costner Lee Van Cleef	6" barrel Colt from "Once Upon A Time In the West" Revolver and rifle from "Dances With Wolves" Derringer from "For A Few Dollars More"
Niagara Falls, New York	"Geronimo" ('93) "Maverick ('94) "Wyatt Earp" ('94)	Full sized "horse" 12 ft. teepee several props
Lake Tahoe, Nevada	Lee Van Cleef	Derringer from "For A Few Dollars More"
Las Vegas, Nevada	Clint Eastwood James Garner Clint Eastwood John Wayne "Lone Ranger" ('56)	Gun from "The Good, The Bad and the Ugly" Revolver from "Maverick" Wood Colt replica from "For a Few Dollars More" Beige shirt and jacket from "The Cowboys" Gray wool tunic

Location	Star	Item
Reno, Nevada	Paul Hogan Roy Rogers "Unforgiven" ('92) Barbara Stanwyck "City Slickers" ('91) "Young Guns II" ('90)	Felt hat from "Lightning Jack" Double-breasted vest Many props Gown worn on "Big Valley" "Little Norman" baby calf Costumes
Myrtle Beach, South Carolina	Jack Palance "Gunsmoke" ('55-'75) "Dances With Wolves" ('90) Clayton Moore Steve McQueen Errol Flynn Robert Redford	Gray shirt from "City Slickers II" photo album Full size buffalo Black cotton robe from "Jesse James Rides Again" serial Black suede pouch from "Tom Horn" Gray/blue jacket from "Virginia City" 3-piece Herringbone suit from "Butch Cassidy and the Sundance Kid"

There are Planet Hollywood restaurants all over the world with more western items—here are only a *few* of the more interesting artifacts:

Cancun	Clayton Moore	Lone Ranger costume
Dubai	John Wayne	Brown shirt from "Rooster Cogburn"
Montreal	Alan Ladd	Brown leather boots from "Shane"
Moscow	"Tales of Wells Fargo" TV series	Rust, black and tan carpet bag
Paris	Clint Eastwood	Navy Colt from "The Good, the Bad and the Ugly"
Singapore	"Gunsmoke" TV series	Canteen

★★★

Ringling Museum of Art

The Ringling Museum of Art in Sarasota combines an art museum with a circus museum which, according to a curatorial assistant, has frequently changing exhibits. They claim to have in their collection posters and circus memorabilia (unnamed) belonging to Tom Mix, Ken Maynard, Tim McCoy, Jack Hoxie and others, but these items are not always on display. Certainly worth investigating but we found the curator of little help to this book.

5401 Bay Shore Rd. (813) 355-5101. Open Monday-Friday 9-10, Saturday 9-5, Sunday 11-6.

★★★

GEORGIA

Audie Murphy Gym

To honor the memory of an outstanding infantryman, the Main Post Gymnasium (Bldg. 2818) at Fort Benning (the U.S. Infantry Center) in Columbus was designated the Audie L. Murphy Fitness Center on March 9, 1973. Although Audie was never assigned to Ft. Benning, he visited the post on at least one occasion in 1955.

★★★

HAWAII

Autry Palm

On August 11, 1956, Gene Autry planted the 46th palm tree in The Lagoon, the largest, oldest coconut grove in all of the Hawaiian Islands. This was at the Royal Grove of Kauai where only very special individuals were granted the privilege of planting a tree. Inscription on the bronze plaque reads "Kumo He Inoa (The Name Tree) Gene Autry, Radio, TV, Motion Picture Star. August 11, 1956."

★★

INDIANA

Henager's Memories and Nostalgia

Specializing in Americana, Henager's Memories and Nostalgia in Buckskin (north of Evansville on State Hwy. 57, just off I-64 in Gibson County in far southwestern Indiana)

A display wall at Henager's.

contains dozens of items of Roy Rogers and Dale Evans given to owner James Henager by Roy "Dusty" Rogers Jr. Other items range from old autos and jukeboxes to records, posters, WWII, Santa Claus and Smokey Bear memorabilia. There are many other collectibles from the likes of Gene Autry, the Rin Tin Tin TV series, "The Rebel," Hopalong Cassidy, as well as western movie and TV comic books. The collection is constantly being supplemented. Officially opened in December '96 by James Henager.

(812) 795-2230. Open on a regular basis, 8-4.

★★★★★★★★★★★★★★★★★★★★★★★★

Ken Maynard's Birthplace

The house in which Ken Maynard was born is clearly marked on Liberty St. in Vevay, located on the Kentucky border in southeastern Indiana on Hwy. 129.

The Vevay welcoming center at 105 West Pike St. has a huge scrapbook on the lives of Ken and Kermit Maynard.

★★★★★★★★★★★★★★★★★★★★★★★★★★★★★★★★★★★★★★

Congressional Medal of Honor Memorial

Second Lieutenant Audie Murphy is included at the Congressional Medal of Honor Memorial in Indianapolis. The Medal of Honor is America's highest award for military valor, bestowed on those who have performed an act of such conspicuous gallantry as to rise "above and beyond the call of duty". The roll of honor includes only 3,432 of the millions of men and women who have served their country since the Civil War.

Audie received the symbol of heroism for his gallantry on January 26, 1945, when he commanded Company B in the 15th Infantry near Holtzwihr, France. Attacked by six tanks and waves of infantry, Lt. Murphy ordered his men to withdraw to the woods while he remained forward, continuing to give fire directions to the artillery by telephone which killed large numbers of advancing enemy infantry. Behind him, one of our tank destroyers was hit and began to burn. Its crew withdrew to the woods. Lt. Murphy climbed aboard the burning tank destroyer, which could have blown up at any moment, and

The Congressional Medal of Honor Memorial.

employed its .50 caliber machine gun, killing dozens of Germans, causing their attack to waver. Losing support, the enemy tanks began to fall back. For an hour the Germans tried to eliminate Lt. Murphy, but he held his position, wiping out the enemy who came as close as ten yards, only to be mowed down by his fire. He received a leg wound, but ignored it, continuing his single-handed fight until his ammunition was exhausted. He then made his way to his company, refused medical attention, and organized his company in a counterattack, forcing the enemy to withdraw. His courage and refusal to give an inch of ground saved his company from possible encirclement and destruction and enabled it to hold the woods which had been the enemy's objective. The medal was presented to Audie June 2, 1945.

Located on the north bank of the Central Canal in White River State Park in downtown Indianapolis, the Memorial is a group of 27 curved glass walls, each between 7 and 10 feet tall. The memorial was dedicated May 28, 1999, the last Memorial Day of the 20th Century. It is a salute to our finest.

★★

James Dean Memorial Gallery

The James Dean Memorial Gallery in Fairmount encompasses a seven room exhibit in an 1890 Victorian home with the world's largest Dean collection including thousands of items from the private collection of Dean archivist David Loehr.

Clothing from all Dean's films (including "Giant"), a rare Warner Bros. life mask, tribute and novelty items and much more. A screening room shows rare film clips. Fully stocked gift shop. Dean was born in Marion, 10 miles north of Fairmount.

425 N. Main St. (765) 948-3326. Open 9-6.

★★

Bracken Library

The Bracken Library at Ball State University in Muncie has around 45 scripts which belonged to B-western player Tex Terry. Terry (1903-1985) worked extensively at Universal and Republic and was quite proficient with a whip.

In addition to the scripts, there are some 8x10" stills and a few other items. Located in the Archives and Special Collections in Bracken Library, some of the script titles are: "Bandits of the Badlands," "Alias Billy the Kid," "Duel at Apache Wells," "Pack Train," "Rock Island Trail" and "Wyoming."

Archives Special Collections librarian, (765) 285-5078.

★★★

Miami County Museum

Peru is known as the Circus Capital of the World. It was once winter headquarters for the Sells-Floto Circus for which Tom Mix was a star performer in 1929, '30 and '31.

The Miami County Museum in Peru displays Tom's stagecoach which was built by the Concord Company of New Hampshire in the 1870s. Mix bought it in 1914 from the U. S. government who had been using it in Yellowstone National Park. Mix used the coach in his movies and while traveling with the circus until 1934, using it for the last time while

Tom Mix Concord stagecoach.

performing with the Sam B. Dill Circus in Kokomo. Afterward, Mix donated it to the Miami County Museum.

In addition to the coach, the museum also displays one of Mix's holsters given to a local man during the Sells-Floto heyday, a model of the Sells-Floto and Tom Mix Circus wagon, a circus souvenir route book, a Christmas card from Tom and Tony and many photos of Mix with the circus. 51 N. Broadway. (765) 473-9183.

There's an annual circus parade in Peru every July. Peru is 70 miles straight north of Indianapolis just off Hwy. 31.

★★★

Circus Hall of Fame

The Circus Hall of Fame in Peru features something (posters, photos, placards, programs) on nearly all the cowboys who were in circuses...Tom Mix, Hoot Gibson, Ken Maynard, Tim McCoy, Cisco Kid, Hopalong Cassidy. They have a case devoted to western cowboys with saddles and posters on exhibit, however, Tom Mix seems to be, technically, the only cowboy inducted into their actual Hall of Fame. Not on display, but available for serious researchers, are many more route books, programs and paper ephemera from the heyday of the movie cowboy on the sawdust trail.

3076 E. Circus Lane in Peru. Closed during the winter. Open April 1 through October 10-5 Monday-Saturday, 1-5 Sunday. (765) 472-7553.

★★★

IOWA

John Wayne Birthplace

Winterset is the birthplace of John Wayne in 1907.

Built in the 1880s, the well-kept four room white frame house exhibits the Duke's movie career (including an eyepatch from his Academy Award winning role in "True Grit" and a suitcase used in "Stagecoach") along with hundreds of rare photos and artifacts. President Ronald Reagan visited the museum in 1984.

Wayne's father, Clyde, was a pharmacist who worked on the south side of Winterset's town square. Wayne described his father as the "kindest, most patient man I ever knew." Wayne's mother was of Irish descent and Wayne called her "a tiny, vivacious red-headed bundle of energy." Perhaps, that's what he saw years later in co-star Maureen O'Hara.

The John Wayne birthplace in Winterset.

The birthplace, restored to its 1907 appearance, with its extensive gift shop (8 page John Wayne catalog) is open seven days a week except Thanksgiving, Christmas and New Year's Day. Guided tours are given from 10-4:30. Take I-80 west from Des Moines about 13 miles to the Hwy. 169 South exit. About 16 miles from there. 216 S. 2nd St. (515) 462-1044.

While you're visiting the John Wayne birthplace in Winterset, watch for John Wayne Dr., which is S. 1st Street.

★★

KANSAS

Dodge City

Dodge City is a magical historic name and that's about all—movie or TV-wise. Certainly steeped in real west history, the dusty, windy west Kansas town does sport a few pictures of James Arness as Matt Dillon (and the rest of the cast), but other than that, "Gunsmoke" is overlooked, although some tour guides at the poorly developed western town will try to make you believe the series was lensed here. Two downtown streets are named Gunsmoke St. and Wyatt Earp Blvd. The Dodge Theatre Building at the corner of Gunsmoke and 1st is the most interesting spot in town. The Cowboy Heritage Festival is held there annually in May. (800) Old-West.

On Hwy. 56 in southwest Kansas.

★★★

Prairie Rose Opera House

The Prairie Rose Chuckwagon Supper and Opera House, about 15 miles east of Wichita, is all about "Great Western Family Entertainment."

One of the fastest growing attractions in Kansas, the 9,000 square foot dining and entertainment complex outside Wichita features a distinct B-western flavor and décor

The Prairie Rose Supper and Opera House.

and is like "an oasis from the realities of life" say owners Cheryl and Thomas Etheredge.

Gates open at 5:30 each evening. As you arrive you'll enjoy horse drawn wagon rides or a Roy Rogers movie at the Happy Trails Theatre. A western mini-museum displays shirts, boots, rifles, watches and other memorabilia that belonged to Roy Rogers, Gene Autry, Hopalong Cassidy, Rex Allen and others. At 6:30 the dinner bell rings as you sit down to enjoy an all-you-can-eat barbecue meal. After dinner, sit back and enjoy the Prairie Rose's hour and a half western stage show featuring the Prairie Rose Wranglers.

In addition to their regular show featuring the Prairie Rose Wranglers, about eight times a year special concerts are presented featuring Roy Rogers Jr., Johnny Western (the writer of the "Have Gun Will Travel" theme song is a resident of Wichita and longtime dj at KFDI radio), Don Edwards, the Sons of the San Joaquin and Rex Allen Jr.

Open Thursday-Saturday 5:30pm-9pm. Reservations required. (316) 778-2121. Special Christmas shows November through December.

The Prairie Rose has been selected to house a Hopalong Cassidy museum with construction to start in 2003. The museum will display memorabilia, posters, photos, novels and feature films and TV episodes in a theatre setting. A Hopalong Cassidy gift shop will feature Hoppy memorabilia and gifts.

From Wichita, take Hwy. K254 east towards El Dorado, 1 mile east of the Butler County Line, turn left on Butler Rd. and go 2 miles north. Turn right on Parallel Rd. and follow the signs.

★★★

Dalton Defenders Museum

A Reb Russell Circus poster from Russell Bros. (no relation) Circus and a couple of other Reb Russell related documents are on display at the "real west" Dalton Defenders Museum at 113 E. 8th Street in Coffeyville where the Daltons were gunned down after attempting to rob two banks simultaneously.

At one time Reb's pistols were housed here but they were stolen several years ago and Reb's son removed other artifacts of his father's so they could not also be stolen.

Open daily except Christmas. 9-7 June, July, August. 9-5 September through May.

★★★

KENTUCKY

Windy Hollow Restaurant

Hal Miller's Windy Hollow Restaurant and Cowboy Museum is a fun place to have your Sunday brunch buffet. But be aware, Sunday is the only day it's open. Hal, along with another fellow, was the producer of the infamous "Marshal of Windy Hollow" movie, the last picture in which Ken Maynard was featured. Sunset Carson was also in the cast. A wrangle over ownership of the film with Hal's former partner has prevented fans from probably ever viewing the film which was shot entirely at Hal's restaurant and surrounding area.

Drop by for Sunday brunch and Hal will tell you all about his experiences with Ken and Sunset. He also has a nice little B-western and WWII memorabilia room adjacent to the dining area. You might also ask about his friend Sam who has an extensive private Roy Rogers collection and will be happy to share it with you by appointment.

10 miles southwest of Owensboro, off KY Hwy. 81. (270) 785-4088. Open Sundays 7-1:30.

★★★

International Museum of the Horse

What's a cowboy without a horse?

The International Museum of the Horse is located at the Kentucky Horse Park, 4089 Iron Works Parkway, Lexington. (800) 678-8813.

If you love horses, this is the place for you. Spread out over 1,032 acres, there are many outstanding exhibition galleries, carriage rides, horsebacking, saddlebred museum, breeds barn, race track, stables and special events throughout the year.

★★★

Fort Knox

On March 23, 1990, Audie Murphy was one of three Medal of Honor recipients to have a building dedicated in his honor at Ft. Knox. Audie's building is designated as Murphy Hall.

★★★

MAINE

John Ford Memorial

The bronze of John Ford at Gorham's Corner.

Nearly 90 years after he left the Irish neighborhoods of Portland, where he was raised, to make movies in Hollywood, John Ford is honored with a 10 ft. bronze statue of him in his director's chair, at Gorham's Corner, where four streets come together in the old Irish section of town. The bronze, by New York City sculptor George Kelly, was donated by philanthropist Linda Noe Laine, a Ford family friend. Longtime Ford friend, Harry Carey Jr. told us, "The statue doesn't look a great deal like John Ford, but if he saw it, he'd like it because it makes him look sorta like Tarzan. (Laughs) You could tell the hat's right but it's not really him, and they don't have the glasses prominent enough. Those glasses were a very prominent part of his persona. Linda Noe Laine redid the whole corner, totally landscaped with rocks from Monument Valley. She's a remarkable woman. It's a beautiful setting." John Mitchum commented, "The sculpture is an exquisite, beautiful representation."

★★

MARYLAND

Baltimore and Ohio Railroad Museum

The Baltimore and Ohio Railroad is the only major railroad that's preserved an extensive collection of antique engines and rolling stock. Certainly, Hollywood has made use of it over the years.

At the Baltimore and Ohio Railroad Museum in Baltimore you'll find three locomotives of interest. The B&O "William Mason" built in 1856 and still operable, was used in "The Great Locomotive Chase," "Raintree County" and the recent "Wild, Wild West" ('99).

The B&O "Thatcher Perkins" on static display, built in 1863, was utilized in Forrest Tucker's "Rock Island Trail" ('50).

The B&O "Lafayette", now on static display, was built in 1926 (an 1837 replica). It appeared in "Wells Fargo" ('37), "Stand Up and Fight" ('39) and "The Great Locomotive Chase" ('56).

The museum collection includes a wide variety of steam locomotives, arguably the most historic collection found in the U.S.

The B&O Railroad Museum is located at the historic site of the B&O's Mount Clare Shops (just 10 blocks west of Baltimore's inner harbor area) at 901 W. Pratt Street. Mount Clare is considered to be the birthplace of American railroading. Open daily 10-5 except major holidays. (410) 752-2490.

Roy Rogers Restaurants

At one time there were 634 Roy Rogers fast food rstaurants primarily on the east coast, with others in California, Oklahoma and Chicago, Illinois. Their cups, napkins, menus, matchbook covers, french fry containers, posters etc. are now extremely collectible items as the restaurants have dwindled to about 35 in three states—Maryland, Pennsylvania and Virginia. The Roy Rogers chain was founded in Fairfax, Virginia, in 1968.

Hardee's bought the chain from original owner Marriott for $365 million in 1990. In 1995 Hardee's sold what they termed "the unprofitable restaurant chain." Some outlets were sold to Wendy's, some to Boston Market and the rest to McDonald's (for 74 million). In July '97, Hardee's sold the remainder to MRO Mid Atlantic Corporation. The following is a list of Roy Rogers restaurants still operational in Maryland. (There may be a few researcher Richard Smith III overlooked; if so, please let us know.)

Valley Mall Hagerstown, Maryland (301) 797-8300	Queen City Drive Cumberland, Maryland (301) 777-8299
1285 National Highway La Vale, Maryland (301) 729-6115	4535 Falls Road Baltimore, Maryland (410) 467-3877
7379 Baltimore/Annapolis Blvd. Baltimore, Maryland (410) 574-6602	8432 Pulaski Highway Baltimore, Maryland (410) 761-6457
1435 Rockspring Road Bel Air, Maryland (410) 893-9283	Route 22 and Campus Hill Drive Churchville, Maryland (410) 879-5315
1930 Pulaski Highway Edgewood, Maryland (410) 679-6044	1438 Liberty Road Eldersburg, Maryland (410) 781-4942
Finksburg Plaza Finksburg, Maryland (410) 526-7183	400 East Ridgeville Blvd. Mount Airy, Maryland (410) 549-2279
Route 140 and Sullivan Road Westminster, Maryland (410) 876-1433	1338 Dorsey Road Hanover, Maryland (410) 684-2111
1240 West Patrick Street Frederick, Maryland (301) 695-8414	5622 Buckeystown Pike Frederick, Maryland (301) 695-8270
191 Thomas Johnson Drive Frederick, Maryland (301) 695-6399	1204 East Patrick Street Frederick, Maryland (301) 695-1464
1990 Riverside Way Frederick, Maryland (301) 695-6465	Francis Scott Key Mall Frederick, Maryland (301) 694-7610
301 Ballenger Center Drive Frederick, Maryland (301) 682-9044	203 Frederick Road (Route 15) Thurmont, Maryland (301) 271-3252
Brunswich Shopping Center (south of Route 340) Brunswich, Maryland (301) 834-8022	7571 South Crain Highway Upper Marlboro, Maryland (301) 627-4770
12525 Laurel Bowie Road Laurel, Maryland (301) 725-1711	11147 New Hampshire Avenue Silver Spring, Maryland (301) 593-2920
11416 Georgia Avenue Wheaton, Maryland (301) 933-9342	*(See also Virginia, Pennsylvania, D.C. for more)*

★★★

MASSACHUSETTS

Cocoanut Grove Fire

Buck Jones was the 481st person of, eventually, 492 who died in the 12-15 minute Cocoanut Grove nightclub fire in Boston on Saturday, November 28, 1942. Buck died Monday, November 30, of critical second and third degree burns to the face, mouth and throat and of smoke inhalation. He would have been 51 on December 12.

At that time, Buck lived at 14050 Magnolia Blvd. in Van Nuys, California. The address of the Cocoanut Grove was 17 Piedmont Street in Boston's Bay Village area. The precise location of the former nightclub is very difficult to find today as the streets have been altered to accommodate a high-rise hotel complex over most of the Cocoanut Grove's dining room and adjacent Melody Street Lounge. Originally, the squat, one and a half story, block long Cocoanut Grove fronted on Piedmont, the rear faced Shawmut Street, one end bordering Broadway, the other adjoining a block of buildings. The Broadway side was about half the width of the rest of the building, an open air parking space occupying the remaining space.

★★★

Gary Cooper's Dusenberg

Gary Cooper's magnificent restored 1930 Dusenberg Model J Derham Tourster is located at the Heritage Plantation Americana Museum of Sandwich at Grove and Pine Streets in Sandwich (on Cape Cod).

The car is the first of only eight ever built and is restored to its original condition in bright yellow and pastel green. It has an enormous, powerful and perfectly balanced straight eight engine. 35 antique and classic cars are housed here in a Shaker Round Dairy Barn.

Open seven days a week, 10-5, mid May–late October. Located 3 miles from the Cape Cod Sagamore Bridge. Exit on Rt. 6A, then take Rt. 130 to Pine St. and Heritage Plantation. (508) 888-1222.

Gary Cooper's 1930 Duesenberg Model J. Tourster.

★★★

MISSISSIPPI

"Jesse James' Women"

Don "Red" Barry's independently produced "Jesse James' Women" ('54) was filmed in the unlikely location of Silver Creek at the junction of Hwys. 84 and 43 in south-central Mississippi.

★★★

MISSOURI

Sky King's Songbird

Sky King's original Songbird, a Cessna T-50 with huge radial engines and a fuselage that seemed almost an afterthought, lays in shambles at an airstrip five miles east of Clinton in three large piles of bent duralumin, decaying wood and ruptured steel. "It just rotted away," says Lawrence Ferro, owner of the Ranch-Aero Airstrip.

The plane has been there over 40 years, ever since Ferro paid $450 for it in 1960. He's the 15th owner of the plane which was built August 16, 1943, and used after the war almost exclusively on the West Coast. It became the Songbird on the "Sky King" TV series in late '51.

Ferro says the Songbird sort of rotted away before his eyes—the skin covering peeling off, the wooden wing spars developed dry rot and the wind one day blew the plane into a nearby pasture. Ferro has voluminous records of ownership of the plane. He claims people have offered him $25,000 just for the paperwork! Despite the plane's wrecked state, Ferro says 99.9% of the pieces are there and it could be rebuilt.

Paul Mantz, the Songbird's fifth owner and technical advisor on the "Sky King" series, was a friend of Ferro's. They were going to work on the plane until Mantz was killed during the filming of "Flight of the Phoenix." Ferro last flew the plane May 3, 1960, the day he picked it up.

A studio mock-up of a T-50 was used for interior shots.

Gloria Winters, niece Penny on the series, told us it was Cessna's idea to replace the T-50 in later episodes with their sleeker 310B.

Clinton is southeast of Kansas City on Hwy. 7.

★★

Branson

The Sons of the Pioneers now perform Tuesday through Saturday at the Braschler Music Theatre, Hwy. 376 in Branson. The current group, headed up by Dale Warren for the last 23 years, carries on the tradition of pure western music developed by Roy Rogers, Bob Nolan, Tim Spencer, Hugh and Karl Farr, Lloyd Perryman, Pat Brady and others. Dale has been with the Pioneers for nearly 50 years and is now the longest running member in Pioneer history. The Roy Rogers/Dale Evans Museum will relocate to Branson in the spring of 2003. (See California entry.)

The current Sons of the Pioneers appear now at Braschler's in Branson.

★★★

Burkett's Hollywood Museum

A John Wayne costume from "Rio Lobo," a rifle from "Young Guns," Bruce Willis' boots from "Sunset," props from "Mask of Zorro," a James Stewart cowboy hat, Ronald Colman's hat and shirt from "The Winning of Barbara Worth," a check written by Zane Grey, props from "Dances With Wolves" and much more are on display at Burkett's Hollywood Museum. Corner of Hwy. 76 and Hwy. 165 in Branson. (417) 334-4855. Open 7 days a week 9am-11pm.

★★★

Hollywood Wax Museum

Roy Rogers, Hoss, Little Joe and Ben from "Bonanza," John Wayne, James Garner and Mel Gibson from the "Maverick" movie are all on display in wax at the Hollywood Wax Museum on Hwy. 76 in downtown Branson. 170 wax figures in all on two floors. Well done. Large "sculpture" outside features John Wayne. (417) 337-8277. Opens year round at 8am.

Hoss, Ben and Little Joe from "Bonanza" in wax.

★★★

Ralph Foster Museum

The Ralph Foster Museum on the campus of the College of the Ozarks has grown from humble beginnings in the '20s to become one of the foremost institutions of historical preservation. The primary focus of the museum today is to collect, preserve and exhibit items relating to the Ozarks region...but that's certainly not all that's displayed in their

40,000 square feet of space spread over three stories. You'll find a shirt Gene Autry wore in "Oh, Susanna!" along with one of Smiley Burnette's black hats.

Their most famous artifact is the original vehicle from Buddy Ebsen's "Beverly Hillbillies" TVer.

Located at the College of the Ozarks Campus in Point Lookout, only two miles south of Branson. Open 9-4:30 Monday-Saturday. (800) 222-0525.

★★

"Little House On the Prairie"

Tour the Laura Ingalls Wilder "Little House On the Prairie" home in Mansfield. The Ingalls family came to Mansfield in 1894 from South Dakota. (See entry for that state.) Laura's adventurous books were adapted for TV by Michael Landon from 1974-1982.

★★

Tom Mix Memorabilia

The Ralston-Purina Company, who sponsored the Tom Mix radio show from 1933-1951 is at Checkerboard Square in St. Louis. They maintain a small display of Tom Mix memorabilia.

★★

Whip Wilson

Whip Wilson was born Roland Charles Meyers in Granite City, Illinois. First attaining notoriety as an opera singer, he appeared in "Gentlemen Unafraid" at the St. Louis Muny Opera which is still in existence and a favorite Summer attraction in the area. Located in Forest Park, St. Louis. (314) 361-1900.

Whip also sang in the Rathskeller Room of the Lennox Hotel at 825-827 Washington Ave., St. Louis, and at the Jefferson Hotel, 415 N. 12th Blvd., St. Louis.

★★

Planet Hollywood

A Planet Hollywood restaurant with many western props is at Laclede's Landing, 800 N. 3rd St. in St. Louis. (314) 588-1717. (See Orlando, Florida entry.)

★★

Big Chief Dakota Steakhouse

While you eat, B-westerns run silently on TV's scattered throughout the Big Chief Dakota Steakhouse, 17352 Manchester Road, Wildwood (about 30 minutes west of downtown St. Louis). (636) 458-4383.

Western music fills the air and the décor is strictly cowboys and Indians. Look for the wagons and teepees out front.

★★

MONTANA

Range Rider of the Yellowstone

William S. Hart is the "Range Rider of the Yellowstone," depicted in a life size bronze statue located in the historical park adjacent to Logan International Airport in Billings.

Hart posed and paid for the statue sculpted by artist C. C. Cristadoro in 1926 which was dedicated July 4, 1927, the 45th anniversary of the founding of the city. Hart wrote the Chamber of Commerce in preparation of his posing, "The subject is a horse with lowered head and dragging reins, nibbling at bunch grass while the man, unconsciously rolling a smoke, is looking out over the prairie, conveying a look of vastness...The bronze

William S. Hart posed for this "Range Rider of the Yellowstone" bronze.

figure gazing out over the Yellowstone as he would have done 40 years ago [1886]. I want it where it belongs—in the old cattle country, to do its bit toward keeping alive the memory of those days that are gone..."

A poem written for the statue by Jack Horan reads:

Range Rider of the Yellowstone
There's a rider up there on the Rimrocks.
He stands by his pony alone,
looking out over this beautiful valley
far beyond the old Yellowstone.
His Fritz horse is nibbling the bunch grass
as Bill rolls a smoke by his side.
And he says, "Old Pardner, you'll need it
for the trail that we have to ride.
For some day the call from up yonder
to leave the rough land you and I know
Then high on the Rimrock silent and still
we'll watch o'er the Yellowstone Valley."

"Warpath" ('51) with Edmond O'Brien was shot in the Billings area...utilizing the fairgrounds and Ft. Lincoln east of Billings which is on I-90 in the southern part of the state.

★★★

NEBRASKA

Nebraskaland Days

Nebraskaland Days are held each June in North Platte, city-wide and at the Wild West Arena where there's a PRCA rodeo with top name entertainers. Each year the week long celebration honors in-person one of our favorite cowboy heroes. Recent honorees have been Will Hutchins, Peter Breck, director Burt Kennedy, Dick Jones, Richard Farnsworth and Nebraska's own B-western badman, Pierce Lyden.

In earlier years, since 1965, honorees have included Dale Robertson, Chuck Connors, Tim McCoy, Andy Devine, Robert Fuller, Ken Curtis, Harry Carey Jr., Ben Johnson, Monte Hale, Gene Autry, Rex Allen and James Drury among others. (308) 532-7939.

North Platte is also home to the Buffalo Bill Cody State Historical Park and Cody Park. Buffalo Bill is the creator of live Wild West shows. (308) 535-8035.

★★

Pierce Lyden Birthplace

B-western screen badman Pierce Lyden was born in Naponee on January 8, 1908. From the early '40s to the early '60s Pierce worked in westerns with Bill Elliott, Johnny Mack Brown, Hopalong Cassidy, Don Barry, Roy Rogers, Gene Autry, Sunset Carson, Jimmy Wakely, Whip Wilson and many others.

Some of Pierce's memorabilia is now housed at the Naponee Historical society in Naponee in Franklin County which is near Harlan County Lake in the very mid-southern part of Nebraska just off Hwy. 136 near the Kansas border. Pierce's hometown is marked by a large wooden sign.

More of Pierce's memorabilia is on exhibit at the Franklin County Museum and Historical Society in Franklin 10 miles east of Naponee.

Movie badman Pierce Lyden (1908-1998) points to a sign outside Naponee.

★★

Sign designates Hooter's Rodeo Arena.

Hoot Gibson Memorial Rodeo

The Hoot Gibson Memorial Rodeo is held in June every year at Hoot Gibson Memorial Rodeo Arena (dedicated in '91) on Hwy. 32W in Tekamah, Hoot's hometown. Bareback, saddle bronc, steer wrestling, calf roping, team roping, bull riding, barrel racing and many other events.

The Burt County Museum in Tekamah has a lot of memorabilia and information on Hooter and puts up an especially big display at the time of the rodeo each year. (402) 374-1505.

Besides being a famous movie cowboy, Hoot rode with Dick Stanley's Congress of Rough Riders in 1910, won his first saddle with silver on it in Bakersfield, California, later that year, won the all around championship in Pendleton, Oregon, in 1912 and the title of World Champion Fancy Roper at the Calgary, Canada, Stampede that same year.

★★

NEVADA

Ponderosa Ranch

You may no longer spot Hoss, Little Joe or Ben at the Ponderosa Ranch but you'll find a great western town complete with a replica of the famous house portrayed in 430 TV episodes of "Bonanza". As a matter of fact, several of the later episodes were actually filmed here at Incline Village, North Lake Tahoe, including "Different Pines, Same Wind," "Little Girl Lost" (the first use of the ranch built there), "Kingdom of Fear," "Lonely Runner," "Winter Kill," "Stallion," "Showdown at Tahoe" and "Desperate Passage". One of Michael Landon's forest-green jackets still hangs in the hallway.

Originally, the Ponderosa ranch house was nothing but a set on the Paramount lot. When Bill and Joyce Anderson saw thousands of "Bonanza" fans coming to Nevada looking for the famous ranch, only to discover it didn't exist, they remedied that problem in 1967, creating the ranch house exactly as it was on the Paramount lot.

Besides the Ponderosa ranch house, the elaborate western street has many stores, a bank, saloon, children's playground, blacksmith shop, petting zoo, horseback rides, church, gold panning and many places to eat including Hop-Sing's Kitchen with the famous Hoss burger. There is also a garage full of vintage vehicles, including chariots from "Ben

Many later episodes of "Bonanza" were filmed at this ranch house in Incline Village, a replica of the famous house on the Paramount backlot.

Hur". The gift shop is extensive. Wild West shows and entertainment daily. This western theme park is open mid-April through October 9:30-5. 100 Ponderosa Ranch Rd., Incline Village on Hwy. 28, N. Shore, Lake Tahoe. (775) 831-0691

★★

Virginia City

A trip to historic nearby Virginia City (where the Cartwrights spent so much "screen time") is also in order. The mining metropolis was once the richest place in the world. Facing the wooden boardwalk in this mountainside town are museums, restaurants, old west saloons and an historic railroad all surrounded by antiques, gift shops and historic mansions.

★★

Nevada State Railroad Museum

Movie studios bought most of their locomotives, rolling stock and other equipment from Nevada's Virginia & Truckee RR, America's richest and most famous short line, originally used for ore shipments from the Comstock Lode. In the '30s, Hollywood discovered five 1870-era V&T locomotives in the company's Carson City engine house and dozens of wooden freight and passenger cars in its yard. Between '37 and '47, movie companies bought four locomotives and more than two dozen cars from the V&T. One of the finest regional railroad museums in the country, the Nevada State Railroad Museum in

Virginia and Truckee locomotive #25 is now housed at the Nevada State Railroad Museum after appearing in 15 movies.

Carson City now houses three of these locomotives: V&T #18, an 1873 Central Pacific built, V&T #22, an 1875 Baldwin built and V&T #25, a 1905 Baldwin built.

No. 18 (owned by Paramount from 1938-1974) was first used in "Union Pacific" ('39) and successively in "Badman's Territory" ('46), "Last Stagecoach West" ('57), "Dakota" ('46), "Whispering Smith" ('49) and Roy Rogers' "Nevada City" ('41) among others. (Scenes from "Nevada City" were later used as the opening to TV's "Stories of the Century.")

No. 22 (owned by Paramount from 1937-1974) can be spotted in "Wells Fargo" ('37), "Showdown" ('40), "Texas" ('41), "The Virginian" ('46), "Duel In the Sun" ('46), "Red River" ('48), "Carson City" ('52), "Great Locomotive Chase" ('56), "Last Train From Gun Hill" ('59), "McLintock!" ('63) and the "Wild Wild West" TV series ('65-'69). It was used in a total of 35 films.

No. 25 (owned by RKO from 1947-1958) appeared in 15 films including "Four Faces West" ('48), "Last Bandit" ('49), "Canadian Pacific" ('49), "Wichita" ('55), "Wyoming Renegades" ('55).

The Nevada RR Museum also displays the ex-Dardanelle and Russellville engine #8, owned by 20th Century Fox between 1945 and 1972 and Short Line Enterprises from 1972-1986. Some of its 15 film appearances include "Jesse James" ('39), "True Story of Jesse James" ('57), "Last Ride of the Dalton Gang" ('78), Kenny Rogers' "Gambler" ('80) and TV's "Bearcats" series ('71).

In all, the Nevada State Railroad Museum houses over 60 pieces of railroad equipment from Nevada's past.

2180 S. Carson St. (U.S. 395) in Carson City. Open daily, year round, 8:30-4:30. (775) 687-6953.

★★★

Rhyolite/Death Valley

One of Nevada's most famous ghost towns is Rhyolite in southern Nevada, near Beatty, the gateway to Death Valley. Founded in 1904, the gold mining community was the third largest city in Nevada by 1908 with nearly 8,000 people. By 1919, with the prosperous gold veins petered out, Rhyolite became a ghost town. Buck Jones' "Desert Vengeance" ('31) used the burning hot location for his desert hideout. John Wayne's "Ride Him, Cowboy" ('32) reused stock footage from Ken Maynard's "Unknown Cavalier", a 1926 First National silent. A second unit crew ventured to the out of the way spot for Roy Rogers' "Rough Riders' Roundup" in 1939. The most famous ruin in Rhyolite is Tom Kelly's Bottle House. Rhyolite is 4 miles southwest of Beatty (which is at the intersection of Hwy. 95 and 374) on 374.

Fewer westerns than you'd think actually filmed in Death Valley (no doubt due to the extreme heat) even though many westerns are "set" there. Films that did lens in Death Valley are "War Paint" ('53) with Robert Stack and Keith Larsen, "One Eyed Jacks" ('61) with Marlon Brando, "Three Godfathers" ('48) with John Wayne, "Twenty Mule Team" ('40) with Wallace Beery and "Law and Jake Wade" ('58) with Robert Taylor.

★★★

Red Rock Canyon

Red Rock Canyon, 18 miles west of Las Vegas on Hwy. 160 is where "Bells of San

Angelo" with Roy Rogers was filmed in 1947.

★★★

Stratosphere Tower

When you visit the Stratosphere Hotel/Casino at the end of the Las Vegas strip, go up in their sky high tower where you overlook Vegas and Nevada for miles. Various 'stations' in the tower relate the history of the area. One includes a production shot of Roy Rogers and Dale Evans when they made "Heldorado" there in 1946. Another kiosk mentions Rex Bell, who married Clara Bow there and was Lt. Governor of the state. (By the way, the revolving restaurant serves excellent food!)

★★★

Planet Hollywood

There are Planet Hollywood restaurants with many western props at Caesar's Casino, 55 Hwy. 50 in Lake Tahoe (775) 588-7828; the Forum shops at Caesar's Palace, 3500 Las Vegas Blvd. in Las Vegas (702) 791-7827 and in Harrah's Casino in downtown Reno, 206 N. Virginia St. (775) 323-7837. (See Orlando, Florida entry.)

★★★

Hoover Dam

As you cross Hoover Dam (aka Boulder Dam) east of Las Vegas (outside Boulder City) remember that Roy Rogers rode there in "Heldorado".

★★★

Valley Of Fire State Park

Valley of Fire State Park, 60 miles northeast of Las Vegas out I-15, has been voted by NEVADA magazine the best park in southern Nevada. A real hotel, complete with furniture, was transported here from Bishop, California, to be Jason Robards' castle in "Ballad of Cable Hogue."

 Sampling of Westerns Filmed in VALLEY OF FIRE STATE PARK

- Black Cyclone ('25)—Big Boy Williams
- Sheriff of Las Vegas ('44)—Bill Elliott
- Heldorado ('46)—Roy Rogers
- Bells of San Angelo ('47)—Roy Rogers
- Professionals ('66)—Burt Lancaster
- Ballad of Cable Hogue ('70)—Jason Robards
- Ulzana's Raid ('72)—Burt Lancaster
- Bite the Bullet ('75)—Ben Johnson/Gene Hackman

★★★

Walking Box Ranch

The historic but isolated Rex Bell Walking Box Ranch is now owned by George Brizendine, a Las Vegas civil engineer.

Rex Bell's Walking Box Ranch is now privately owned.

The 38.5 acre ranch is desolately located seven miles west of Searchlight on Hwy. 164. The fabled two story, 12 room Walking Box Ranch was founded 70 years ago by '30s cowboy star Rex Bell and his actress wife, Clara Bow, who married in '31 and stayed on the ranch until the late '40s. The ranch originally covered 400,000 acres with 1,800 head of cattle and thousands of desert Joshua trees. The seller (and previous owner) of the ranch, Viceroy Gold Corporation, a gold mining company, bought the ranch in 1989. They spent more than $750,000 restoring the Walking Box, adding a tennis court and terra cotta tile on the lower level of the house. The ranch is surrounded by 120 acres of land owned by the Nature Conservancy.

To view the privately owned red-tile-roofed rancho, take Hwy. 95 to 164W, go 6.5 miles.

★★★

NEW JERSEY

Fort Lee

Fort Lee, from the early 20th Century to the early teens, was the site of numerous studios. Solax, Eclair, Peerless-World and Champion made many films in the area for major release through Fox, Metro and Goldwyn. Champion, built in 1909, turned out an incredible number of westerns including "At Double Trouble Ranch" (1911), "Caught By Cowboys" (1910), even "Cowboy and the Squaw" (1910). Certainly, not all the films made there and at adjoining Coytesville were westerns, but there were plenty of early shoot 'em ups shot there including "A True Indian's Heart" (1909) with Charles French (father of Ted French, grandfather of Victor French), released through Bison. Portions of the silent serial classic "Perils of Pauline" were shot on the Palisades at Coytesville's eastern edge. In 1907-1908 Sidney Olcott directed westerns for Kalem in the Coytesville area.

Portions of Rambo's Hotel, used as a set for many westerns, was perfectly preserved until a fire gutted the place in 1998. Gloria Limone, now in her 70s, whose grandfather once ran the Rambo, and her husband still live in the rear of the building which was untouched by the blaze.

Portions of "The Great Train Robbery" (1903), the hold up and chase action, were shot on the Erie Lackawanna railroad around West Orange. Interiors were shot at Edison's New York studio.

A museum dedicated to the Ft. Lee film industry is scheduled to open in the Spring of 2002.

★★

Planet Hollywood

A Planet Hollywood restaurant with many western props is in Caesar's Casino across from Ocean Mall at 2100 Pacific Ave. in Atlantic City. (609) 347-7827. (See Orlando, Florida entry.)

★★

NEW MEXICO

El Rancho Hotel

Formally opened on December 17, 1937, the El Rancho Hotel in Gallup was built by the brother of movie magnate D. W. Griffith. Drawn by the many films made in the area, Tom Mix, Ronald Reagan, Wayne Morris, Dick Foran, Errol Flynn, Dick Jones, Alan Ladd, Kirk Douglas, Joel McCrea, Robert Taylor, Richard Boone, and Ben Johnson were among the many stars listed as hotel guests. All the rooms are not only numbered, but designated with a star's name, such as Richard Boone, Dale Robertson, Barbara Payton etc. Autographed movie photos adorn the magnificent two story open lobby with its circular staircase, heavy beams and Navajo rugs. Autographed photos include Tom Mix, John Russell, Dick Foran, Wayne Morris, Dale Robertson, Peter Graves, Ben Johnson, John

Lobby of the palatial El Rancho Motel.

Wayne and Alan Ladd. The historic hotel is located on the south side of Hwy 66 just off I-40 at exit 22. (505) 863-9311. On the National Register of Historic Places.

Dick Jones tells me, while shooting "Rocky Mountain", his dog, Spot, was the only dog ever allowed in the hotel. Incidentally, the El Rancho Hotel restaurant features such fare as the John Wayne (half pound burger with guacamole and cheese), the Roy Rogers (half pound burger with garnish), the Tom Mix (BBQ beef sandwich on a French roll) and the Leo Carrillo taco plate.

Sampling of Westerns Filmed in GALLUP AREA

- Great Divide ('15)—House Peters Sr.
- Redskin ('29)—Richard Dix
- Pursued ('47)—Robert Mitchum
- Ambush ('49)—Robert Taylor
- Streets of Laredo ('49)—Macdonald Carey
- Rocky Mountain ('50)—Errol Flynn
- Only the Valiant ('51)—Gregory Peck
- Fort Defiance ('51)—Dane Clark
- New Mexico ('51)—Lew Ayres
- Raton Pass ('51)—Dennis Morgan
- Red Mountain ('51)—Alan Ladd
- Fort Massacre ('58)—Joel McCrea
- Hallelujah Trail ('65)—Burt Lancaster

★★

Inscription Rock

The massive sandstones of El Morro.

Inscription Rock near Gallup plays a major role in Joel McCrea's "Four Faces West". The historic site, technically named El Morro National Monument, is famous for its "Paso Por Aqui" (Passed this way) phrase inscribed in the massive sandstone rock, rising over 200 feet from the valley floor, El Morro, named such by the Spaniards. A Spanish governor carved an inscription on it in 1605, as did other travelers after him. Off I-40 between Grants and Gallup. Follow the signs.

★★★★★★★★★★★★★★★★★★★★★★★★★★★

Eaves Movie Ranch

One of New Mexico's most frequently used locations is the Eaves Movie Ranch. Eaves, who died at 85 August 8, 2001, stopped running cattle on the ranch in the early '60s and shortly afterward a town set was built on his ranch for "Cheyenne Social Club" ('70). Over the years, the ranch and townsite grew in size incorporating two main streets. In recent years, as westerns were produced less and less, the Texas born Eaves opened the ranch to tourists and corpo-

Crowds explore Eaves Movie Ranch during a film festival.

rate parties. The official name for the 1,600 acre property is Rancho Alegre, about 14 miles southwest of Santa Fe, halfway between Santa Fe and Cerrillos. (Incidentally, Cerrillos on Hwy. 14, south of there, was used for the TV series "Nine Lives of Elfego Baca" in 1958 with Robert Loggia as well as "Young Guns" in '88.) It was Eaves' ranch that really helped bring the film industry into New Mexico.

Sampling of Westerns Filmed at EAVES RANCH

- Cheyenne Social Club ('70)—James Stewart
- Gatling Gun ('71)—Robert Fuller
- A Gunfight ('71)—Kirk Douglas
- The Cowboys ('72)—John Wayne
- Santee ('73)—Glenn Ford
- Adios Amigo ('75)—Fred Williamson
- Silverado ('85)—Kevin Kline/Kevin Costner
- Gambler III: The Legend Continues (TV)—Kenny Rogers ('87)
- Independence (TV)—John Bennett Perry ('87)
- Return of the Desperado (TV)—Alex McArthur ('88)
- Where the Hell's That Gold (TV)—Willie Nelson ('88)
- Longarm (TV)—John Terlesky ('88)
- Wild Times (TV)—Sam Elliott ('80)

Bonanza Creek Ranch

The Bonanza Creek Ranch was called the Jarrett Ranch when Hollywood first showed an interest in 1955 for James Stewart's "Man From Laramie". There still exists a door that has Stewart's name and all of the other cast members' names on it. "The Legend of the Lone Ranger" production company built a townset there but demolished it upon completion of filming. Many of the buildings (ranch house, barns) were constructed for "Silverado" and used in later productions. In the early '90s, Terence Hill's "Lucky Luke" production company built an all new townsite (Daisy Town) on

The western street at Bonanza Creek Ranch during the filming of "Lucky Luke" in 1990.

the Bonanza Creek Ranch site, which is only a few miles from the Eaves Ranch.

Sampling of Westerns Filmed at BONANZA CREEK RANCH

- Man From Laramie ('55)—James Stewart
- Cowboy ('58)—Glenn Ford
- Cheyenne Social Club ('70)—James Stewart
- The Cowboys ('72)—John Wayne
- Wild Times (TV)—Sam Elliott ('80)
- Legend of the Lone Ranger ('81)—Klinton Spilsbury
- Silverado ('85)—Kevin Kline/Kevin Costner
- Return of the Desperado (TV)—Alex McArthur ('88)
- Young Guns ('88)—Emilio Estevez
- Lonesome Dove ('89)—Robert Duvall
- Lucky Luke ('90)—Terence Hill
- Gunsmoke IV: Long Ride (TV)—James Arness ('93)
- Desperate Trail (TV)—Sam Elliott ('94)
- Last Stand at Saber River (TV)—Tom Selleck ('96)
- Lazarus Man (TV) ('96)

★★★

Cook Ranch

Feed and grain building used for a climatic stunt in "Silverado" on the Cook Ranch. (Photo by Ken Taylor.)

The "Silverado" townsite on the Cook Ranch was built from scratch for that 1985 film. Located on 16,000 acres about 24 miles outside of Santa Fe (near Galisteo which is on Hwy 41 where parts of "Young Guns" were lensed), the site is not generally open to the public. Building the town set there for "Silverado" was all by coincidence. Bill and Marian Cook were not in the location business when filmmakers came to them looking for a large pasture in which to build their town. When filming ended, Cook nearly burned the town down. Luckily, he didn't as "Lonesome Dove" and many others made use of it a few years later. Unfortunately, much of the townsite burned following a planned explosion for "Wild Wild West" in 1998 which went wrong.

Sampling of Westerns Filmed at COOK RANCH

- Silverado ('85)—Kevin Kline/Kevin Costner
- Gambler III: Legend Continues (TV)—Kenny Rogers ('87)
- Longarm (TV)—John Terlesky ('88)
- Return of the Desperado (TV)—Alex McArthur ('88)
- Lonesome Dove (TV)—Robert Duvall ('89)
- Young Guns II ('90)—Emilio Estevez
- Gunsmoke IV: Long Ride (TV)—James Arness ('93)
- Wyatt Earp ('94)—Kevin Costner
- Lazarus Man (TV)—Robert Urich ('96)
- Last Man Standing ('96)—Bruce Willis
- Walker Texas Ranger (TV): Last of a Breed—Chuck Norris ('97)
- Wild Wild West ('98)—Will Smith

★★★

Tom Mix Home

There is a controversy to this day which house on Gallinas Street in Las Vegas Tom Mix lived in while he made films there in 1915-1916 ("Local Color," "Race For a Gold Mine," "How Weary Went Wooing," "Bad Man Bobbs," "Range Girl and the Cowboy," "Never Again" etc.) It was either 912 Gallinas (now 920 Gallinas) or 906 Gallinas. According to Marva McGee who now lives at 906, that house was built in 1901. Tom lived there approximately six months while making films in Las Vegas. When a later owner moved down the street, he took his "house number" with him (you could do that back then in a small New Mexico community) so as not to change his address, hence the "correct" Mix house confusion.

The rest of the crew were housed at the Plaza Hotel downtown, which is still in existence.

Portions of "Hazards of Helen," the Helen Holmes 1915 serial, were also shot in Las Vegas. In recent years, "Last Stand At Saber River" with Tom Selleck was shot in the area.

If you take Rt. 3 north out of Las Vegas a few miles to man-made Storrie Lake State Park, you'll find the location for several Selig Mix films in this period. At least 15 one-reelers were shot in the Las Vegas area around this time.

Las Vegas is on I-25, 64 miles north of Santa Fe.

906 Gallinas Street is where Tom Mix reportedly lived while making silent westerns circa 1915-1916.

★★★

Cumbres and Toltec Scenic Railroad

The world's highest and longest scenic train ride is the Cumbres and Toltec Scenic Railroad. Built in 1880 by the Denver and Rio Grande Railway, this is America's most authentic steam railroad, just as it was for a century from the coal tipple to the conductor's smile. Twisting and turning through the beautiful San Juan Mountains on tracks that tamed the West, you'll cross the Colorado–New Mexico border eleven times. Count them as you look down from Windy Point, up at the spires of Phantom Curve, or into the depths of Toltec Gorge. This ride captures a moment in time that's genuine fun.

The Denver & Rio Grande sought to abandon a branch of their line in 1967 (as they'd done in Colorado between Durango and Silverton earlier in the '60s) with Colorado and New Mexico jointly purchasing 64 miles of track between Chama, New Mexico, and Antonito, Colorado, creating the Cumbres and Toltec Scenic RR in 1970.

Still operable are three ex-Denver and Rio Grande Western Railroad locomotives that were featured in "Good Guys and the Bad Guys" ('69), "Bite the Bullet" ('75), "White Buffalo" ('77) and "Legend of the Lone Ranger" ('81).

178

Your best ride on this train is to go only halfway to the lunch and water stop at Osier and return that afternoon, as the second leg of the journey on to Antonito is nowhere near as beautiful. And you certainly don't need to spend the night in a seedy hotel in Antonito. Inquire about the half-way or half-day trip at the station in Chama. Reservations necessary. (888) 286-2737. (505) 756-2151.

PO Box 789, Chama, New Mexico 87520.

Open Memorial Day weekend to mid October.

Waiting to board the train in Chama.

 Sampling of Westerns Filmed on CUMBRES / TOLTEC RR

- Good Guys and the Bad Guys ('69)—Robert Mitchum
- Shootout ('71)—Gregory Peck
- Showdown ('73)—Dean Martin
- Bite the Bullet ('75)—Ben Johnson, Gene Hackman
- Missouri Breaks ('76)—Jack Nicholson
- Butch and Sundance, The Early Years ('79)—Tom Berenger
- Where the Hell's That Gold ('88)—Willie Nelson
- Wyatt Earp ('93)—Kevin Costner

★★

Lincoln
The historic town of Lincoln where the real Billy the Kid rode in the late 1870s has

changed little over the years. A walking tour will acquaint you with his life and times there. The tour begins at a museum which houses many Billy the Kid movie related items and shows film clips in their theatre.

Take I-25 south of Albuquerque 75 miles to Socorro, turn east on State Hwy. 380, then about 100 miles to historic Lincoln near the Capitan Mountains.

★★★

Roswell

Roy Rogers (then Leonard Slye), 24, and Grace Arline Wilkins, 21, were married in ceremonies at a private residence at 920 E. 2nd in Roswell on June 11, 1936. The house is now Michelet Homestead Realty.

Photos from the wedding are in the archives (open 1-4 on Fridays) of the Historical Society for Southeast New Mexico, 200 N. Lea Ave., Roswell. (505) 622-8333.

★★★

Carlsbad Caverns

"Cave of Outlaws" ('51) with Macdonald Carey was filmed in the world famous Carlsbad Caverns in Carlsbad. The caverns, 83 separate caves forming the world's largest underground caverns, can be visited on varying tour lengths. Southeastern New Mexico on Hwy. 285. The caves made their debut in 1931's "White Renegade" with Tom Santschi, unfortunately a lost film.

★★★

NEW YORK

Roy Rogers/Dale Evans Children's Center

The Roy Rogers/Dale Evans Children's Center, a state of the art medical facility at Our Lady of Mercy Medical Center in the Bronx, was dedicated in June 1996. Roy and Dale helped raise $6 million for the children's wing and were honored with the Terence Cardinal Cooke Humanitarian Award at New York's Waldorf Astoria Hotel in September 1995. 600 East 233rd St. in the Bronx.

★★★

Bronx Walk of Fame

Guy Williams, who played "Zorro" on TV, is immortalized with a permanent street plaque on the Grand Concourse, the most famous street in the Bronx.

Williams, from Bedford Park, died in 1989 at 65. His posthumous induction into the Bronx Walk of Fame (which was started in 1997) took place in 2000.

★★★

Planet Hollywood

A Planet Hollywood restaurant with many western props is at 1540 Broadway (Times Square) in New York City. (212) 333-7827. (See Orlando, Florida entry.)

★★★

Planet Hollywood

A Planet Hollywood restaurant with many western props is at 4608 Bender St. in Niagara Falls, on the Canadian side in Ontario. (905) 374-8332. (See Orlando, Florida entry.)

★★★

NORTH CAROLINA

Tweetsie Railroad

The Tweetsie Railroad, complete with wild west town, near Blowing Rock, was allegedly purchased from Gene Autry for $1 by the Robbins family.

Apparently, Gene was going to move the train to California but the transportation cost was excessive. In checking with Autry Entertainment, they could find no record of this transaction, but some old records have long been destroyed.

Open all of June and July with most of May, August and September on their schedule. Music, dancing, gunfights. Riders In the Sky and other groups often appear in concert.

On U.S. 321 between Boone and Blowing Rock. (800) 526-5740.

All aboard the Tweetsie Railroad.

★★★

Tastee Freeze B's

Stop by the Tastee Freeze just off Blue Ridge Parkway in Wilkesboro and enjoy the B-western memorabilia while you enjoy a cool delight.

★★★

Tom Mix Road

Howard Collins, 78, remembers, as a youngster, his father relating to him about a man named Tom Mix who was working as an inmate on the road around 1930 along with other convicts. The story goes, Tom told the guard he was going to run for his freedom. The guard replied, "Yea, if you do, I will shoot you." That day Tom broke away and ran. The guard went after him and killed him near a farm pond just off the rural road now named for him...not the movie cowboy as one would surmise.

Truly odd that a road would be named for a prisoner killed there, but that's the story related to Empire Publishing's Don Key by two long time residents of Tom Mix Road.

Empire Publishing's Don Key beside the oddly named Tom Mix Road in Stokes County.

Tom Mix Road is located in rural Stokes County, just a short distance from the Virginia state line. From Winston–Salem, drive approximately 20 miles to Walnut Cove, take Hwy. 89 West 18.3 miles from Walnut Cove where Hwy. 89 begins (through Danbury). Look for Tom Mix Road on the right side of 89 West.

★★★

Randolph's Ride Red Ale

A red ale named after Randolph Scott, Randolph's Ride Red Ale, is sold only on the premises at the Rock Bottom Charlotte Brewery and Restaurant, 401 N. Tryon Street, Suite 100, in Charlotte.

Most of the brewery's beers are named for something or someone relating to the Charlotte area. Brewer David Gonzales tells us Randolph's Ride Red Ale is a medium-bodied beer combining a rich malty flavor from British Crystal Malt with a distinct citrus aroma of Cascade Hops.

A ceramic picture of Scott, who attended the University of North Carolina and graduated with a degree in textile engineering and manufacturing, hangs on one of the brewery walls. (704) 334-2739.

★★★

Old Time Western Film Club

The Old Time Western Film Club meets the 4th Saturday of January, March, May, August and October at Charlie's Music Barn. Go 8 miles east of Siler City on Hwy. 64, turn left on Buckner/Clark Road. Or from Pittsboro, go west 6 miles on Hwy. 64, turn right on Buckner/Clark Road. From either, go half mile, turn left on Hillside Music Road. The club welcomes new members or even just the curious. At each meeting they screen three B-westerns and a serial chapter. Crowds usually range from 100 to 200 people.

Sponsored for many years by Milo Holt (PO Box 142, Siler City, NC 27344).

★★★

Western Film Preservation Society

The Western Film Preservation Society meets at 7 pm on the third Thursday of each month at The McKimmon Center on the Campus of North Carolina State University in Raleigh, North Carolina. The club has been ongoing for 22 years and new members are welcome to attend any meeting. B-Western films and serials are viewed each month. Free newsletter available upon request. Write to: Nikki Ellerbe, President, 2404 Rock Ridge Court, Raleigh, NC 27613. Phone (919) 787-6013.

★★★

OHIO

Duck Run

Roy Rogers' boyhood home, built in 1922, is a two bedroom, one and a half story frame home located on 1.28 acres of land at the junction of Roy Rogers Road (formerly Duck Run Road, changed in 1982) and Sly Road in Rush township in the northwest part of Scioto County.

Roy learned to play the guitar and sing in this house and lived there for close to 10 years until the family moved to Cincinnati. Farrell and Mary Lou Crabtree have owned the house for the last 24 years. The house has undergone extensive remodel-

Ohio Historical Marker indicating Roy Rogers' boyhood home.

ing since Roy lived there. When the house was put up for auction on August 3, 1996, the minimum bid of $70,000 was never reached. As a guide, a more realistic value for homes in this area of similar size would be $25-30,000.

Go north on U.S. 23 from Portsmouth to Lucasville. At the last traffic light in Lucasville turn left on State Route 348 (going west) and drive 3.75 miles to Mohawk Drive. Turn north on Mohawk Drive. Take Mohawk Drive 0.3 miles to Roy Rogers Road. Turn right on Roy Rogers Road and drive 700 feet to the property.

Roy "Dusty" Rogers Jr. sits on the steps of his Dad's boyhood home. (Photo by Doug Miller.)

★★★

Roy Rogers Mural

As you enter Portsmouth, you'll note signs directing you to several huge, colorful murals painted on an outdated 2,000 ft. long concrete flood wall off Sun Street along the river. The most popular of these is an over 12x12 foot mural of Roy Rogers rearing up on Trigger. Roy's mural and others were painted by world renown artist Robert Dafford of Lousiana over a nine year period.

Roy Rogers' sister, Cleda, stands beside the flood wall mural of her brother in Portsmouth.

Roy Rogers Hospital Wing

The Scioto Memorial Hospital (in Portsmouth) Children's Wing was dedicated in February 1960 as the Roy Rogers Children's Wing. At that time it was the Portsmouth General Hospital. At one time there was a sign to this effect over the Argonne Street entranceway to the hospital. Roy sent a statue of himself and Trigger for placement in the lobby which is now gone. The hospital, having undergone remodeling and renaming, may also no longer display the Argonne Street sign.

Roy Rogers Field

The athletic field of Northwest High School in Portsmouth was named Roy Rogers Field in 1959 with Roy attending the dedication ceremony. There is a maker-stone with "Roy Rogers Field" on it.

Northwest High School is at 914 Mohawk Dr., McDermott (approximately 11 miles from Portsmouth).

Roy Rogers Hometown Exhibit

There is a nice display of Roy Rogers memorabilia at the Portsmouth post office, however, it can be viewed by appointment only . Call Georgia Furr (740) 372-4851 or Nancy and Larue Horsley (740) 353-0900.

Reno's Roadhouse

Reno's Roadhouse has many paintings and repros of lobby cards of Roy Rogers and Trigger, Hopalong Cassidy, Gene Autry and others. We believe this is a chain of several around the area. Comfortable western in style, you know, with peanuts on the table and you toss the shells on the floor.

2844 U.S. Hwy. 23 in Portsmouth.

Korean War Memorial and All Veterans Walkway

Audie Murphy is remembered with an inlaid brick at the Korean War Memorial and All Veterans Walkway in Dayton, located in Riverbend Park, on the north bank of the Great Miami River just east of the Riverside Dr. Bridge (130 Riverside Dr.). A thirteen foot tall granite statue represents all of the armed forces of the U.S. The well-lighted 475 foot All Veterans Walkway leads to the main memorial. Audie's inlaid brick reads: "Audie L. Murphy, Major, MOH 1-26-45. Army WWII."

The memorial, for which planning began in 1988, was formally dedicated in 1995.

★★★

Zane Grey

Topping all western writers in popularity at the time of his death in '39 was Zane Grey, whose work was maligned by critics but somehow had a knack for storytelling that clicked with the public. But even his literary critics acknowledge his popularity. How could one not—85 books have sold in excess of 40 million copies and 112 movies have been filmed since 1918 based literally or liberally on his works.

The Zanesville author has a museum in his honor at 8850 East Pike in Norwich (10 miles east of Zanesville on Hwy. 40).

The museum displays several movie posters of Grey films and has some photos of Grey on movie sets.

Open May-September 9:30-5 seven days a week, October-November 9:30-5 (Wednesday-Sunday). (800) 752-2602.

★★★

Hopalong In Cambridge

In 1991 Everett and Laura Bates purchased the Cambridge boyhood home of William Boyd—who would become Hopalong Cassidy. A plaque identifies the now rented house at 1141 Steubenville Ave. The same year, Laura instigated the Hopalong Cassidy Festival in Cambridge (see film festival listings).

The City of Cambridge dedicated a brick sidewalk to Hopalong Cassidy in 1992 near Park Elementary School (corner of Highland and Wheeling Ave.) where William Boyd attended school as a youth. Boyd contributed money in the '50s for playground equipment to the school

Hoppy memorabilia fills the room of the Hopalong Cassidy Museum in Cambridge.

which he considered his alma mater. Later in '92, a stone monument with Hoppy's picture was erected near the Hoppy sidewalk. The school designed a reading room in which a number of Hoppy items are displayed.

There is a fabulous collection of Hopalong Cassidy artifacts at the Hopalong Cassidy Museum located as part of the 10th Street Antique Mall at 127 S. 10th St., in Cambridge.

Road signs at all four entrances to the city of Cambridge, located in the southern part of the state on I-70, indicate Hopalong Cassidy lived here.

Monument to William Boyd at Park School.

★★

William (Hopalong Cassidy) Boyd's Birthplace

The state of Ohio recently put up road signs at both ends of William (Hopalong Cassidy) Boyd's birthcity in Hendrysburg, about 25 miles east of Cambridge just off I-70 on Hwy. 800.

In 1993, Hoppy's birthplace house at 35584 Hendrysburg Rd. was purchased by Ingeborg Wrede of Germany. A marker on this house is only evident during the time of the Hopalong Cassidy Festival.

★★

Guernsey County Hall of Fame

William Boyd was inducted into the Guernsey County Hall of Fame on May 27, 1975. A plaque honoring Hoppy hangs in their Historical Museum, located next block behind the Courthouse at 218 North Eighth St. (740) 432-3145. Open 1-5 Sunday afternoons Memorial Day through Labor Day. Open other times by appointment. Also on display is a doll reportedly owned by Boyd.

★★

Longhorn Steakhouse

If you're in the area, have lunch or dinner at the Longhorn Steakhouse. There are photos of many of our cowboy heroes and a display of some of the old movies. 953 Boardman-Poland Road, Boardman on I-76 near Youngstown. (330) 729-9730.

★★

OKLAHOMA

Sheb Wooley

Sheb Wooley is best known to western fans as scout Pete Nolan on "Rawhide" from '61-'65. Sheb was honored in his hometown of Erick in August 1994 when Main Street was renamed Sheb Wooley Ave.

The 100th Meridian Museum on the corner of Sheb Wooley Ave. and Roger Miller Blvd. is an area history museum with several items relating to Sheb. The 100th Meridian of longitude was once Oklahoma's western most boundary. (580) 526-3221.

Erick is just off I-40 in western Oklahoma.

★★

Old Town Museum

The Old Town Museum in Elk City is worth a visit. A Hollywood cowboy heroes section has a small display of Roy Rogers, Buck Jones, Lone Ranger, Ken Maynard and John Wayne memorabilia.

Beutler Rodeo Hall of Fame features many photos of celebrities who were at rodeos of which Beutler Brothers were stock contractors. Photos include Bill Cody (signed in 1932), Jimmy Wakely, Clint Walker, Rex Allen, Forrest Tucker, Clu Gulagher, Terry Wilson and Frank McGrath (of "Wagon Train"), Jack Lord (of "Stoney Burke"), Doug McClure (Trampas on "The Virginian"), Dale Robertson, Roy Rogers, Dale Evans, Dennis Weaver, Amanda Blake, Milburn Stone, Ken Curtis, Dan Blocker, Michael Landon, Lorne Greene, Sheb Wooley and Paul Brinegar (of "Rawhide"), John Smith (of "Laramie"), Chill Wills and Fess Parker. A group of buildings known as Old Town includes one in which is planned to house the Rex Theater, patterned after an old Elk City theater. The plan is to screen B-westerns on Saturdays on a big screen TV. Other displays in the museum are of dust bowl days in the '30s, a native American room, a Stars and Stripes room and much more. Elk City is just off I-40 in western Oklahoma. Museum is on the corner of old Hwy. 66 and Pioneer Road. Open 9-5 Monday-Saturday except major holidays. (580) 225-6266.

★★

Will Rogers Bust

There is a 30 ft. x 30 ft. bust of Will Rogers carved out of blocks of granite at the Willis Granite Products Quarry, 900 Quarry Dr., Granite. It is all that was completed of a project that was also intended to depict Jim Thorpe's full figure in granite. The wooden framework has allowed some of the granite blocks to shift so they are no longer flat. (580) 535-2184. Granite is on Hwy. 6 south of I-40 from Elk City.

★★★★★★★★★★★★★★★★★★★★★★★

National Cowboy Hall of Fame

You can easily spend a day at the National Cowboy Hall of Fame (recently renamed the National Cowboy and Western Heritage Museum) in Oklahoma City, a 9,220,000 square foot facility which honors our big and small screen heroes as well

Will Rogers grins in granite.

as rodeo stars, artists and real cowboys.

John Wayne's gun and holster are in the National Cowboy and Western Heritage Museum.

The Western Performers gallery houses "The West of John Wayne" which includes Duke's western stock saddle; his saddle, gun and holster, spurs and rifle scabbard used in "True Grit"; his pistol from "The Shootist"; the renowned 1892 modified Winchester Carbine with large loop first used in "Stagecoach"; his extensive Katchina doll collection; many paintings and bronzes including works by Charlie Russell, Olaf Weighorst and Edward Borein; many jade, ivory and ebony carvings; a Bowie knife with an Alamo scene carved on the blade; a selection of books from Wayne's library and much more.

You'll also see a Tom Mix saddle, a Will Rogers hat, outlaw and sometimes actor Al Jennings' saddle, a large bronze of Ronald Reagan by Glenna Goodacre, a Tom Selleck saddle, the monumental End of the Trail statue by James Earle Frazer, fabulous Remington, Russell (and others) paintings as well as paintings of all our cowboys who've been inducted into the Hall of Fame—Joel McCrea, James Arness, Roy Rogers, Gene Autry, Dale Robertson, Tim Holt, Barbara Stanwyck, John Wayne, Amanda Blake, etc. Robertson served as MC for their first awards banquet in 1961. The National Cowboy Hall of Fame and Western Heritage Center officially opened in 1965. The annual Western Heritage Awards began in 1960.

John Wayne in the Hall of Fame.

Open daily (except major holidays) 9-5. Atop Persimmon Hill at 1700 NE 63rd in Oklahoma City. (405) 478-2250.

★★★

Guthrie

The town of Guthrie is designated a National Historic Landmark.

Tom Mix worked as a bartender at the Blue Belle saloon at the corner of Harrison and 2nd Street. It's still in operation with a historical marker on the sidewalk in front of the saloon attesting to Tom's employment. The back bar of the joint is inlaid with a TM brand.

The Oklahoma Territorial Museum at 406 East Oklahoma Ave. focuses on the 1889 land run but has a painting of Mix on the second floor. Tom once taught physical fitness classes in the basement of this building. (405) 282-1889. Open Tuesday-Friday 9-5, Saturday 10-4, Sunday 1-4. On I-35 north of Oklahoma City.

★★

Jim Thorpe Museum

Famed Indian athlete Jim Thorpe, winner of the pentathlon and decathlon in the 1912 Olympics, played both Indian chiefs and renegade Indians in scores of '30s and '40s westerns such as "White Eagle," "Wagon Wheels," "Arizona Frontier," "Outlaw Trail" and "Prairie Schooners." A member of the Sac and Fox tribe, he later participated in both professional baseball and football. Born in 1889, he died of a heart attack in 1953. Burt Lancaster portrayed him on screen in "Jim Thorpe—All American" in '51.

Thorpe's home and museum is at 706 E. Boston in Yale (about 17 miles east of Stillwater). On display are Thorpe's track and field awards and family items. Thorpe lived there from 1917-1923.

Only open weekends...Saturday 10-5, Sunday 1-5. (918) 387-2815.

Thorpe's portrait and Olympic medals are on display at the Oklahoma State Capitol Building in Oklahoma City.

Thorpe was recently immortalized on a Wheaties (Breakfast of Champions) cereal box.

★★

Simpson's Mercantile

When you walk into Simpson's Mercantile in Enid, it's as if you stepped back in time. Among the fancy wearing apparel and working cowboy pants/shirts/jackets are walls filled with real west and reel west memorabilia. Brothers Rick and Larry Simpson are the owners who also operate Skeleton Creek Productions. They produced a full length western for video, "Trail To Abilene," in 1997. Open Monday-Saturday 8:30-5:30. 228 E. Randolph Street in Enid. (580) 234-4998.

★★

101 Ranch Memorial

The 101 Ranch Memorial south of Ponca City is a National Historic Landmark that commemorates the ranch that was home to the hundreds of participants of the famous 101 Wild West Show. This show, which traveled throughout the world in the '20s, featured sharp shooters, trick riders, ropers, Indians and—western movie stars such as (at one time or another) Tom Mix, Jack Hoxie, Art Acord, Ken Maynard, Buck Jones, Mabel

Normand, Montie Montana, character player Tex Cooper and Bill Pickett.

The ranch once stretched over four counties and covered 101,000 acres, hence the name. The self-contained ranch had its own tannery, dairy, school, ice plant, electric power plant, cannery, cider mill and 25,000 Long Horn steers. They even had their own money! The ranch was in operation for over 50 years (from 1879) before being split up into small farms in 1931. Only remnants of huge concrete silos and the foundation for the old company store which burned in a mysterious 1987 fire remain. Just south of the store remains is Cowboy Boot Hill where owner Zack Miller is buried. A picnic area commemorates several acres of land on the original 101.

The famed 101, once in Bliss, now Marland, is outside of Ponca City. Go south on Hwy. 177 and turn west on 156.

Oil was discovered on the ranch and marketed as 101 Oil. Later Marland Oil Company, it's now better know as Conoco.

Artifacts and memorabilia from the 101 are on view on the lower level of the Ponca City Cultural Center and Museum at 10th and Grand in Ponca City. Open Monday-Saturday 10-5. (800) 475-4400.

There are also some 101 items at the small museum adjacent to the historic Pioneer Woman Statue on 14th Street (Hwy. 177) and Lake Road in Ponca City. Will Rogers unveiled the statue in 1930 before a crowd of 40,000 people.

In addition, the Western History Collection at Oklahoma University in Norman has a Miller Brothers 101 Ranch manuscript collection. (405) 325-3641.

While you're in Ponca City, stop by Ray Falconer's Glass Negative at 104 N. First. He has over a thousand glass plate negatives of the old 101 with many rare photos of Tom Mix.

The PRCA 101 Ranch Rodeo with world champion contenders is held annually in August in Ponca City.

★★

Tom Mix Saddle at Woolaroc

One of Tom Mix's 101 Ranch saddles is on view at the often overlooked, splendid Woolaroc Museum near Bartlesville. Often called "a living monument to the Old West" or the "Smithsonian of the West," it was originally the country retreat of oilman Frank Phillips. The world class musuem is an Indian heritage center, has a rustic lodge and is a 3,600 acre wildlife preserve with a herd of roaming buffalo. The interior, including the stunning dome room, is filled with a variety of art and artifacts depicting the life and times of the Old West. Many Miller Brothers 101 ranch items are on display.

Saddle used by Tom Mix on the 101 Ranch.

Open in Winter Tuesday-Sunday 10-5, Summer daily 10-5. Closed on major holidays. Take Hwy. 60 east from Ponca City and turn south on Hwy. 99 to Hwy. 11 east then north on 123 to Woolaroc. 12 miles southwest of Bartlesville. (918) 336-0307.

★★

The steel suitcase that hit Tom Mix in the back of the neck and killed him is on display, along with boots and other Mix memorabilia, at the Tom Mix Museum in Dewey.

Tom Mix Museum

The Tom Mix Museum is situated at 721 N. Delaware in Dewey. Opened in 1968, the museum houses the largest collection of personal Mix belongings in the world—hats, a $15,000 silver mounted saddle, guns, ropes, boots...even the steel suitcase that broke Tom's neck when his Cord crashed in Arizona in 1940. An in-museum theatre constantly plays Tom Mix westerns. There is an excellent gift shop with many Tom Mix collectibles available nowhere else.

Open 10-4:30 Tuesday-Saturday, 1-4:30 Sunday. Closed Mondays and holidays and all of January. 5 miles north of Bartlesville on U.S. 75. (918) 534-1555.

A block away is the small one-room jailhouse utilized by Tom when he served as night marshal in Dewey. The museum will direct you.

★★

Ben Johnson

Pawhuska's Ben Johnson is remembered around his hometown in northeastern Oklahoma. Although the respondents at the Osage County Historical Society Museum as well as at the Visitors Center in Pawhuska were quite vague, there is apparently a display on Ben at their museum. 700 Lynn Ave., Pawhuska (Hwy. 60 between Ponca City and Bartlesville) (918) 287-9924.

★★

Will Rogers' Birthplace

Will Rogers' birthplace is two miles east of Oologah on Hwy. 169 north of Tulsa. Built in 1875, Will was born here November 4, 1879, the son of a Cherokee senator, judge and cattleman. The home is authentically conserved. Open to the public 365 days a year dawn to dusk, the ranch has always been under the ownership of the Rogers family or as a donated icon.

Clem Rogers' original spread was 60,000 acres with up to 10,000 head of Texas Longhorn cattle. Today's ranch is 400 acres with 50 Texas Longhorns. (918) 275-4201. Tours are at 10 and 2 daily. RV hookups available on the ranch grounds.

★★

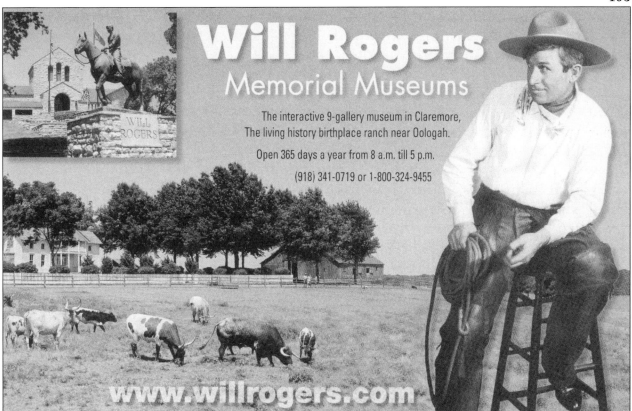

Will Rogers Memorial Museum

America's beloved cowboy humorist is remembered at the Will Rogers Memorial Museum in Claremore housing Will's saddle collection, artifacts, ropes and memorabilia pertaining to his vaudeville and Ziegfeld Follies career, his film and radio career as well as his syndicated newspaper column. The 16,652 sq. ft. nine gallery museum was opened in 1938 with the east wing added in 1982. The entire museum was remodeled in the early '90s. The museum frames the family tomb in the sunken garden. The 21-acre museum grounds, purchased by Will in 1911 for $500 an acre, was his planned retirement homesite. Following his untimely death in a plane crash at Point Barrow, Alaska, the land was donated by his widow and children to the state. The 2,400 sq. ft. library serves as an office of the Will Rogers Memorial. Included in the library are more than 2,000 volumes by, about or referencing Will Rogers. The archives house 15,000 photographs and thousands of original manuscripts, private letters, contracts and personal papers. In all, there are nine galleries, 3 theaters and interactive television.

Will Rogers Spring Water, which is bottled in Oologah, is only sold presently at the Will Rogers Memorial.

Located at 1720 W. Will Rogers Blvd. in Claremore (a few miles northeast of Tulsa on Hwy. 86). Open 365 days a year from 8-5. No charge. (918) 341-0719 or (800) 828-9643.

★★

Will Rogers Statue

In the middle of the 300 W. Will Rogers block in Claremore, you will want to stop, grab your camera and visit the life-size bronze statue of Will Rogers, sitting on a park bench reading the CLAREMORE PROGRESS. The Rogers County Historical Society presented this statue, "All I know is what I read in the papers," to the City of Claremore in '96. The Will Rogers Story is being presented in the form of statues to be placed throughout the city. Sit with Will and have your picture taken.

Incidentally, Will Rogers Downs Racetrack is 2.5 miles east of Claremore on State Hwy. 20 while Will Rogers Raceway is at 21601 E. Hwy. 20.

★★★

Old Will Rogers Library

The Old Will Rogers Library is now occupied by the City of Claremore on the southwest corner of 4th St. and Weenonah. A year before his death, Will donated his lots in downtown Claremore with the understanding they were to be sold with the proceeds of the sale going to build a city library.

★★★

Will Rogers Hotel

The former Will Rogers Hotel at Lynn Riggs (Rt. 66) and Will Rogers Blvd. in Claremore was dedicated in 1930 and is now the site of the Will Rogers Senior Center and Apartments.

There is a statue of Will in the lobby.

★★★

Will Rogers Monument

A seven foot granite marker signifying the 75th year of Route 66, also known as Will Rogers Hwy., was unveiled in February 2001. The marker has a likeness and brief bio of Will Rogers and has been placed at the J. M. Davis Arms and Historical Museum on U.S. 66 in Claremore.

The monument was created by Darrell Ray of Joplin, Missouri.

★★★

Cain's Ballroom

Cain's Dancing Academy, commonly referred to as Cain's Ballroom, where Bob Wills and the Texas Playboys first played on New Year's Night in 1935, still stands at 423 N. Main in Tulsa. Wills played Cain's Academy more than 90 times every year for eight years, approximately 720 times. His popularity was greater in 1942, at the end of those appearances, than it was in 1935.

A two to three block section of Main St. is named Bob Wills Main St. directly in front of Cain's which still operates as a ballroom. (918) 747-0001.

★★★

Scullin Area

Hereford Heaven where Dale Evans arrives in "Home In Oklahoma" ('46) is actually Scullin (just southeast of the Chickasaw Turnpike in south-central Oklahoma.

The overpass where Roy and Trigger take off after George Meeker is in Byars (intersection Hwys. 102 and 59 north of Scullin).

State Hwy. 1 parallels a railroad track where fight scenes on the train were done between Scullin and Mill Creek to the south.

Locations for Walter Wanger's "Tulsa" ('49) were shot at the ranch of Oklahoma Governor Roy Turner near Sulpher in the same general area (Hwy. 177 west of Scullin and east of Davis).

Roy Rogers and Dale Evans were married December 31, 1947, on the Flying L Ranch in Murray County near Sulphur.

★★

Gene Autry Museum

Dedicated to the Singing Cowboy of B-Western Movies, the Gene Autry Museum in the town of Gene Autry offers not only a magnificent display of Gene Autry memorabilia, but toys and collectibles on Roy Rogers, Tex Ritter, Eddie Dean, Jimmy Wakely and other singing cowboys as well. More than 10,000 people have visited the museum with many commenting "...the best museum of its kind in the country."

Over 1,000 people gather each September to honor the singing cowboys at an annual film and music festival.

Inauspicious front of the Gene Autry, Oklahoma Museum. Inside is an amazing display of Autry memorabilia.

In the fall of 1939, while he was on the radio with "Melody Ranch," Gene Autry bought a 1,200 acre ranch two miles west of Berwyn. Veteran lawman Cecil Crosby proposed the town change its name to Gene Autry, honoring the state in which Gene was reared. With the approval of the post office, the name change became official November 4, 1941. Gene broadcast his radio show from the town on November 16th, the 34th anniversary of Oklahoma statehood. The broadcast went on the air before a live audience of 35,000 people.

Gene Autry is located in southern Oklahoma, just north of Ardmore on State Hwy. 53. Of course, there's a Gene Autry Road in town.

Opened in 1990, the museum, located in the former Gene Autry school building on a hill with a view of the Arbuckle Mountains, is open Monday-Saturday 10-4. Admission is free. Elvin Sweeten (580) 294-3047.

★★

Achille

Although Gene Autry once lived in the former railroad town of Achille (pronounced a-SHEEL according to Gene), which is stated in his own words in his autobiography, the time frame is hazy at best. He apparently operated a theater projector at the long-extinct

Dark Feather Theater which was opened in 1913 (next to the bank) and, according to town records, closed before 1920. Apparently, Gene lived there from sometime in 1919 through 1921 and attended school there. Quick math will tell you Gene would only have been 12 or 13 years old which seems quite young to be operating a theater projector. Around 1921 the family moved back to Tioga where Gene lived until around 1924. (See Tioga, Texas, entry.)

These days, the theater building no longer exists with old Achille being mostly abandoned as the town has moved about a half mile down to Highway 78, 12 miles south of Durant.

Autry Private Collection

Albert Frazier's private collection of Gene Autry and Roy Rogers memorabilia can be seen by appointment only by calling the Idabel Chamber of Commerce (580) 286-3305.

Albert's collection encompasses films, posters, collectibles, and a few personal Autry items such as one of Gene's hats. Most "private" collections are not included in this book for security reasons, but Albert asked us to include his collection and it is consistently listed in the Kiamichi County, Oklahoma, travel guide.

Idabel is in the far southeastern corner of Oklahoma.

★★

OREGON

Bend

The area around Bend was used several times on "Have Gun Will Travel" episodes—"The Race," "The Hunt" and "Silent Death". "Oregon Passage" ('57) with John Ericson and "Rooster Cogburn" ('75) with John Wayne were also lensed in the area. Although I cannot guide you to specific locations, checking with elderly locals and the Chamber of Commerce often proves rewarding.

Bend is on Hwy. 97 in Central Oregon.

★★★

PENNSYLVANIA

Jimmy Stewart

James Stewart's outfit from "Night Passage".

Jimmy Stewart was born and grew up in Indiana, a town that may have inspired many of the All-American roles that earned him international acclaim. Indiana is on Route 422, northeast of Pittsburgh. A bronze plaque marks the doorstep of the house where Jimmy was born. A Jimmy Stewart statue is in front of the courthouse.

The Jimmy Stewart Museum at 845 Philadelphia St. highlights its namesake's accomplishments in film, radio and TV through displays, film presentations and gallery talks. You can view Jimmy's films and career retrospectives in the museum's vintage 1930s theatre. The Hollywood Gallery displays something from all of Stewart's 80 features, a costume, a poster or script, including the sweat-stained cowboy hat Jimmy wore in seven westerns and a jacket from "Night Passage." The museum also sports two flight outfits worn by Brig. General Stewart as well as a dress blue uniform and military tuxedo. The Awards Gallery displays numerous awards including his Golden Boot Award and National Cowboy Hall of Fame Award, a testament to the 18 westerns Stewart made. A desk and chair from his office are also in the museum.

The museum gift shop handles T-shirts, paperweights, posters, videos, mugs, Christmas ornaments and Jimmy Hawkins' book, IT'S A WONDERFUL LIFE. In addition to being in the film, Hawkins was Tagg on TV's "Annie Oakley." Museum is open Monday-Saturday 10-5; Sundays and holidays Noon-5. Closed on Monday and Tuesday in January, February and March. (800) 83-JIMMY.

★★

Roy Rogers Restaurant

Roy Rogers Restaurant still operational. (See details under Maryland.)
Pennslyvania Turnpike, Newburg, Pennslyvania (717) 423-5592.

★★★

Tom Mix Home

Tom Mix once lived at 524 Orient Ave. in DuBois. The house is now easily spotted by it's green siding.

★★★

Tom Mix Birthplace

The birthplace of Tom Mix is at Mix Run. Renovation of the land began a few years ago and now picnic tables and a parking area are provided with a river flowing nearby the clearly marked site.

From I-80 take 255 north. When it splits into two roads, take 555 east to the right. Between Weedville and Driftwood watch for the signs which will direct you along Red Run Road to the Mix birthplace site.

★★★

Zane Grey's Home

Zane Grey's home in Lackawaxen is now a National Historic site administered by the National Park Service.

For "serious researchers" they have stills, movie posters and newspapers on Grey novels turned into film.

Their opening hours, *generally* 10-5 Thursday through Sunday only, seem to be erratic. It all seems to depend on staffing, so be sure to call ahead. (570) 685-4871.

Lackawaxen is right on the Delaware River bordering New York State—upriver from Port Jervis.

★★★

SOUTH CAROLINA

Planet Hollywood

A Planet Hollywood restaurant with many western props is at 2915 Hollywood Dr. in Myrtle Beach. (843) 448-7827. (See Orlando, Florida entry.)

★★★

SOUTH DAKOTA

Deadwood

Hollywood is in Deadwood! The Celebrity Hotel and Casino at 629 Main and the Mint across the street at 638 Main house a vast array of western movie memorabilia along with non-western items such as James Bond's Aston Martin and the Batmobile from "Batman Returns." Don Nelson's collection at the Mint includes John Wayne's 1978 Ford Pickup, John Wayne's vest from "The Cowboys" and "Cahill, U.S. Marshal," John Wayne's pants and shirt from "The Cowboys," Michael Landon's spurs from "Bonanza," a Spencer rifle used as a prop in "Unforgiven" with Clint Eastwood, Clint Eastwood's outfit from "Joe Kidd," Rock Hudson's shirt from "Undefeated," Brian Keith's leather togs from "The Mountain Men," Dan Haggerty's shirt from "Grizzly Adams," Andie McDowell's dress from "Bad Girls," Keifer Sutherland's western outfit from "Young Guns II" and a screen dress worn by Maureen O'Hara. On display at the Celebrity are John Wayne's shirt from "Rooster Cogburn," Clint Eastwood's Sharps 45/70 rifle with brass scope from "Outlaw Josey Wales," Gene Hackman's silk shirt from "Unforgiven," Tom Selleck's shirt and longjohns from "Quigley Down Under," Yul Bynner's shirt from "The Magnificent Seven" and Glenn Ford's hat and holster used in many westerns.

Other non-western items abound—Herbie the Love Bug Volkswagon, Charlton Heston's tunic from "Ben Hur," a "M*A*S*H" jeep and much more.

Hotel reservations (888) 399-1886. Children are welcome on the casino floors to see the movie memorabilia.

Deadwood is located in the historic Black Hills north of Rapid City in the western part

Clint Eastwood's Spencer rifle from "Unforgiven", John Wayne's vest from "The Cowboys", "Cahill, U. S. Marshal" and "The Train Robbers" along with much more is on display at the Celebrity Hotel and Casino.

of the state.

★★★

Ft. Hays

Examine the movie set buildings of Fort Hays, built for filming Kevin Costner's "Dances With Wolves." Chuckwagon supper and western music variety show nightly at 6:30.

Four miles south of Rapid City at 8181 Mt. Rushmore Rd./Hwy. 16 West. Open free to visitors from May 15 to September 15. (888) 394-9653.

Costner's winter camp in the film was in Spearfish Canyon, north of Rapid City on Hwy. 90.

The headquarters building built for "Dances With Wolves", along with many others used in the Academy Award Winner, still stands at Fort Hays.

★★★

"Dances With Wolves" Buffalo Herd

3,500 buffalo constitute the world's largest privately owned herd at the Triple U Standing Butte Ranch outside Pierre in the center of the state. It was here, by necessity, Kevin Costner brought his film crew for much of "Dances With Wolves" in 1990. The Tennessee Civil War battle was filmed outside Pierre.

Pierre is right in the middle of the state where U.S. 14 crosses U.S. 83.

★★★

Tom Mix Packard

Tom Mix's white 1931 four-door convertible Packard Sport touring car is currently housed at the Pioneer Auto Museum in Murdo, midway across the state on I-90, exit 192. There's over 100 different "collections" from nickelodeons to band organs in this 10 acre, 39 building antique town.

Open in the summer only, 8-9. (605) 669-2691.

★★★

Ingalls Homestead

Enjoy hands-on 1880s activities on the homestead Laura Ingalls lived on and wrote about in her famous "Little House" books which were so successfully adapted for TV by Michael Landon. Horse drawn wagon rides, 1880s classroom, 90 acres of prairie grass, much more. The largest collection of memorabilia and artifacts of the family in existence.

Tour hours are daily 9-6 Memorial Day through Labor Day. Open other times during the year, but call first. The Laura Ingalls Pageant recreates scenes from the pioneering days, 9pm, Friday, Saturday and Sunday for three weekends each summer. (605) 692-2108.

Ingalls Homestead, 20812 Homestead Rd., De Smet (Hwy. 14 between Huron and Brookings). (800) 776-3594. (See Missouri for another entry.)

★★★

TENNESSEE

Country Music Hall of Fame

Election to the Country Music Hall of Fame is the highest honor in country music. The Hall of Fame award was created in 1961 by the Country Music Association (CMA), the country music industry's leading trade organization. The award recognizes persons who have made outstanding contributions to country music over the length of their careers.

The Hall of Fame honors performers, promoters, music publishing and recording leaders, broadcasters and others in the music industry, reflecting country music's stature as both art and enterprise. Hall of Fame members are selected annually by an anonymous panel of 200 electors, each of whom has been an active participant in the country music business for at least 15 years.

The first Hall of Fame members were elected in 1961. Hall of Fame plaques were displayed at the Tennessee State Museum in Nashville until 1967, when the first Country Music Hall of Fame Museum building was opened on Music Row in Nashville. The

The Country Music Hall of Fame.

plaques are now housed in the Country Music Hall of Fame and Museum in downtown Nashville.

Included are Tex Ritter (elected in 1964), Bob Wills (elected in 1968), Gene Autry (elected in 1969), Jimmie Davis (elected in 1972), Pee Wee King (elected in 1974), the Sons of the Pioneers (elected in 1980), Roy Rogers (elected in 1988) and Johnny Bond (elected in 1999).

The Country Music Hall of Fame and Museum also displays instruments, costumes and memorabilia from the lives of Gene Autry, Roy Rogers, Tex Ritter, Rex Allen, Eddie Dean, Roy Acuff, Carolina Cotton, Bob Wills, Tex Williams, Pee Wee King and many others. Over one million artifacts, recordings, films and state of the art exhibits. Now open in their new $37 million home of nearly 40,000 sq. ft. of exhibit space in a thriving area of Nashville only a short distance from Music Row where the city's music industry operates.

Roy Rogers is in the Country Music Hall of Fame by himself as well as with the Sons of the Pioneers.

The original museum, opened in 1967, was a dream of Tex Ritter and record producer Owen Bradley. Along with the Country Music Association, they led the fund raising drive to build and establish the enterprise.

There's live entertainment daily as well as numerous interactive features. There's a 214 seat acoustically sound theatre with a digital film presentation of country music around the world. A 5,500 sq. ft. gift shop offers the best selection of vintage and contemporary tapes, CDs, books, videos, collectibles and apparel. A display entitled "Friends and Neighbors" features old country music radio programs including the WLS National Barn Dance. Gene Autry, Ray Whitley, Tex Ritter, Sons of the Pioneers and others are in the "Singing Cowboys" display including Gene's beautiful Martin 000-45 guitar, Whitley's Gibson J-200 guitar, the original handwritten lyrics to "Back In the Saddle Again" written in '38 by Whitley and a Patsy Montana Vogue picture disk from the '40s. The "Tennessee Saturday Night" exhibit includes Pee Wee King's accordion. Pee Wee was in several Johnny Mack Brown, Charles Starrett and Gene Autry westerns. There's a "Hollywood Barn Dance" exhibit featuring a fiddle owned by Bob Wills, Merle Travis' original Paul Bigsby-made solid body guitar and outfits made by Nudie and Turk, the penultimate B-western outfitters. There are also plenty of Roy Rogers/Dale Evans items throughout the vast museum of history and artifacts.

Open daily 10-6. 222 5th Ave. South. (800) 852-6437, (615) 416-2001.

★★★

Grand Ole Opry Museum

Tex Ritter's Gibson J-200 and Fender Kingman guitars, cowboy outfits, posters and his '52 record of "High Noon" are on display at the Grand Old Opry Museum on the grounds of the Opry House at 2804 Opryland Dr. in Nashville. Exhibits are free and also include a Tex Ritter saddle, Marty Robbins costumes, instruments and racing awards, show posters from various artists and much more. (615) 889-3060.

★★

Audie Murphy at Willie's Museum

Did you know Willie Nelson was a fan of Audie Murphy? In fact, he has devoted a portion of his museum which is located near Opryland in Nashville to exhibit Audie Murphy memorabilia.

Like Audie Murphy, Willie is a Texan. Other similarities can be noted including the fact Audie Murphy was also a published song writer with his "Shutters and Boards" sung by Jerry Wallace being a big hit.

Some of the items on display at the museum which belonged to

Audie Murphy display at the Willie Nelson Museum

Audie include a pair of cowboy boots, a guitar, movie lobby cards and clothing. Copies of some of Audie's medals are also on display as well as a uniform and helmet.

Willie Nelson's Museum is at 2613-A McGavock Pike in Nashville. (615) 885-1515.

★★

Roy Acuff Museum

The Roy Acuff Museum and Library in Maynardville is mostly the history of Maynardville and Union County. Apparently, Acuff donated $25,000 to the museum along with much of his memorabilia which is now housed there. They have a picture of his birthplace in the museum. Now gone, it was located about a quarter mile up the road from the museum. It's so designated by a historical highway marker.

Acuff starred in several country or semi-westerns at Republic and Columbia in the '40s. The museum also has a display on Carl Smith, the country singer who was featured in "Badge of Marshal Brennan" and "Buffalo Gun."

Display in the Roy Acuff Museum that pays tribute to Acuff, as well as Carl Smith with the large painting on right and a "Badge of Marshal Brennan" poster.

★★

TEXAS

Dan Blocker Bust

In a downtown park in O'Donnell, hometown of Dan Blocker (Hoss Cartwright on TV's "Bonanza"), there is a bronze bust of him complete with his Hoss hat. Located across the street from the local museum, which may have some Blocker memorabilia. We were unable to confirm this.

O'Donnell, a cotton farming town, is on Hwy. 87, 25 miles south of Lubbock in the Texas panhandle. A large sign on the highway celebrates it as Dan's hometown.

★★

Turkey

Granite monument to Bob Wills in Turkey. Note twin fiddles atop the spire.

Bob Wills, referred to as "the best damn fiddle player in the world," by Merle Haggard, is the legendary band leader and composer from Turkey. Wills became the "King of Western Swing" with his dynamic combination of New Orleans Jazz, blues, and folk fiddle music. He and his Texas Playboys swept the country off its feet with favorites like "San Antonio Rose," "Faded Love" and "Take Me Back to Tulsa." His music was so popular in the early '40s that his records sold better than other mainstream recording artists at that time. Wills was inducted into the Country Music Hall of Fame in Nashville and was voted into the National Cowboy Hall of Fame in Oklahoma City. Wills' legendary status was not only achieved through his music but also on the big screen. His popularity escalated in the early '40s when he and his band made eight B-westerns with Russell Hayden and others with Tex Ritter, Glenn Ford and Charles Starrett. Although Bob Wills died on May 13, 1975, his musical influence lives on in much of today's country music.

Established by the Wills family, the Bob Wills Museum in Turkey exhibits many wonderful momentos of Bob's career—fiddles, photos, clothes, all pay tribute to the legend. Take note too of the large octagonal granite monument to Bob which sports pictures of him all around the base with twin fiddles atop a steel spire.

The museum, at 6th St. and Johnson St., is open Monday-Friday 8-noon, 1-5. (806) 423-1253 or (806) 423-1033.

Turkey is 100 miles southeast of Amarillo and 100 miles northeast of Lubbock, at the junction of Hwys. 86 and 656, off I-27 in the Texas panhandle.

★★★

"Giant"

"Giant" was filmed near Marfa in 1955. Here stood the Reata ranch mansion, ancestral home of the fictional Benedict clan in "Giant," until most of it crumbled away in the

'80s. Only the white slumprock gateway now remains to the Evans Ryan Ranch about 18 miles west of Marfa on I-90 toward Valentine (left side of the road). The windmill remnants of Little Reata can also be seen about 8 miles west of Marfa on the right of I-90. The Paisana Hotel in Marfa contains a few items of memorabilia from the classic film in their lobby.

It's also reported that "Flashing Spurs" and "Texas Battler" were filmed in the area in 1929 with Art Acord, but those films may have never been distributed.

Remnants of entranceway to Reata Ranch.

Marfa is south of historic Ft. Davis on Hwy. 17 in west Texas.

★★★

Fort Davis

Fort Davis is now a National Historic Site about 30 miles down Hwy. 17 off of I-10 at exit 206. The restored frontier fort was once owned by Jack Hoxie in 1929 with plans to turn it into a dude ranch and filming site. However, at the depths of the depression, this didn't work out. Texas turned the beautiful area into a state park in 1933.

★★★

Garner Memorial Museum

Dale Evans was born in Uvalde.

The dress Dale wore when she appeared at the Uvalde Centennial in 1956 was on display at the Garner Memorial Museum, former home of John "Cactus Jack" Garner, vice president under Franklin D. Roosevelt, but is now in storage until the new city library is completed. At that time, Dale's dress will be on display there along with other area artifacts.

The house in which Dale was

Dale Evans' birthplace in Uvalde.

born at 726 Fort Clark St. (corner of Shook St.) still stands but is a private residence.

★★

Brackettville

The late Happy Shahan's Alamo Village is where an exact replica of the real 1836 Alamo (in San Antonio) was constructed for John Wayne's $7,500,000 epic, "The Alamo" ('60).

Actually, "Arrowhead" ('53) was the first film shot in the area—in Brackettville (on Hwy. 90, 30 miles east of Del Rio) and at nearby Fort Clark (also utilized in "The Alamo"). In 1955, Sterling Hayden's Alamo epic, "The Last Command," was shot on the nearby Hobbs Ranch where an Alamo set was constructed. That ranch has since been sold several times. Parts of "Arrowhead" were also shot on that ranch.

Originally planned to shoot in Mexico, the Daughters of the Republic of Texas convinced John Wayne to lens "The Alamo" in Texas. Wayne struck a deal with Shahan and work was begun to construct the Alamo set on Shahan's 22,000,000 acre ranch in 1957. The full-size facsimile took two years to build. Filming began in 1959.

Over the years, with more films coming in, Shahan's Alamo Village began to expand about 300 yards away from Wayne's Alamo set. That excellent western street is now operated by Shahan's daughter, Virginia, with a John Wayne museum (not well cared for) on the property as well as a cantina for a lunch break. The museum exhibits some original props from "The Alamo", dozens of construction photos, photos from the film—even original cannons.

Alamo Village is open 9-5 Labor Day to Memorial Day (Winter season) and 9-6 Memorial Day to Labor Day (Summer season). Trail rides are offered in Spring and Fall. During the Summer there are cowboy music shows, gunfights and other events.

Seven miles north of Brackettville on Hwy. 674. (830) 563-2580.

Entrance to Brackettville's Alamo compound as it looks today. *(Photo by Ken Taylor.)*

210

Sampling of Westerns Filmed at ALAMO VILLAGE / BRACKETTVILLE

- Arrowhead ('53)—Charlton Heston
- Last Command ('55)—Sterling Hayden
- Five Bold Women ('58)—Merry Anders
- The Alamo ('60)—John Wayne
- Two Rode Together ('61)—James Stewart
- Bandolero ('68)—James Stewart
- Centennial (TV)—Robert Conrad ('78)
- Barbarosa ('80)—Willie Nelson

- Six Gun Heroes (TV)—Sunset Carson ('82)
- Thirteen Days To Glory (TV)—James Arness ('86)
- Lonesome Dove (TV)—Robert Duvall ('89)
- Gunsmoke: The Last Apache (TV)—James Arness ('90)
- Rio Diablo (TV)—Kenny Rogers ('92)
- Gambler V (TV)—Kenny Rogers ('94)
- Streets of Laredo (TV)—James Garner ('95)

★★

Audie Murphy VA Hospital

By far the most prestigious memorial erected in Audie Murphy's memory is the Audie L. Murphy Memorial Veteran's Hospital, 7400 Merton Minter Blvd., part of the South Texas Medical Center in San Antonio. Dedicated November 17, 1973, the complex is seven stories high with 646,000 square feet of hospital space providing surgical and care facilities to 420 patients. Only four of the 171 VA Hospitals have been named by public law in honor of individuals such as Audie. This is the *only*

Audie Murphy Bronze in front of San Antonio VA hospital.

hospital in the entire VA system named after a soldier, for being a soldier.

An eight foot, one ton bronze of Audie in battle dress and position is located in a garden area on the grounds in front of the hospital's main entrance. Dedicated May 21, 1975, the massive, realistic statue is the work of Ms. Jimilu Mason of Virginia who spent 18 months on the project. On the same day the bronze statue of Audie was dedicated, the Audie Murphy Memorial Room (actually the main lobby) was opened to the public. This area contains artifacts and memorabilia associated with Audie, both the actor and the soldier. On display is the AutoLite metal spark plug sign Audie used for target practice as a youth; a letter to Pam Murphy, Audie's widow, upon Audie's death from President Richard Nixon; movie posters; MOTION PICTURE EXHIBI-

Portrait of Audie Murphy at VA hospital by Nielsen.

TOR award; scripts; a hat; photos; Audie's WWII dress uniform and a 1975 painting of Audie by T. Nielsen.

★★

Plaza Theatre of Wax
John Wayne at the Alamo is immortalized in wax at the Plaza Theatre of Wax, 301 Alamo Plaza in San Antonio (across from the real Alamo). (210) 224-9299.

★★

Joe Gish's Old West Museum
Joe Gish's Old West Museum has over 600 lobby cards from silent westerns, many on display along with a large amount of autographed western star photos, fancy chaps, a

photo of Yakima Canutt receiving the Roosevelt Trophy and much more.

Call (830) 997-2794 for an appointment. Located at 502 N. Milam in Fredericksburg. No admission, contributions accepted.

★★★★★★★★★★★★★★★★★★★★★★★★★★★★★★★

Camp Mabry
The Texas Military Forces Museum at Camp Mabry in Austin has a number of excellent displays on Audie Murphy and the Texas National Guard.

A six foot bronze statue, suggested to be Audie Murphy although it appears more as a generic soldier, stands outside the museum. It was sculpted by artist Bill Leftwich of Ft. Davis and dedicated November 3, 1984.

Camp Mabry is the headquarters of the state military forces, named after General Woodford Mabry, Adjutant General of Texas from 1891-1898.

This bronze at the Texas Military Forces Museum is reputed to be of Audie Murphy but bears little resemblance.

Painting of Audie Murphy, the soldier, by Kipp Soldwedel hangs in the Texas State Capitol in Austin.

★★★★★★★★★★★★★★★★★★★★★★★★★★★★

Audie Murphy Paintings
Two oil paintings were made of Audie Murphy while he was alive. One by Kipp Soldwedel, a Dallas artist, was presented to the state of Texas on April 17, 1951, and now hangs in the State Capitol building in Austin. (The other

painting by Dimitri Vail is owned by one of Audie's sisters.)

★★

John Kimbrough display at the Texas Sports Hall of Fame.

Texas Sports Hall of Fame

Two Texas sports legends also had a fling at western movie fame.

Slingin' Sammy Baugh was perhaps the world's greatest quarterback, throwing footballs for more than 23,000 yards in gains while he was field general for the Washington Redskins of the NFL for 16 seasons. Before that, he was an All-American quarterback for the Texas Christian University Horned Frogs, played in the inaugural Cotton Bowl game and is a charter member of both the College Football Hall of Fame and the Pro Football Hall of Fame. Sammy was also named to the modern all-time team, encompassing a 50 year period from 1919-1969. The boy who played high school ball in Sweetwater, Texas, never leaves his ranch outside Rotan in West Texas.

Fellow Texan and longtime friend Jolting John Kimbrough played fullback for Texas A&M, 1938-1940, and was unanimous All-American in '40 and the runner-up for the Heisman Trophy that year. In the 1940 Sugar Bowl, John rushed for 152 yards on 26 carries, scored two touchdowns, one on a 10-yard run ending an 18 yard pass-lateral play.

Collegiate totals: 1,357 yards rushing on 375 carries, 24 receptions for 197 yards, 12 interceptions for 198 yards, 21 touchdowns, 126 points. He played for the New York Americans in the AFL in '41 and the L.A. Dons of the AAFC from '46-'48. Kimbrough is in the National Football Hall of Fame.

Baugh starred in Republic's "King of the Texas Rangers" serial in 1941.

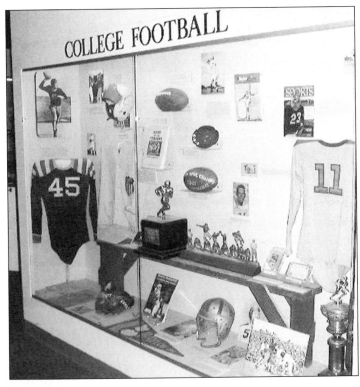

Sammy Baugh display at the Texas Sports Hall of Fame.

Kimbrough signed a contract to star in Zane Grey westerns for 20th Century Fox but WWII interrupted the series after two, "Lone Star Ranger" and "Sundown Jim" (both '42). After the war, John returned to Haskell and ranching. Baugh laughingly chides his friend, "I guess I was the world's worst actor, unless it was John Kimbrough."

The Texas Sports Hall of Fame in Waco honors both these gridiron/movie heroes along with over 350 other Texas sports heroes. Not only memorabilia is on display, but the Tom Landry Theatre shows films that preserve memorable moments in Texas College and pro-sports.

John Kimbrough's 1936 Abilene High School Sweater is there along with a pair of his football cleats and several "Sundown Jim" lobby cards and stills.

The display for Baugh is more extensive, exhibiting a 1936 TCU game ball, a 1937 Cotton Bowl football, 1953 All-American ball, #45—1937 College All-Star jersey, Washington Redskins jersey, football pants, Texas All-Time Pro-Football Team plaque from 1975, Texas Sports Hall of Fame plaque from 1954, NCAA plaque from 1969, a 1927 TCU vs AMC program, a cast of Sammy's hand trophy and several other items including photos from his Republic serial.

Open Monday-Saturday 10-5, Sunday Noon-5 (til 6 in summer). 1108 S. University Parks Dr., Waco. (254) 756-1633.

★★★

Audie L. Murphy Gun Museum

The Audie L. Murphy Gun Museum is on the Campus of Hill Junior College in Hillsboro. The name of the museum was changed in 1975 from the Hill College Gun Museum to honor "the most highly decorated soldier in American history."

Besides having some of the finest gun collections in Texas, it contains the most complete library on weaponry in the Southwest.

The Audie Murphy Marksmanship Award is given annually to the best marksman at Hill Junior College and in both the Fort Worth and Dallas Junior ROTC programs.

Hillsboro is between Fort Worth and Waco on I-35.

★★★

Morgan Woodward Way

Morgan Woodward has established himself over the years in such westerns as "Gun Hawk," "Gunsight Ridge," "Gun Point," "Yuma" and TV episodes of "Gunsmoke," "Tales of Wells Fargo," "Wagon Train," "Bonanza" and many others including a run as Shotgun Gibbs on "Life and Legend of Wyatt Earp" from '58-'61.

His hometown of Arlington has honored him with a street, Morgan Woodward Way.

★★★

National Cowgirl Hall of Fame

Dale Evans, singer Patsy Montana (who sang her million seller "I Want to Be a Cowboy's Sweetheart" in Gene Autry's "Colorado Sunset"), songwriter Cindy Walker (who wrote over 500 songs including nearly all the songs performed by Bob Wills and His Texas Playboys in the B-westerns Bob co-starred in with Russell Hayden from 1942-'43), stuntwoman Alice Van Springsteen (who doubled Dale Evans among others and was married to B-western director R. G. "Buddy" Springsteen), stuntlady Polly Burson, and the Queen of the trick ropers Texas Rose Bascom (who was featured in Johnny Carpenter's "Lawless Rider" in 1954) are among the over 150 inspiring honorees in the National Cowgirl Museum and Hall of Fame at 1720 Gendy St. in Fort Worth. The Hall also includes vocalist Louise Massey cited for her song "My Adobe Hacienda," bronc riders Alice Greenough Orr and Alice Ione Anderson Adams Holden who both did stuntwork in films. Orr worked in "The Californian" and later on "High Chaparral" among others.

The Hall of Fame began in Hereford in 1975 and recently opened up $21 million digs in the cultural district of Ft. Worth. It's the only museum dedicated to honoring and documenting the lives of distinguished western women. The 33,000 sq. ft. museum encompasses five galleries—Spirit of the Cowgirl, Ranching, Ranch Life, Rodeo, Wild West shows and Popular Culture. The museum features costumes, saddles and rodeo trophies plus a mechanical bronco you can ride as a 1930s rodeo film runs behind you. (800) 476-3263. Open 10-8 Tue., 10-5 Wed.-Sat., 12-5 Sun. Closed Mondays.

★★

Texas Trail of Fame

The Texas Trail of Fame at the Fort Worth Stockyards includes stars with the names of Roy Rogers, Dale Evans, Gene Autry, Clayton Moore, and Tex Ritter. The names of those honored are on bronze markers laid in the stockyards walkways. John Wayne, Will Rogers and writers such as Will James and Elmer Kelton are other inductees along with real pioneers such as Charles Goodnight and Oliver Loving who blazed the cattle trail that bore their names.

The historic Fort Worth Stockyards district (which also includes the Cowtown Coliseum and more) is on East Exchange Ave. off N. Main St.

★★

"Gunsmoke" Bar

The bar used on TV's "Gunsmoke" is now in the Pavestone Sales Office in Grapevine.

Too large for normal storage, the legendary bar behind which Glenn Strange as bartender Sam served drinks to Matt, Doc, Chester, Miss Kitty, Festus and all the patrons on "Gunsmoke" had resided in an airplane hanger for years. While at auction in 1998, Bob Schlegel bid on and won the magnificent 11x24 ft. mahogany bar.

Schlegel designed the lobby of Pavestone to accommodate the showpiece. Drop by 3215 State Hwy. 360 in Grapevine. (Between Dallas and Ft.Worth.)

(No, they don't serve drinks.)

The bar Glenn Strange tended on "Gunsmoke" is now in Grapevine.

★★

Palace of Wax

John Wayne, Clint Eastwood and Audie Murphy are the only three western stars among 175 celebrities memorialized in wax at the Palace of Wax, 601 E. Safari Parkway in Grand Prairie. Open Monday-Friday, 10-5, Saturday and Sunday, 10-6, from Labor Day to Memorial Day. Summer: seven days a week 10-9. (972) 263-2391.

★★★

Dovie's Restaurant

The building that is now Dovie's Restaurant in Dallas was built in the early '30s and

used as a house. Audie Murphy purchased the home in the '50s. It was converted to Dovie's in May 1980. A large courtyard room was added and the kitchen was expanded by using the garage. Open for lunch Monday-Friday 11-2; Dinner Monday-Saturday 5:30-9. Sunday brunch 10:30-2. 14671 Midway Rd., Dallas. From I-35, get off the Beltline Rd. exit in the Addison area. Drive east. Turn right on Midway Rd. (972) 233-9846.

Dovie's Restaurant used to be a home owned by Audie Murphy.

★★★

Audie Murphy VFW

Dallas VFW Post 1837 is designated as Audie L. Murphy Memorial Post 1837.

★★★

Gene Autry Theaters

Gene Autry once owned eight movie theaters in Dallas, as well as six others in the deep South (one each in Little Rock, Arkansas; Montgomery, Alabama; Mobile, Alabama; Columbia, South Carolina; Roanoke, Virginia and Charlotte, North Carolina) when movie going was at its peak in the late '40s and early '50s. All the Texas theaters were in the Oak Cliff area of Dallas.

Autry Enterprises opened their first, the Hill, at the small island city of Cockrell Hill (4334 West Jefferson) on July 10, 1946. Cockrell Hill is surrounded by Oak Cliff. Gene joked he'd always have a place to run his pictures in Dallas. The building's life as a theater was relatively short, it closed in 1952. It later became an auto parts store before it burned in December 1998. The area is now a vacant lot.

The other theaters Gene owned in the Oak Cliff area were The Rosewin, now Amador Auto Insurance and a religious articles shop; the Beckley (2111 S. Beckley) opened in 1946 and closed around 1956. It's now Shekinah Tabernacle Baptist Church; the Beverly Hills was demolished in 1953 with the property now a Spanish Assembly of God Ministries building; the Kessler (1230 W. Davis), building still standing, looking much as it did; the Midway (nothing known); the Cliff Queen (616 E. Jefferson) now a Pan-African bookstore in a very seedy section of town and the Heights which was on Jefferson somewhere between the Midway and the Cliff Queen.

None of Gene's theaters were first run houses—and Gene's pictures were treated no differently than those of Roy Rogers or Charles Starrett. Not only had Gene become big on TV but overall theater attendance was dwindling by 1952 when Gene decided to sell off his Dallas theaters and invest in television stations. The Robb and Rowley (later United Artists) chain purchased the Autry theaters.

★★★

Texas State Fair Grounds

Gene Autry's "Big Show" was partially filmed at the Texas Centennial in Dallas in 1936 on the state fairgrounds. Some of the buildings which show in the exteriors can still be seen.

★★★

Gene Autry Hometown

This sign welcomes you to Gene Autry's "hometown."

Tioga is the "home of the best mineral water in Texas" and the birthplace of Gene Autry. The small town, population 625, about 50 miles north of Dallas on Hwy. 377, now sports a large sign announcing it as Gene's birthplace. Technically, Gene was born about six miles west of Tioga at Indian Creek.

Quiet and serene, Tioga's residential streets are bordered with comfortable, livable homes on streets such as Gene Autry Dr., Gene Autry Trail and Gene Autry Street. Back in 1937, the town even toyed with the idea of renaming itself Autry Springs. Tioga was founded in 1851 when the Texas and Pacific Railroad came through. It later became a popular health resort due to its healthy mineral springs. Gene always said he had fond memories of Tioga, the place where he used to shine shoes, bale hay and slop hogs.

The Tioga Chamber of Commerce also mentions Tioga the "home of Gene Autry" and is adjacent to Campaign Headquarters for the Tioga Museum and Heritage Association, featuring Gene Autry.

★★★

Yellow Jacket Boat Company

Roy Rogers was vice president of the Yellow Jacket Boat Company in Denison from 1955-1961. He (and Dale) made regular visits to the city over that period. He used his own Yellow Jacket speedboat in such TV episodes as "Fishing For Fingerprints" and "Mountain Pirates."

Richard McDerby established and operated the firm over a decade until the advent of fiberglass took over the industry. At the end of WWII McDerby joined Harry Frye in opening a small marina at 701 N. Houston in Denison. They soon picked up a couple of partners. The firm grew and in 1948 made a move to the corner of South 75 at Bullock. In 1949 the Yellow Jacket Boat Company began operations in the back of 216 West Woodard. The company prospered but exploded nationwide in 1955 when Roy Rogers bought out McDerby's partner, Lee Siebert of Kansas City. Siebert had bought out McDerby's other partners in 1952.

At the time Roy said, "I became interested in Yellow Jacket boats ever since the first time I acquired my first boat. I had been racing in marathons and hadn't found a boat that would hold together until I tried a Yellow Jacket. I won four straight races with my first boat." Roy's initial visit to Denison was to explore the possibility of lining up either a dealership or distributorship on the west coast. He ended up a partner in the company.

Roy Rogers in his Miss Yellow Jacket speedboat in the late '50s on Lake Texoma near Denison.

New names were now showing up on the boats, the Trigger series, the Bullet series, even President Eisenhower had his own Yellow Jacket. Roy and McDerby appeared on numerous radio and TV shows promoting the company. In 1956 Yellow Jacket expanded by erecting a new facility near Lake Texoma with Roy turning the first shovel of dirt. McDerby eventually returned to his Louisiana home. Roy stayed until the firm went under in 1961.

The old plant, which has been closed for 40 years, is still in Denison just off Hwy. 91 at the Denison Dam. As resident Billy Holcomb explains, "It's not really a tourist attraction but people can go by the old plant. Which few people realize Roy Rogers was VP of."

★★

Audie Murphy American Cotton Museum

The Audie Murphy American Cotton Museum in Greenville contains much of Audie's memorabilia…a 3rd grade report card, a plaque from the Texas Music Hall of Fame, scrapbooks, oil paintings, family photos, photos of former houses Audie lived in and various other exhibits and personal effects. Much of the material once housed at the Greenville Public Library is now at this museum as the library was not large enough to accommodate and care for the expanding exhibits.

Founded in 1987 as the

Audie Murphy display at the Audie Murphy American Cotton Museum.

Hunt County Museum to preserve the history of Hunt County, the museum was expanded in the mid '90s. The Audie Murphy section was dedicated in 1998.

An 11 foot bronze statue of Audie Murphy, by artist Gordon Thomas, will sit on a five foot granite base.

Open 10-5 Tuesday through Saturday. Located at 600 I-30 East in Greenville. (903) 450-4502.

A Texas State Historical Marker is located in front of the old post office on Lee Street in downtown Greenville. Audie Murphy joined the Army in this building on June 20, 1942.

The X indicates where Audie Murphy was born on the W. R. Boles farm near Greenville.

Audie Murphy Birthplace

Although the house in which Audie Murphy was born in Hunt County no longer stands, there is a Texas State Roadside Historical Marker designating his birthplace on U.S. 69 about eight miles north of Greenville and a mile and a half south of Kingston. The marker indicates Murphy was born on the W. R. Boles farm, 400 yards east of the marker near a large tree. What was once a field of cotton during Audie's youth is now a field of grass.

Audie Murphy—Farmersville

Farmersville was the town listed as Audie Murphy's hometown during WWII because of his sister Corinne's residence there. Murphy was actually born on a farm in rural Hunt County, in which Farmersville is located.

Audie Murphy Memorial Plaza in the middle of the town square was dedicated in Farmersville on May 28, 1973, the second anniversary of his death. A verse of Audie's poem, "Dusty Old Helmet, Rusty Old Gun", is inscribed on one side of a marble tablet in the plaza. A dedication to Audie is inscribed on the other side.

Audie Murphy Plaza was erected where the speaker's platform stood on June 15, 1945, when the entire town turned out to welcome Lt. Murphy home from Europe.

Audie Murphy Memorial Highway (Rt. 69) runs through Farmersville, Celeste and Greenville in Hunt County. It also includes Audie L. Murphy Memorial Overpass.

The Charles J. Pike Memorial Library (203 Orange St.) in Farmersville has Audie Murphy film posters and an ex-

Audie Murphy Memorial Highway runs through Farmersville.

tensive collection of newspaper clippings and photographs.

★★★

Audie Murphy Memorial Park

In 1926 when Audie Murphy was about two years old, his family moved from the Boles farm near Kingston, where Audie was born, to the John Warren farm east of Celeste (on Rt. 69 north of Greenville) where they lived for a few years. Following another move, the family lived on the Nickles farm west of Celeste. Still later, from 1933-1937 the family actually lived in the town of Celeste so the children could attend school.

Audie Murphy Memorial Park, with a flower garden, flags and a large bronze plaque, is in Celeste. There is a Texas State Historical Marker on U.S. 69 on the eastern edge of Celeste.

★★★

Tex Ritter Museum

The Tex Ritter Museum and Texas Country Music Hall of Fame is located on the second floor of the historical Hawthorne-Clabaugh-Patterson House which also serves as the Chamber of Commerce in Carthage. Here you'll learn about not only Tex Ritter but the musical legacy of the Lone Star state.

A huge 8 ft. tall bronze of Tex playing guitar beside his horse, White Flash, is erected outside the museum. The artist is Bob Harness. The museum itself houses several Ritter guitars, two saddles, several guns and holsters, shotguns, rifles and other personal items.

Inducted into the Texas Country Music Hall of Fame besides Ritter, have been Dale Evans, songwriter Cindy Walker (she wrote nearly all the music for the Russell Hayden/Bob Wills Bs at Columbia as well as "Blue Canadian Rockies" and others for Gene Autry, etc.), Bob Wills, Stuart Hamblen and Gene Autry.

Located two blocks from downtown Carthage, 300 W. Panola St. Open Monday-Friday 8:30-4:30, Saturday 1-4. (903) 693-6634.

Bronze of Tex Ritter and White Flash outside the Ritter Museum and Texas Country Music Hall of Fame.

★★★

Tex Ritter Windmill Museum

Tex Ritter, although born in Murvual (about 12 miles from Carthage in eastern Texas), attended his last couple of years of high school in the Dutch Community of Nederland (near Beaumont) after his family relocated there. In "Sing, Cowboy, Sing," Tex tries to cheer up his pal Al St. John by saying, "Do you know what I tell folks down in my home town of Nederland, Texas, when they get to feeling blue?" Then he sings "Cowboy Medicine."

After Tex began touring regularly in the '30s, he always tried to visit family members in Nederland. He often sang at the First Methodist Church there. It was in Nederland he chose to be buried.

Nederland honors Tex at the Windmill Museum in Tex Ritter Park (1500 Boston Ave.) with a large display on the first floor that showcases a suit, hat, boots and other items owned by Tex. Many photos, songbooks, etc. are also in the display presented by his family. Free admission. Open 1-5 Tuesday-Sunday from March to August, Thursday-Sunday from September to February. (409) 722-0279.

This Windmill welcomes you to Tex Ritter Park in Nederland.

★★★

Stuart Hamblen

Singer/songwriter/sometime Republic actor Stuart Hamblen ("Arizona Kid," "In Old Monterey." "Sombrero Kid," "King of the Forest Rangers" etc.) is immortalized with a plaque honoring his memory in Jefferson.

It reads:

STUART HAMBLEN
1908–1989
SONGWRITER
Remembered for his many songs and hymns, including
"This Ole House," "Until Then" and
"It Is No Secret (What God Can Do)."
Born in nearby Kellyville, Texas,
Marion County, October 20, 1908
Died in Los Angeles, California, March 8, 1989

The plaque is on a pedestal in the city park area at the corner of Market and Lafayette.

Incidentally, some of Hamblen's memorabilia occupies a corner of the Roy Rogers/Dale Evans Museum in Victorville, California. Hamblen was a close friend of the Rogers family and appeared in several of Roy's B-westerns.

★★★

UTAH

St. George

It was Mormon prophet and colonizer Brigham Young who saw the possibilities in the rugged area known today as St. George and sent 309 families to settle the area in 1861. Today, the city in the far southwestern corner of the state boasts over 45,000 residents.

For filming, the area became infamous when John Wayne's "The Conqueror" was shot there only four months after several nuclear bomb tests had been set off in the Nevada desert. There have been claims over the years that numerous cast and crew members on "The Conqueror" died of cancer caused by the blasts—including Wayne, Susan Hayward, Pedro Armendariz, director Dick Powell and Agnes Moorehead. Almost half the residents of St. George developed cancer in the years since the Yucca Flats A-tests.

St. George is a historical gold mine of old homes, churches, buildings and roads that lead to crumbling, hidden-away ghost towns, including Grafton off Hwy. 9 near Rockville (east of St. George). This is where Katherine Ross' farmhouse, in "Butch Cassidy and the Sundance Kid," site of the "Raindrops Keep Falling On My Head" musical interlude in which Paul Newman rides a bicycle, was shot. The house, built for the film, still stands.

Stop by the Chamber of Commerce, 97 East St. George Blvd. for more specific information on filming sites.

Sampling of Westerns Filmed in ST. GEORGE

- Painted Stallion ('37)—Ray "Crash" Corrigan (serial)
- Toughest Man In Arizona ('52)—Vaughn Monroe
- Road to Denver ('55)—John Payne
- Santa Fe Passage ('55)—John Payne
- A Man Alone ('55)—Ray Milland
- Run of the Arrow ('57)—Rod Steiger
- They Came to Cordura ('59)—Gary Cooper
- Seven Ways From Sundown ('60)—Audie Murphy
- Six Black Horses ('62)—Audie Murphy
- Bullet For a Badman ('64)—Audie Murphy
- The Appaloosa ('66)—Marlon Brando
- Gunpoint ('66)—Audie Murphy
- Butch Cassidy and the Sundance Kid ('69)—Paul Newman / Robert Redford
- Jeremiah Johnson ('72)—Robert Redford

★★★

Kanab

Kanab, in southern Utah near the Arizona border, clearly deserves its reputation as the "Little Hollywood" of non-California western filming sites, owing its significant place in film history largely to the efforts of three men: Chauncey (Chaunce), Gronway and Whitney (Whit) Parry.

Chaunce, the eldest of the Parry brothers, and Gronway first attracted outsiders to the area in 1916, when they began hauling tourists by bus from Cedar City to Bryce Canyon, Zion National Monument, the north rim of the Grand Canyon and other scenic wonders of the region. Eventually, the brothers turned to the ultimately more lucrative venture of bringing moviemakers to the area.

Tom Mix starred in the first title filmed at Kanab, "Deadwood Coach" ('24). According to local lore, Mix convinced the Parrys to induce other production crews to come there as well. Armed with photos, including aerial shots, Chaunce Parry went to Hollywood for meetings with studio executives, persuading them he and his brothers could not only provide splendid vistas and unusually varied terrain, but also livestock, wagons and other rolling stock, ample lodging, a large company of willing extras, even Paiute and Navajo Indians from nearby reservations.

Soon, movie crews were beating a path to Kanab. Portions of John Wayne's "Big Trail" ('30) are said to have been filmed there, although it's difficult to spot distinctive Kanab locales in that title. MGM took a crew to Kanab and Zion for the Wallace Beery entry "Bad Man of Brimstone" ('37). The same studio did some Kanab shooting for Robert Taylor's "Billy the Kid" ('41), although much of that film used Monument Valley and Sedona, among other locales, and the actors' scenes were mainly shot in front of a process screen rather than on location.

In the late '30s and early '40s, Kanab played host to a number of B-westerns, including Tim Holt's "Wagon Train" and Bob Steele's "Feud of the Range," for which Chaunce and Whit Parry, albeit with their nicknames misspelled, are listed in the credits as associate producers.

Wartime restrictions hardly dampened Hollywood's enthusiasm for the area as Republic brought a crew to Kanab for the Duke's "In Old Oklahoma" ('43) and Fox filmed exteriors there for Joel McCrea's "Buffalo Bill" ('44).

In '30-'31, the Parrys built Parry Lodge. About that same time, Guy Chamberlain, whose family later purchased Moqui Cavern, a filming site north of town, opened the Kanab Hotel. An abandoned gasoline station was converted into a casting office.

When Chaunce Parry was killed in an automobile accident on Kanab's main street, Gronway and Whit continued as Hollywood's principal Kanab contacts. Gronway provided transportation and food for casts and crews, while Whit ran the lodge. At times, Gronway also supervised construction of replicas of period rolling stock, such as those used in Joel McCrea's "The Outriders" ('50).

Kanab Canyon. This road can be distinctly seen in "Red Canyon" ('49) with Howard Duff, among others.

By 1949, with a population in Kanab of only 1,365, movie companies were spending an estimated $20,000 a day on shoots. Cowboys were getting $55 daily, citizen extras $35 and children $10.

Much filming was done in area canyons, especially winding Kanab Canyon a few miles north of town off Hwy 89, with its overhanging house rock formations and other familiar settings.

Another frequent site was Johnson Canyon,

Johnson Canyon townset.

about five miles east of Kanab, which featured more even terrain surrounded by beautiful white cliffs.

Put to extensive use was Paria Canyon, farther east from Kanab and surrounded by hills and gorgeous cliffs of brown, red and white hues, includes at one point a winding narrow canyon floor bordered by steep cliffs. The steep cliffs and canyon floor of Paria Canyon were used effectively in "Buffalo Bill" and Tim Holt's "Wagon Train", among other titles. (Turn north off Hwy. 89 about 30 miles east of Kanab. Go 4.7 miles down in the canyon to find the rebuilt buildings of Paria.)

About a mile down Johnson Canyon Road to the right is a distinctive natural landmark serial fans find especially familiar. Eagle Gate, an arch rock used first perhaps in George O'Brien's "Dude Ranger" as the entrance to a cattle rustling hideout, was featured in Chapter 4 of "Great Adventures of Wild Bill Hickok", as well as chapters of "Overland With Kit Carson."

Paria townset.

The overhanging (or house rock) formations in Kanab Canyon, as well as similar ones in Paria Canyon and House Rock Valley southeast of Kanab, also figured prominently in the Elliott serials and other titles. Kanab Canyon's most distinctive house rock formation and an adjoining corral were given prominent play not only in the "Carson" serial but also in Rod Cameron's "Ride the Man Down" ('53), which includes a rare overhead shot of the corral area. Another cliff overlooking Kanab Canyon furnished the setting for the opening scene of Clayton Moore's "The Lone Ranger" ('56), while the canyon itself hosted exciting fight scenes in that title as well as many other films.

The Coral Pink Sand Dunes northwest of Kanab were another filming site, whether for desert epics such as "Arabian Nights" and "Sudan," or westerns, including "The Outriders."

One of the many slot canyons dotting the countryside, chiseled into rock by water over millions of years, extremely narrow and winding with steep sides, was used in 1956's "Lone Ranger" feature. It's located at the end of a winding dirt road in Red Canyon, just north of the north entrance to Kanab Canyon (now home to the Best Friends Animal Sanctuary).

Three Lakes, a collection of tiny lakes on the left side of Hwy. 89 a few miles north of Kanab, was yet another area star (just past Moqui Cavern).

The most beautiful lake in the area is Aspen Mirror Lake at Duck Creek, an hour or so drive northwest of Kanab. (Locals can direct you.) Mirror Lake, as well as the area's white barked aspen trees, meadows and nearby Strawberry Point and Navajo Lake, probably made their first film appearance in Henry Fonda's colonial epic "Drums Along the Mohawk" ('39) but were also put to scenic use in "Black Bart" ('48), "Oh, Susanna" ('51), "My Friend Flicka" ('43), "Best of the Bad Men" ('51) and "The Outriders," among other titles.

According to ace stuntman and Kanab resident Neil Summers, the tiny village of Alton, north of Kanab near the entrance to Zion National Park, appeared in Joel McCrea's "Ramrod."

Other sites in the Kanab vicinity appeared in pictures, too. The Kaibab Forest and Jacob Lake near the north rim of the Grand Canyon (which appears itself in the climax to "Dude Ranger"), as well as House Rock Valley east of there were often utilized.

Until enclosed and converted into a gift shop, Moqui Cavern, 9 miles north of Kanab on the right, also appeared in features and episodes of such TV series as "Death Valley Days". The cave, now a tourist stop/museum displays wood carvings of Roy Rogers and Ronald Reagan.

Bottomland just north of Kanab on the left side of Hwy 89 served as a military encampment for "Bugles In the Afternoon" ('52).

Kanab streets and other sites made occasional film appearances as well. Main Street had a brief role in "Dude Ranger", the local rodeo grounds with bleachers embedded in a hillside (now the site of the local hospital) was used in "Calamity Jane and Sam Bass" ('49) as well as "Red Canyon" ('49). Parry Lodge itself, sporting its actual name, appeared in "Girl in Black Stockings" ('57).

Located at 89 East Center St., the walls of Parry Lodge's restaurant are studded with over 150 photos (most of them autographed) of the stars that worked in the area over the years—Randolph Scott, Roy Barcroft, Walter Reed, Fess Parker, John Smith, Gabby Hayes, Clayton Moore, Ben Johnson, John Wayne, Jack Elam, Glenn Ford, Johnny Western, Gregory Peck, James Arness, Rhonda Fleming, etc. Many of the cabins at Parry Lodge are named for the stars who stayed there—John Wayne, Arlene Dahl, James Garner and Robert Taylor for example. John Wayne stabled his horse in the Barn behind Parry's Lodge, now converted into a playhouse. Call (800) 748-4104 for reservations.

The Tourism Center and Film Commission across the street from Parry Lodge at 78 S. 100 East is another valuable stop to pickup a list of films made in the area as well as stills and posters from many of the films on display. (800) 733-5263.

Production companies did not rely entirely on natural locales. They also built a variety of movie sets. Among the first were the fort set, houses and out-buildings constructed at Duck Creek and Strawberry Point for "Drums Along the Mohawk"

Another fort, first built probably for "Buffalo Bill," was set in Johnson Canyon, on the left of the current road there, about a mile

Fort Kanab today as seen looking through the remains of the main gate.

north of the only remaining Kanab area street set which is on the right.

The Kanab fort set, which is most familiar to movie and TV fans, was Ft. Kanab itself. First built for "Pony Express" ('53) and situated on private property southwest of town, it also appeared in "Yellow Tomahawk" ('54), "Fort Yuma" ('55), "Quincannon, Frontier Scout" ('56), "Fort Bowie" ('58), Glenn Ford's "The Long Ride Home" (aka "A Time for Killing") ('67) and Don Knotts' "The Apple Dumpling Gang Rides Again" ('79), among other features, as well as in numerous TVers (e.g., "Boots and Saddles," "Daniel Boone").

The locations of town and settlement sets, used in "Wagon Train", "Badge of Marshal Brennan" etc. are generally more difficult to pinpoint. However. two area town sets are easily identified. A western street set in Johnson Canyon, which may have first been constructed for Robert Taylor's "Westward, the Women" ('52) and also appeared the next year in "Pony Express," was later enlarged and remains relatively intact. "Gunsmoke" used it for the two-parter "Island In the Desert" as well as other features and TV series, including color entries for the "Lone Ranger" TV show.

Dale Robertson was inducted into the Kanab Walk of Fame in 2001.

South of the town set is the site where the Macahan Ranch for the "How the West Was Won" TV pilot, another James Arness project, once stood.

A town set stood for years in Paria Canyon

as well. Apparently first built for Frank Sinatra's "Sergeants Three" ('62), that set also appeared in James Garner is "Duel at Diablo" ('66) and Jack Nicholson's "Ride in the Whirlwind" and "The Shooting" ('66), but most notably in Clint Eastwood's "The Outlaw Josey Wales" ('76). Unused apparently after the Eastwood shoot, the Paria set became so dilapidated it was recently torn down and replaced with several replicas of the original buildings. Several Paria structures were moved and are now on display at Kanab's Frontier Movie Town (297 West Center) along with buildings used in "One Little Indian" and "Outlaw Josey Wales" that were moved from Kanab Canyon.

A barn still standing at the base of one of Kanab Canyon's overhanging house rocks was originally built for "Fort Dobbs."

At one place on Center St. in Kanab are several plaques mounted on 3 ft. steel pedestals honoring stars who worked there over the years—Tom Mix, Ben Johnson, Dale Robertson, Robert Fuller, Buck Taylor and the cast of "Gunsmoke," producer Howard Koch, director Earl Bellamy and Ronald Reagan. More are added each year during an annual film festival.

Sampling of Westerns Filmed in KANAB

- Deadwood Coach ('24)—Tom Mix
- Bad Man of Brimstone ('37)—Wallace Beery
- Dude Ranger ('34)—George O'Brien
- Feud of the Range ('39)—Bob Steele
- Wagon Train ('40)—Tim Holt
- Fargo Kid ('40)—Tim Holt
- Westbound Stage ('40)—Tex Ritter
- Roll Wagons Roll ('40)—Tex Ritter
- Great Adventures of Wild Bill Hickok ('38)—Bill Elliott (serial)
- Overland With Kit Carson ('39)—Bill Elliott (serial)
- In Old Oklahoma ('43)—John Wayne
- Desperadoes ('43)—Randolph Scott
- Thunderhead, Son of Flicka ('45)—Roddy McDowall
- Red Canyon ('49)—Howard Duff
- Stallion Canyon ('49)—Ken Curtis
- Sierra ('50)—Audie Murphy
- The Outriders ('50)—Joel McCrea
- Oh, Susanna ('51)—Rod Cameron
- Cattle Drive ('51)—Joel McCrea
- Westward the Women ('52)—Robert Taylor
- Ride, Vaquero! ('53)—Robert Taylor
- Ride the Man Down ('53)—Rod Cameron
- Pony Express ('53)—Charlton Heston
- Yellow Tomahawk ('54)—Rory Calhoun
- Lone Ranger ('56)—Clayton Moore
- Stagecoach To Fury ('56)—Forrest Tucker
- Lone Ranger (TV): Ghost Canyon ('56)
- Ghost Town ('56)—John Smith
- Tomahawk Trail ('57)—Chuck Connors
- Copper Sky ('57)—Jeff Morrow
- Dragoon Wells Massacre ('57)—Barry Sullivan
- Raiders of Old California ('57)—Jim Davis
- Lone Ranger (TV): Quarter Horse War ('56)
- Lone Ranger (TV): White Hawk's Decision ('56)
- Badge of Marshal Brennan ('57)—Jim Davis
- Dalton Girls ('57)—John Russell
- Revolt at Fort Laramie ('57)—Gregg Palmer
- Boots and Saddles (TV)—series ('57-'58)
- Fort Bowie ('58)—Ben Johnson
- Fort Dobbs ('58)—Clint Walker
- Sergeants 3 ('62)—Frank Sinatra
- Fort Courageous ('65)—Don Barry
- Convict Stage ('65)—Don Barry
- Branded (TV): opening scene to series ('65-'66)
- Duel At Diablo ('66)—James Garner
- Bandolero ('68)—Dean Martin
- MacKenna's Gold ('69)—Gregory Peck
- Death Valley Days (TV): How To Beat a Badman ('69)
- One Little Indian ('73)—James Garner
- Gunsmoke (TV): Island In the Desert ('74)
- Outlaw Josey Wales ('76)—Clint Eastwood
- How the West Was Won (TV): series ('77-'79)

★★★

Monument Valley

Monument Valley is simply breathtaking! John Ford's movie location home-away-from-home for "Stagecoach," "My Darling Clementine," "Fort Apache," "The Searchers" and others was a Piute Indian Reservation in 1921 when Harry and Leone (nicknamed "Mike") Goulding wandered into the valley searching for some of their lost sheep. The land was not for sale for private ownership until two years later when the state of Utah offered the Piutes more fertile land further north and opened Monument Valley to homesteading in 1923. Harry quickly staked out claim to 640 acres at a paltry fifty cents an acre. $320 to own one of the most impressive parcels of territory in the U.S. The museum is open daily April through October.

Captain Brittle's headquarters in "She Wore A Yellow Ribbon" with John Wayne still stands today adjacent to the main lodge at Monument Valley.

Over the ensuing years the couple established a trading post for the Navajo Indians of the region. In 1927, they built a two-story trading post which still stands today as a museum that traces the history of the valley and houses dozens of movie artifacts including the saloon doors from "She Wore a Yellow Ribbon." The building itself was used as the cavalry post in "She Wore a Yellow Ribbon." The nearby Captain Brittle's cabin is a set from "She Wore a Yellow Ribbon," originally Goulding's potato cellar.

The tale goes that Harry Goulding learned through a friend that John Ford was searching for a new and picturesque location in which to film his upcoming "Stagecoach". So, in 1938, Goulding traveled to Hollywood and eventually convinced Ford Monument Valley was what he needed. The rest is history.

Virtually unchanged from its glory days, you will see the dusty dirt road towards El Capitan peak used in "Stagecoach" and "My Darling Clementine". The town of Tomb-

I'm admiring the vistas of spectacular Monument Valley on (John) Ford's Point.

stone for "Clementine" was constructed on the Valley floor only a few hundred yards in front of the original trading post. It stood for nearly five years before being torn down. You'll find distinct and memorable formations such as the Mittens, Rock Door Mesa (just above the new Goulding's Lodge), the Totem Pole, Camel Butte, Big Indian, Three Sisters, the North Window, Mexican Hat Rock and especially Ford's Point. (In "The Searchers" Wayne and others lower Jeffery Hunter over the edge so he can enter the Indian camp.)

Reservations at the on-site Goulding's Lodge should be made well in advance as it stays booked up with tour buses and other visitors. Otherwise, you'll need to stay in Kayenta, Arizona, about 20 miles south. Goulding's operates half day and all day tours into Monument Valley in open air trucks or jeeps. All day tours depart at 9am for eight hours of adventure. Half day tours depart at 9am, 1:30 and 4pm and last 3 hours. One or the other is recommended as your first course of action to acquaint yourself with "the lay of the land". Your next day should be an investigation of specific sites on your own. Air tours are also available. There is a laundromat, car wash, Stagecoach Restaurant (where you can get a 16 oz. John Wayne cut sirloin), pool, gift shop and even campgrounds adjacent to the Lodge and motel rooms. (435) 727-3353 or 3287. Write Goulding's Tours, PO Box 1, Monument Valley, Utah 84536. Open April through October.

Monument Valley is just off Hwy. 163 in the southeastern corner of Utah.

 Sampling of Westerns Filmed in MONUMENT VALLEY

- Stagecoach ('39)—John Wayne
- Kit Carson ('40)—Jon Hall
- My Darling Clementine ('46)—Henry Fonda
- Fort Apache ('48)—John Wayne
- She Wore a Yellow Ribbon ('49)—John Wayne
- Wagonmaster ('50)—Ben Johnson
- Rio Grande ('50)—John Wayne
- The Searchers ('56)—John Wayne
- How the West Was Won ('62)—John Wayne
- Cheyenne Autumn ('64)—Richard Widmark
- The Villain ('79)—Arnold Schwarzenegger
- Legend of the Lone Ranger ('81)—Klinton Spilsbury

★★

Moab

The Moab area has been a filming location since 1949 when John Ford came to the sleepy little town in eastern Utah to film "Wagonmaster" with Ben Johnson. Since then, literally hundreds of films and TV shows have been lensed in the area, incorporating a vast array of locations.

In fact, because the entire area is so picturesque, filmmakers were all over the area from Professor Valley to the Colorado River, from White's Ranch to Castle Valley, from Dead Horse Point State Park to Arches National Park—and all points in between. Therefore, your first stop needs to be the Moab Visitors Center at 805 N. Main Hwy. (Hwy. 191) in Moab. (800) 635-6622. Or the Moab Film Commission at 50 E. Center #1, (801) 259-6388, to pick up a copy of the "Moab Area Movie Locations Auto Tour" brochure. Also, if any copies are left, purchase Bette Stanton's WHERE GOD PUT THE WEST, a book on Moab and Monument Valley movie history. This brochure and book will pinpoint and guide you to specific locations. Incidentally, Bette's father put together Kanab Picture Corp. and produced "Stallion Canyon" ('49) with Ken Curtis, filmed in the Kanab area where Bette went to school.

I'm dwarfed by the magnificent scenery of Moab. This shot was taken in 1994, right after "Geronimo" was filmed here.

The Moab to Monument Valley Film and Movie Museum is scheduled to open in the Red Cliffs Adventure Lodge (and Restaurant) in Moab by the Fall of 2002. Many of the dozens of westerns filmed in the immediate area are already displayed in the lobby and other areas of the lodge. The Movie Museum room itself will represent dozens of Moab-lensed titles. Mile 14 on Scenic Hwy. 128, 16 miles east of Moab on the Colorado River. (800) 325-6171.

 Sampling of Westerns Filmed in MOAB

- Wagonmaster ('50)—Ben Johnson
- Rio Grande ('50)—John Wayne
- Battle at Apache Pass ('52)—Jeff Chandler
- Border River ('53)—Joel McCrea
- Siege at Red River ('53)—Van Johnson
- Taza, Son of Cochise ('53)—Rock Hudson
- Smoke Signal ('54)—Dana Andrews
- Fort Dobbs ('56)—Clint Walker
- Warlock ('58)—Henry Fonda
- Gold of the Seven Saints ('60)—Clint Walker
- Comancheros ('61)—John Wayne
- Cheyenne Autumn ('63)—Richard Widmark
- Rio Conchos ('64)—Richard Boone
- Wild Rovers ('66)—William Holden
- Alias Smith and Jones (TV): series ('72)
- Against A Crooked Sky ('75)—Richard Boone
- Geronimo ('93)—Jason Patric
- City Slickers II ('93)—Billy Crystal

★★

Heber Valley Railroad

The Great Western Railway is a 61 mile common carrier headquartered in Loveland, Colorado. Purchasing diesel engines starting in 1951, they eventually sold off all the steam locomotives.

The Heber Valley Railroad in Heber City (southeast of Salt Lake City on Hwy. 40/189) maintains the still operable ex-Great Western Railway #75 locomotive, built in 1907. Trains leave daily for a two hour ride at 11am. A few of its 15 film appearances are "The Professionals" ('66), "Breakheart Pass" ('76), "Centennial" mini-series ('78) and "Far and Away" ('92).

Visit the Heber Valley Historic Railroad at 450 S. 600 W. in Heber City. (435) 654-5601.

★★

VIRGINIA

Roy Rogers Restaurants
Roy Rogers Restaurants still operational. (See details under Maryland.)

4707 Columbia Pike Arlington, Virginia (703) 521-4692	1100 South Hayes Street Arlington, Virginia (703) 415-4242
1506 Belleview Blvd. Alexandria, Virginia (703) 660-1264	7265 Arlington Blvd. Falls Church, Virginia (703) 560-9442
Merrifield Plaza Merrifield, Virginia (703) 560-3570	11170 South Lakes Drive Reston, Virginia (703) 620-2249
451 South King Street Leesburg, Virginia (703) 777-5551	540 East Market Street Leesburg, Virginia (703) 777-6322

★★★

The most decorated hero of WWII, Audie Murphy, is buried at Arlington National Cemetery.

Arlington National Cemetery

Audie Murphy was buried with full military honors at Arlington National Cemetery June 7, 1971. A large black oak tree towers above the gravesite just west of the Amphitheater of the Tomb of the Unknown Soldier, near Memorial Drive. In 1973 a flagstone walk was laid from Memorial Drive to Audie's grave (#366-11, section 46) with a post and chain link fence erected around the walk and gravesite to provide a viewing platform for visitors.

Arlington National Cemetery is on Memorial Drive on the Virginia side of the Arlington Memorial Bridge.

★★

True Grit Restaurant

The True Grit Restaurant in Dumfries opened in 2000 and contains a host of John Wayne memorabilia. Their sign features a painting of the Duke wearing a "True Grit" eye patch. Owner Frances Dent's father, who had a rental car business in the '40s, once rented a Packard to Wayne. When the car broke down, the two men exchanged some heated words, then became very good friends. That's when her father started collecting the Wayne memorabilia now filling the restaurant.

On Route 1 in Dumfries, north of Fredericksburg. (703) 221-1064.

★★

Audie Murphy Monument

Three years and a day after Audie Murphy was killed in a tragic plane crash, the government issued a permit to VFW Post 5311 of Christiansburg for a monument on Brushy Mountain in the Jefferson National Forest where Murphy's plane crashed. The plane went down on Brushy Mountain a few miles from the West Virginia line in Craig County, 15 miles southwest of New Castle, 20 miles west of Roanoke.

Audie, 46, and four business associates were flying from Atlanta to Martinsville on May 28, 1971, to visit a manufacturing plant in which Audie was interested in investing. The last contact from the plane was a call to Roanoke asking about weather conditions on that rainy, foggy morning.

Following the fatal crash, people came up the mountain and took the wreckage away piece by piece as souvenirs. Many of those pieces are now at the VFW in Christiansburg.

Because the accident was on government land, it took some time for the granite rock monument in Audie's memory to be erected on the Appalachian ridge. It was dedicated on Veteran's Day, 1974.

For several years afterward, nobody could get to it because a nearby landowner refused public access across his property. Eventually, the Forest Service bought some land and right-of-way access, realigning the Appalachian Trail to swing by the monument.

★★

WASHINGTON

Yakima Canutt

Stunt legend Yakima Canutt is at home on the third and fourth level of Hickman Boot and Saddlery in Colfax which features four full floors (10,000 sq. ft.) of working cowboy equipment. An Old West Museum with artifacts dating back to the 1860s is on the second floor. The Yak museum houses over 300 photos as well as posters and memorabilia of the legendary cowboy who began in silents and eventually won an Academy Award for his work on "Ben Hur" with Charlton Heston. Other personal items of Yak's are also included.

At 203 N. Main in Colfax, 60 miles south of Spokane on Hwy. 195. (888) 397-2022.

★★★

WISCONSIN

The Buck Jones Wild West Show wagon #49 is at Circus World. It dates to Buck's ill-fated 1929 season which folded after only 40 shows.

Circus World Museum

The Circus World Museum in Baraboo founded in 1959 holds the largest repository of big top memorabilia in the world. 149 circus wagons, railroad cars, route books, programs, photos, heralds and banners, posters, artifacts and extensive circus and wild west research material on the many celluloid cowboys who also rode the sawdust trail. There's the Ken Maynard Air Calliope used in Ken's 1936 show and later owned by Disney who presented it to Circus World. The Buck Jones Wild West Wagon #49 came from his 1929 season on the road. The show's equipment ended up at the Lancaster, Missouri, farm of Billie Hall, a circus dealer, who donated it and a Buck Jones baggage wagon to the museum. There's also Ken

Maynard's ticket wagon #130 and at least six varying types of wagons from the historic Miller Brothers 101 Ranch in Oklahoma. The authentic train cars owned by Circus World include some used by Tim McCoy.

There is an extensive library and research center, films, live circus performers, parades, calliope concerts and much more. Open mid-May to mid-September daily 9:30-6. 426 Water Street, Baraboo (north of Madison). (608) 356-8341.

The museum occupies the site of the original winter quarters of Ringling Brothers Circus from 1884-1918.

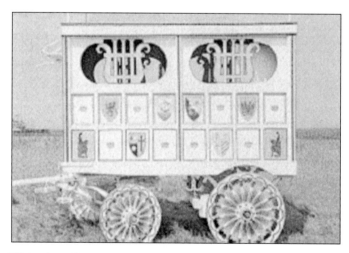

This Air Calliope originated with Ken Maynard's short-lived Diamond K Ranch Wild West Circus and Indian Congress of 1936. It's over 10 feet tall.

★★

WYOMING

Nelson Museum of the West

The Nelson Museum of the West in Cheyenne features 11,000 square feet of displays

including real west artifacts along with an array of western stars' personal items. Included are George Montgomery; a Tom Mix hat; Ken Maynard hat; Jock Mahoney hat, coat, spurs; Rex Allen coat, hat, boots, spurs; Guy Madison guns, spurs, boots; Richard Farnsworth; Roy Rogers boots; Gene Autry suit, hat and more.

Open Monday-Friday 8-noon and 1-5 September-May; 8-5 Monday-Saturday June-August. 1714 Carey Ave. in downtown Cheyenne. (307) 635-7670.

Only part of the excellent displays at the Nelson Museum.

★★

Mabel Strickland Cowgirl Museum

Mabel Strickland was an early rodeo star, beautiful, vivid and daring. Mabel was probably the most photographed cowgirl ever, inspiring the likes of Faye Blackstone and other female rodeo performers to enter the sport of rodeo. She and her husband, Hugh, who was a bronc rider, steer roper and rodeo producer, helped mold rodeo into the sport it is today. Mabel won recognition in relay racing, trick riding and steer roping, often competing alongside men. She was awarded the McAlpin Trophy as the all around cowgirl at Cheyenne Frontier Days and was crowned queen of the Pendleton Roundup in 1927. When films called, Mabel and her trick horse Sunday appeared in "Border Vengeance" with Reb Russell and "Custer's Last Stand" serial with her biggest role coming in "Rough Riding Ranger" ('35) with Rex Lease. Later in life, Mabel helped in the formation of the American Appaloosa Horse Association.

The Mabel Strickland Cowgirl Museum is being established in Cheyenne with not only Mabel's memorabilia but the records and collections of other special heroines. The present exhibits are at the Texas Trail Museum in Pine Bluffs, located at 3rd and Market.

(307) 245-3713.

★★

American Heritage Center University of Wyoming

The American Heritage Center (AHC) at the University of Wyoming (at Laramie) is a major research facility and repository of manuscripts, rare books and artifacts (including saddles donated by Hopalong Cassidy and the Cisco Kid). The AHC curently maintains more than 7,000 collections from such westerners as William Boyd, Tim McCoy, Barbara Stanwyck, director Frank McDonald and hundreds more. The AHC holds extraordinarily rich resources—scripts, promotional material, correspondence, industry records, contracts, musical scores—a researcher's dream. Photocopies of collections are available at reasonable fees. Contact Leslie Shores, Assistant Archivist/Reference at University of Wyoming, PO Box 3924, Laramie, Wyoming 82071. (307) 766-2582.

Hopalong Cassidy's saddle now resides at the American Heritage Center at the University of Wyoming.

Their 125 page "Guide To Popular Culture History Resources" booklet is available for a nominal fee (about $8).

Here is a listing of some of the more noteworthy western film related files maintained:

- Margaret Armen—scripts from her TV westerns "Big Valley," "Rifleman" etc.
- William Beaudine Sr.—scripts and miscellaneous material relating to this prolific director's career
- William Boyd—saddle, correspondence files, scripts for Hopalong Cassidy film, TV and radio productions, press kits and promotional material, product labels, toys and clothing, comic books and strips, scrapbooks, sheet music and phonograph records, layouts and photographs, extensive business files, ledgers, accounting reports, contracts, copyright documents. 192 boxes.
- Borden Chase—screenplays and outlines from "Red River," "Winchester 73" and numerous TV series.
- Frank Davis—scripts he wrote such as "Springfield Rifle".
- Albert Dekker—newspaper clips, correspondence, playbills, photos, scrapbook.
- Irving Gertz—composer. Scores to "Overland Pacific," "Lone Gun," "Top Gun" etc.
- Albert Glasser—composer for "Cisco Kid," "Hopalong Cassidy" TV series. Reel to reel tapes, music scores, cue sheets, correspondence, miscellaneous material.
- Walter Greene—composer, orchestrator. Much Gene Autry material.
- Percy Helton—scripts, correspondence, audio tapes of the noted character actor.
- Rochelle Hudson—co-starred in "Beyond the Rockies," "Scarlet River," "Konga, the Wild Stallion." Contracts, newspaper clips, photo albums, handwritten reminis-

cence, baby clothes.

- I. Stanford Jolley—audio tape interview, list of all films.
- Harris Katleman—scripts from TV's "The Rebel."
- Leon Klatzkin—scores for 10 episodes of "Gunsmoke."
- Gene Levitt—scripts to "Bat Masterson" etc.
- Pierce Lyden—manuscripts, correspondence, scrapbooks, serial scripts, miscellaneous material.
- Tim McCoy—contract files on his Wild West Show, movies and TV series, correspondence, financial files from the Wild West Show, research files, stills, scrapbooks.
- Frank McDonald—correspondence, promotional material, scripts, stills, 5 scrapbooks, set plans for "Wyatt Earp" episodes, manuscript for his unpublished autobiography for the noted director.
- Dudley Dean McGaughey—radio scripts for "Gene Autry," "Hopalong Cassidy."
- Robert Pirosh—scripts, research material, clippings, stills from such series as "Laramie."
- Maudie Prickett—character actress in dozens of B-westerns and TV shows. Correspondence, clippings, scrapbooks, scripts.
- Duncan Renaldo—correspondence, legal papers relating to citizenship, "Cisco Kid" TV and radio scripts, publicity material for "Cisco Kid," contracts, costumes and a saddle.
- Barbara Stanwyck—scripts, her Oscar and Emmy Awards.
- Paula Stone—appeared in "Hopalong Cassidy" and two Dick Foran westerns. Two radio interviews on audio, clippings, photos, home movies, scrapbooks.
- Al Ward—scripts to "Rawhide," "Virginian," others.
- Marie Windsor—correspondence, articles, photos.

Two of the biggest collections of personal memorabilia at the American Heritage Center at the University of Wyoming are from Duncan "Cisco Kid" Renaldo and William "Hopalong Cassidy" Boyd. This historic meeting of the two took place in the early '50s when both were quite popular on TV.

★★

Medicine Bow

From Laramie take U.S. 30-287 and follow the original route of the historic Lincoln Highway as it loops through the community of Medicine Bow, the town and wide open spaces that inspired Owen Wister to write his famous 1902 western novel THE VIRGINIAN, which was adapted into three films and a TV series. Here is cowboy country at its best, little changed from those earlier rawhide days Wister lived and recorded. According to legend, one-time deputy sheriff of Carbon County, James Davis, was playing poker when one of the other players made an insulting remark about Davis' immediate canine ancestry. Davis' reply was reportedly, "When you call me that, smile." Wister, gathering material for his novel, overheard the remark and incorporated it into his book, immortalizing the phrase.

★★

Little Wind River

The famous scene of Indians crossing a river with bluffs in the background was filmed on the Little Wind River Indian Reservation, a few miles north of Lander in the west central part of the state.

The scenes were originally filmed for Tim McCoy's MGM silent, "War Paint ('26). They were later used in McCoy's "End of the Trail" ('32) at Columbia and turned up in stock footage countless times in westerns and serials.

Little Wind River area today.

Sampling of Westerns Filmed in LITTLE WIND RIVER

- War Paint ('26)—Tim McCoy
- End of the Trail ('32)—Tim McCoy (stock)
- Singing Vagabond ('35)—Gene Autry (stock)
- Overland Express ('38)—Buck Jones (stock)
- Roll Wagons Roll ('39)—Tex Ritter (stock)
- Overland With Kit Carson ('39)—Bill Elliott (serial) (stock)
- Prairie Schooners ('40)—Bill Elliott (stock)
- Pioneers of the West ('40)—3 Mesquiteers (stock)
- Frontier Fury (43)—Charles Starrett (stock)
- Law Rides Again ('43)—Trail Blazers (stock)
- Daredevils of the West ('43)—Allan Lane (serial) (stock)
- Little Big Horn ('51)—Lloyd Bridges (stock)
- Wild Dakotas ('56)—Bill Williams (stock)

★★

Jackson Hole

Jackson Hole's film history is discussed by historian Walt Farmer once a week from early June to October 1 on Thursday nights at 4:30pm at Jenny Lake Lodge in Jackson Hole. The primary western lensed there is "Shane" with Alan Ladd. Other films include "The Big Sky," "Close Encounters of the Third Kind," "Bad Man of Wyoming," "The Wild North," "Jubal," "Spencer's Mountain," "Mountain Man," "Any Which Way You Can", "The Big Trail" (where the wagons were lowered down the sheer slope), "Three Bad Men" and Tex Ritter's "Down the Wyoming Trial". Some 30 films in all were made in the area and Farmer is available, with advance notice, to take you (or your group) on a guided eight hour tour (with a lunch break). Based on your desire and capabilities, you can hike to several location sites including the "Shane" Cemetery Hill/townsite/Starrett home-

Although in considerable disrepair, this still-standing house was used as the Ernie Wright homestead in "Shane". It belonged to a local family that still lives in Jackson and wasn't built specifically for "Shane". It was used where Torrey (Elisha Cook Jr.) talks to Wright (Leonard Strong) who was fixing to move out. The Ryker boys drive some cattle through his place towards the mountains.

stead locations. $75 per adult, minimum of two adults plus entrance fee to Grand Teton National Park and Yellowstone (usually $20 per family). Children 10-18 are half price, under 10 are free. Half day tours are $50. Call (307) 690-6909 or (307) 733-2173 or write to Box 1821, Jackson, Wyoming 83001. Jackson is in the western part of Wyoming near the Idaho border.

★★

Buffalo Bill Historical Center

America's finest western museum, the Buffalo Bill Historical Center in Cody, 52 miles from Yellowstone National Park, offers four museums under one roof: The Whitney Gallery of Western Art, the Buffalo Bill Museum, the Plains Indian Museum and the Cody Firearms Museum. They safeguard historical spoils of the past and documents of the Old West unmatched by any other in the world. The Harold McCracken Research Library is a bibliophile's paradise.

The museum dates from 1917, when citizens of Cody wished to create a monument to their fellow townsmen. The museum has become an important center devoted to the American West. The Firearms Museum contains the world's most comprehensive collection of American arms. John Wayne was there in 1976 to help dedicate the Winchester Museum.

Open every day from May through September 30. Opening hours vary month to month. During March, April, October and November it is open on a partial schedule. 720 Sheridan Ave. (307) 587-4771.

Cody Wild West Days are held in Stampede Park each May with the real blowout coming the 4th of July weekend, which includes fireworks, a parade and the Cody Stampede, often said to the best outdoor rodeo in America.

A bronze Buffalo Bill welcomes visitors to his western museum in Cody.

★★

CANADA

Calgary Stampede

Relive the glory days when Hoot Gibson won the title of World Champion fancy roper in 1912 at the Calgary Stampede. Hoot Gibson returned to Calgary to make a silent western about the most famous rodeo in the world in 1925. To this day, every July the best of the best saddle up for a ground shaking showcase of world class rodeo action. Saddle bronc and bareback riding, bull riding, wild cow milking, rodeo clowns, the wild horse race, chuckwagon races as well as a 90 minute grandstand outdoor show. Hotel rooms are at a premium, so plan in advance.

For Stampede information contact Calgary Stampede, Box 1060, Station M, Calgary, Alberta, Canada T2P 2L8. (800) 661-1260

★★★

ORAL HISTORIES

Columbia University has an extensive oral history section with recordings and un-published interviews by Gene Autry, Walter Brennan, Richard Boone, Joel McCrea, John Wayne and others.

Other significant oral histories:

Yakima Canutt, Arizona Historical Society
Harry Carey Jr., Southern Methodist University
Donald Curtis, Southern Methodist University
Gene Autry, Southern Methodist University
Jack Elam, Arizona Historical Society
John Ford, American Film Institute
Earl Holliman, Southern Methodist University
Ben Johnson, Arizona Historical Society; Southern Methodist University
Adele Mara, Southern Methodist University
George Montgomery, Southern Methodist University
Hank Worden, Southern Methodist University
Jack Williams, Arizona Historical Society
John Wayne, Arizona Historical Society
Hal Taliaferro, Arizona Historical Society
Gil Perkins, Southern Methodist University
Peggy Stewart, Southern Methodist University
Dean Smith, Southern Methodist University
Ella Raines, Southern Methodist University

ANNUAL WESTERN FILM FESTIVALS

As dates for festivals change annually, you'll need to call for dates, brochures or flyers offered and accommodations.

★ The **Roy Rogers/Dale Evans Film Festival** is held in February at Victor Valley's Cinemark Valley Theater in Victorville, California. (760) 240-3330. Proceeds benefit Happy Trails Children's Foundation.

★ The **Williamsburg, Virginia, Film Festival** is held annually in February or March in this historic Colonial village. (757) 482-2490.

★ **Festival of the West** is in March at WestWorld in Scottsdale, Arizona, celebrating all facets of Western history and living. (602) 996-4387

★ **Santa Clarita (California) Cowboy Poetry and Music Festival.** Held annually at Gene Autry's Old Melody Ranch (formerly the Monogram Ranch) and William S. Hart Park. Usually in late March-early April. (800) 305-0755, (661) 286-4021.

★ Many western names are usually in attendance along with other film personalities, young and old, at the **Hollywood Collectors and Celebrities Show** at the Beverly Garland Hotel in North Hollywood, California. Held four times a year. (352) 683-5110.

★ **Bob Wills Day** in Turkey, Texas, is the last Saturday in April. (806) 423-1253.

★ **End of the Trail** celebrates cowboy action shooting. Many western film personalities are usually in attendance. (877) 411-SASS. Usually around April.

★ The **Hopalong Cassidy Festival** each May in Cambridge, Ohio, keeps his legend alive and well. William Boyd was born (June 5, 1895) in Hendrysburg, 25 miles east of Cambridge. Laura Bates (740) 826-4850.

★ **Gene Autry Days** are held in June at the Harden County Fairgrounds in Kenton, Ohio, where many of Gene's cap guns were manufactured. (419) 673-4131.

★ The **Roy Rogers Festival** rides around in early June in Portsmouth, Ohio, near Roy's birthplace of Duck Run. (740) 353-0900.

★ The **Buck Jones Film Festival** memorializes the great cowboy's life in Rochester, New York, each year. Dom Marafioti (716) 359-8987.

★ **Gabby Hayes Day** in Wellsville, New York, is the last Saturday of July. Hayes was born there May 7, 1885. (716) 593-5080.

★ The **Memphis Film Festival** began in 1972. Usually in late June or early July. PO Box 111347, Memphis, Tennessee 38111.

★ The long running **Charlotte Western Film Festival** is held annually in July in the picturesque North Carolina city. (704) 365-2368.

★ The western equivalent to the Academy Awards, the **Golden Boot Awards** are held in late July or early August at Merv Griffin's Beverly Hilton Hotel in Beverly Hills, California. Seats are $200 up. (818) 876-1900. Proceeds benefit the Motion Picture and Television Fund Home and Hospital.

★ **Western Legends Days** are in August in Kanab, Utah, where scores of westerns were filmed. Bonnie Riding (800) 644-5094.

★ **Iverson's Wild West Days** at the famous western film location ranch are usually held in September to raise money for the Happy Trails Children's Foundation. (805) 527-5343.

Two superb character players in westerns, Myron Healey and Walter Reed, were awarded Golden Boots an August 5, 2000.

★ **Gene Autry, Oklahoma, Film and Music Festival** is always in late September. Elvin Sweeten (580) 294-3047.

★ Visit the famous Alabama Rocks where so many westerns were lensed during the **Lone Pine, California, Film Festival** in October. (760) 876-9103.

★ **Rex Allen Days** are held in Rex's hometown of Willcox, Arizona, in October. (520) 384-4583 or (877) 234-4111.

★ The **Western Music Association** celebrates with hundreds of western musical acts, including many top name entertainers, every November. (520) 743-9794.

★ The guest list is usually smaller but the **Asheville, North Carolina, Film Festival** is well run. In November. (828) 524-5251.

★ **Audie Murphy Days** are held annually in Greenville, Texas. Contact the Audie Murphy American Cotton Museum, (903) 450-4502.

★ A **"Bonanza" Friendship Convention** is held irregularly at Lake Tahoe, Nevada. Box 135, 13170B Central Ave. SE, Albuquerque, New Mexico 87123.

BIBLIOGRAPHY

Autry, Gene. BACK IN THE SADDLE AGAIN. Doubleday, 1978.

Fernett, Gene. AMERICAN FILM STUDIOS: AN HISTORICAL ENCYCLOPEDIA. McFarland, 1988.

Jensen, Larry. THE MOVIE RAILROADS. Darwin Pub., 1981.

Magers, Boyd and Fitzgerald, Michael. WESTERNS WOMEN. McFarland, 1999.

Magers, Boyd. WESTERN CLIPPINGS #1-44 (1994-2001).

Norris, M. G. "Bud". THE TOM MIX BOOK. World of Yesterday, 1989.

Rainey, Buck. THE REEL COWBOY. McFarland, 1996.

Reeves, Tony. WORLDWIDE GUIDE TO MOVIE LOCATIONS. Acappella, 2001.

Rothel, David. AN AMBUSH OF GHOSTS. Empire, 1990.

Simpson, Col. Harold B. AUDIE MURPHY, AMERICAN SOLDIER. Alcor Pub. Co., 1982.

Stanton, Bette. WHERE GOD PUT THE WEST. Four Corners, 1994.

Yarbrough, Tinsley. THOSE GREAT B-WESTERN LOCATIONS. Western Clippings Pub., 1998.

INDEX

ABOUT THE AUTHOR

Boyd Magers has always felt he grew up in the right time and place for a full appreciation of all westerns...the late '40s–early '60s. Born in Kansas City, Kansas, he grew up with a western influence in Independence, Kansas (near where the Dalton and James Gangs rode) and Ponca City, Oklahoma (the site of the famed 101 Ranch). Beginning in late 1946 he attended the Beldorf in Independence and the Center in Ponca City, riding the range with the current crop of B-western heroes—Roy Rogers, Gene Autry, Rex Allen, Monte Hale, Tim Holt, Eddie Dean, Jimmy Wakely, Durango Kid, Johnny Mack Brown and others. By 1953 the new medium of television offered him a steady hour upon hour education in the early screen cowboys—Buck Jones, Bob Steele, Hoot Gibson, Ken Maynard, George O'Brien, Rex Bell, Tim McCoy and the rest. The early '50s was also the time for the dawning of the TV western—"Hopalong Cassidy", "Kit Carson", "Cisco Kid", "Stories of the Century" and the others which slowly matured into the so-called adult TV western of the late '50s early '60s, "Gunsmoke", "Cheyenne", "Sugarfoot", "Restless Gun" and dozens more. Therefore, he came to appreciate all eras of westerns.

Following military service in Korea, and during a fifteen year career in radio ('62-'77), Boyd began to contribute articles on westerns to publications such at COUNTRY STYLE and others.

In 1977 he established VideoWest which soon became the most respected source for western movies and TV episodes on video for over 25 years. From 1987 to 1994 he contributed a regular column on westerns to THE BIG REEL. Over the ensuing years he wrote regular columns or contributed articles to COUNTRY AND WESTERN VARIETY, UNDER WESTERN SKIES, CLASSIC IMAGES, FILM COLLECTOR'S REGISTRY, among several others. Over the years he's also provided research data and material to over 30 books and several TV/video documentaries. He wrote hundreds of B-western film reviews still being used annually in VIDEO MOVIE GUIDE.

In 1994 he began self-publishing WESTERN CLIPPINGS which has become *the* primary source and authority for western readers over the last nine years. He also publishes SERIAL REPORT.

Knowledgeable about all phases of western films, over the last twelve years Boyd has moderated over 100 western celebrity guest star discussion panels at western film festivals all over the country. In addition, Boyd currently has over 1,000 reviews and observations ("The Best and Worst of the West") of western films online at Chuck Anderson's Old Corral <www.surfnetinc.com/chuck/magers.htm>

Boyd's first book, WESTERNS WOMEN, was published by McFarland in 1999 and was followed in 2002 by LADIES OF THE WESTERN. SO YOU WANNA SEE COWBOY STUFF is his third book, soon to be followed by THE FILMS OF AUDIE MURPHY and THE FILMS OF GENE AUTRY.

Boyd is dedicated to preserving the rich heritage and enduring memories of small and big screen westerns and the people who populated them.

Boyd Magers

262

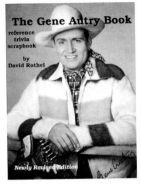

THE GENE AUTRY
Reference-Trivia-Scrapbook
BOOK
by David Rothel

HERE IS EVERYTHING YOU EVER WANTED TO KNOW ABOUT AMERICA'S FAVORITE SINGING COWBOY, GENE AUTRY!

- **One Man's Life—Another Man's Trivia.** A giant, comprehensive compendium of questions and answers—little-known facts about a well-known cowboy.
- **The Wit and Wisdom of Gene Autry.** Memorable quotes on a wide range of subjects.
- **The Films of Gene Autry.** A complete Filmography!
- **Gene Autry on Tour.** Gene, Champion, and a whole entourage of entertainers played as many as 85 dates on a single tour. The stories they have to tell!
- **Gene Autry—On the Record.** A complete discography!
- **"The Gene Autry Show" TV Series.** This is the FIRST publication of the credits for Gene Autry's TV Series—ALL 91 episodes!
- **"Melody Ranch Theater."** During the 1980s, Gene was back on TV hosting his classic Western films.
- **The Autry Museum of Western Heritage**—Gene's long-time dream comes true!

ALL OF THIS AND MUCH MORE! $25.00 (+ $3.00 shipping/handling)

- **A conversation with The King of the Cowboys.**
- **One Man's Life—Another Man's Trivia.** A giant, comprehensive compendium of questions and answers—little-known facts about a well-known cowboy.
- **The Films of Roy Rogers.** A complete filmography!
- **Roy Rogers—On the Record.** A complete discography!
- **"The Roy Rogers Show" TV Series.** This is the FIRST publication of the credits for Roy's TV series—all 100 episodes!
- **A Roy Rogers Scrapbook of Clippings.** Rare fan magazine reprints of Roy Rogers articles!
- **Collecting Roy Rogers Memorabilia.** From lunchboxes to cap pistols, you'll see photos and current values of these hard-to-find collectibles.

THE ROY ROGERS
Reference-Trivia-Scrapbook
BOOK
by David Rothel

HERE IS EVERYTHING YOU EVER WANTED TO KNOW ABOUT "THE KING OF THE COWBOYS," ROY ROGERS!

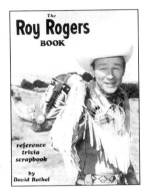

ALL OF THIS AND MUCH MORE! $25.00 (+ $3.00 shipping/handling)

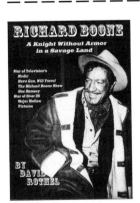

RICHARD BOONE
"A Knight without Armor in a Savage Land"
by David Rothel

- MILESTONES AND MINUTIAE
- IN-DEPTH INTERVIEWS WITH FAMILY MEMBERS
- IN-DEPTH INTERVIEWS WITH FRIENDS AND CO-WORKERS:
- THE WIT AND WISDOM OF RICHARD BOONE.
- *MEDIC* Episode Guide.
- *HAVE GUN, WILL TRAVEL* Episode Guide.
- *THE RICHARD BOONE SHOW* Episode Guide.
- *HEC RAMSEY* Episode Guide.
- TV MOVIES & ANTHOLOGY TV PROGRAMS Episode Guide.

Each copy of *RICHARD BOONE, "A Knight without Armor in a Savage Land"* is packaged (at no extra cost) with a Johnny Western CD featuring "The Ballad of Paladin" and "The Guns of Rio Muerto," the only commercial recording Richard Boone made.

FREE *Johnny Western* **CD**

ORDER YOUR COPY NOW!
only $30.00 postpaid
Includes *FREE* Johnny Western CD

EMPIRE PUBLISHING, INC. • PO BOX 717 • MADISON, NC 27025 • PH 336-427-5850 • FAX 336-427-7372

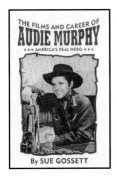

THE FILMS AND CAREER OF
AUDIE MURPHY

by Sue Gossett

$18⁰⁰
+ $2.00 shipping

A Film-by-film Synopses of this Legendary Hollywood Star / War Hero

This book reflects all of Audie Murphy's movie career of 44 films. Also included are two of his three made-for-television movies and one episode of his 1961 series, "Whispering Smith."

Along with acting and producing films, Audie's brilliant and well-documented war record is highlighted for those who want a thumb-nail account of what he endured while in the service of his country. This young man was not yet old enough to vote when he was awarded every combat medal for valor this nation had to offer.

Audie Murphy loved country music and expressed himself through the lyrics of dozens of songs, some of which were recorded by famous artists. Some of his poetry and songs are included in a special chapter. Order today!

To celebrate the movie career of Audie Murphy, Sue Gossett and Empire Publishing are delighted to present this volume of *Audie Murphy: Now Showing*. It contains 200+ pages and more than 500 photo illustrations of advertising materials used to promote the 44 films given to Audie's credit. The contents include photos of movie 1-sheet posters, lobby and window display cards, half sheets, publicity items, author's comments, and more. *A must-have for the true Audie Murphy fan!*

Contents include:
- The movie magic of this legendary giant as illustrated via theatrical promotional materials.
- 200+ pages
- More than 500 photo illustrations
- Complete filmography
- Foreign items and testimonials
- Interviews with actors who appeared in his films
- Locations where movies were filmed
- Brief synopsis of each film
- Much more!

Audie Murphy:
NOW SHOWING

by Sue Gossett

Author Sue Gossett is a true Audie Murphy historian, having followed his career since 1954.

$30⁰⁰
+ $3.00 shipping

Those Great
COWBOY SIDEKICKS
by David Rothel

- 8-1/2 x 11
- 300+ PAGES
- BEAUTIFUL COLOR COVER
- OVER 200 PHOTOS
- $25.00 (+ $3.00 s/h)

This book features in-depth profiles of such fondly-remembered character actors as George "Gabby" Hayes, Smiley Burnette, Andy Devine, Al "Fuzzy" St. John, Pat Buttram, Max Terhune, Fuzzy Knight, and many other sidekicks of the B-Westerns—thirty-nine in all! Much of *Those Great Cowboy Sidekicks* is told through the reminiscences of the sidekicks themselves and the cowboy stars who enjoyed the company of these often bewhiskered, tobacco-chewing saddle pals. Mr. Rothel provides the reader with the rare opportunity to go behind the scenes to discover the manner in which Western screen comedy was created.

Author David Rothel is a Western film historian who has also written An Ambush of Ghosts, Tim Holt, and Richard Boone, A Knight Without Armor in a Savage Land, among several other titles.

EMPIRE PUBLISHING, INC. • PO BOX 717 • MADISON, NC 27025 • PH 336-427-5850 • FAX 336-427-7372

Other Fine Western Movie Books Available from Empire Publishing, Inc:

ABC's of Movie Cowboys by Edgar M. Wyatt. $5.00.

Audie Murphy: Now Showing by Sue Gossett. $30.00.

Back in the Saddle: Essays on Western Film and Television Actors edited by Garry Yoggy. $24.95.

Bill Elliott, The Peaceable Man by Bobby Copeland. $15.00.

Bob Steele, Stars and Support Players by Bob Nareau. $20.00.

B-Western Actors Encyclopedia by Ted Holland. $30.00.

Buster Crabbe, A Self-Portrait as told to Karl Whitezel. $24.95.

B-Western Boot Hill: A Final Tribute to the Cowboys and Cowgirls Who Rode the Saturday Matinee Movie Range (revised edition) by Bobby Copeland. $15.00.

The Cowboy and the Kid by Jefferson Brim Crow, III. $5.90.

Duke, The Life and Image of John Wayne by Ronald L. Davis. $12.95.

The Films and Career of Audie Murphy by Sue Gossett. $18.00.

The Films of the Cisco Kid by Francis M. Nevins, Jr. $19.95.

The Films of Hopalong Cassidy by Francis M. Nevins, Jr. $19.95.

From Pigskin to Saddle Leather: The Films of Johnny Mack Brown by John A. Rutherford. $19.95.

The Gene Autry Reference-Trivia-Scrapbook by David Rothel. $25.00.

The Golden Corral, A Roundup of Magnificent Western Films by Ed Andreychuk. $29.95.

The Hollywood Posse, The Story of a Gallant Band of Horsemen Who Made Movie History by Diana Serra Cary. $16.95.

Hoppy by Hank Williams. $29.95.

In a Door, Into a Fight, Out a Door, Into a Chase, Movie-Making Remembered by the Guy at the Door by William Witney. $32.50.

John Ford, Hollywood's Old Master by Ronald L. Davis. $14.95.

John Wayne—Actor, Artist, Hero by Richard D. McGhee. $25.00.

John Wayne, An American Legend by Roger M. Crowley. $29.95.

Last of the Cowboy Heroes by Budd Boetticher. $32.50.

The Life and Films of Buck Jones, the Silent Era by Buck Rainey. $14.95.

The Life and Films of Buck Jones, the Sound Era by Buck Rainey. $24.95.

More Cowboy Movie Posters by Bruce Hershenson. $20.00.

More Cowboy Shooting Stars by John A. Rutherford and Richard B. Smith, III. $18.00.

The Official TV Western Roundup Book by Neil Summers and Roger M. Crowley. $34.95.

Quiet on the Set, Motion Picture History at the Iverson Movie Location Ranch by Robert G. Sherman. $14.95.

Randolph Scott, A Film Biography by Jefferson Brim Crow, III. $25.00.

Richard Boone: A Knight Without Armor in a Savage Land by David Rothel. $30.00.

Riding the (Silver Screen) Range, The Ultimate Western Movie Trivia Book by Ann Snuggs. $15.00.

Riding the Video Range, The Rise and Fall of the Western on Television by Garry A. Yoggy. $75.00.

The Round-Up, A Pictorial History of Western Movie and Television Stars Through the Years by Donald R. Key. $27.00.

Roy Rogers, A Biography, Radio History, Television Career Chronicle, Discography, Filmography, etc. by Robert W. Phillips. $65.00.

The Roy Rogers Reference-Trivia-Scrapbook by David Rothel. $25.00.

Saddle Gals, A Filmography of Female Players in B-Westerns of the Sound Era by Edgar M. Wyatt and Steve Turner. $10.00.

Saddle Pals: A Complete B-Western Roster of the Sound Era by Garv Towell and Wayne E. Keates. $5.00.

Singing in the Saddle by Douglas B. Green. $34.95.

The Sons of the Pioneers by Bill O'Neal and Fred Goodwin. $26.95.

Television Westerns Episode Guide by Harris M. Lentz, III. $95.00.

Tex Ritter: America's Most Beloved Cowboy by Bill O'Neal. $21.95.

They Still Call Me Junior by Frank "Junior" Coghlan. $37.50.

Those Wide Open Spaces by Hank Williams. $29.95.

Tim Holt by David Rothel. $30.00.

The Tom Mix Book by M. G. "Bud" Norris. $24.95.

Trail Talk, Candid Comments and Quotes by Performers and Participants of The Saturday Matinee Western Films by Bobby Copeland. $12.50.

The Western Films of Sunset Carson by Bob Carman and Dan Scapperotti. $20.00.

Western Movies: A TV and Video Guide to 4200 Genre Films compiled by Michael R. Pitts. $25.00.

Westerns Women by Boyd Magers and Michael G. Fitzgerald. $36.50.

Whatever Happened to Randolph Scott? by C. H. Scott. $12.95.

White Hats and Silver Spurs, Interviews with 24 Stars of Film and Television Westerns of the 1930s-1960s. $38.50.

Ask for our complete listing of 300+ movie books!